IMAGES
of America

CHICKASHA

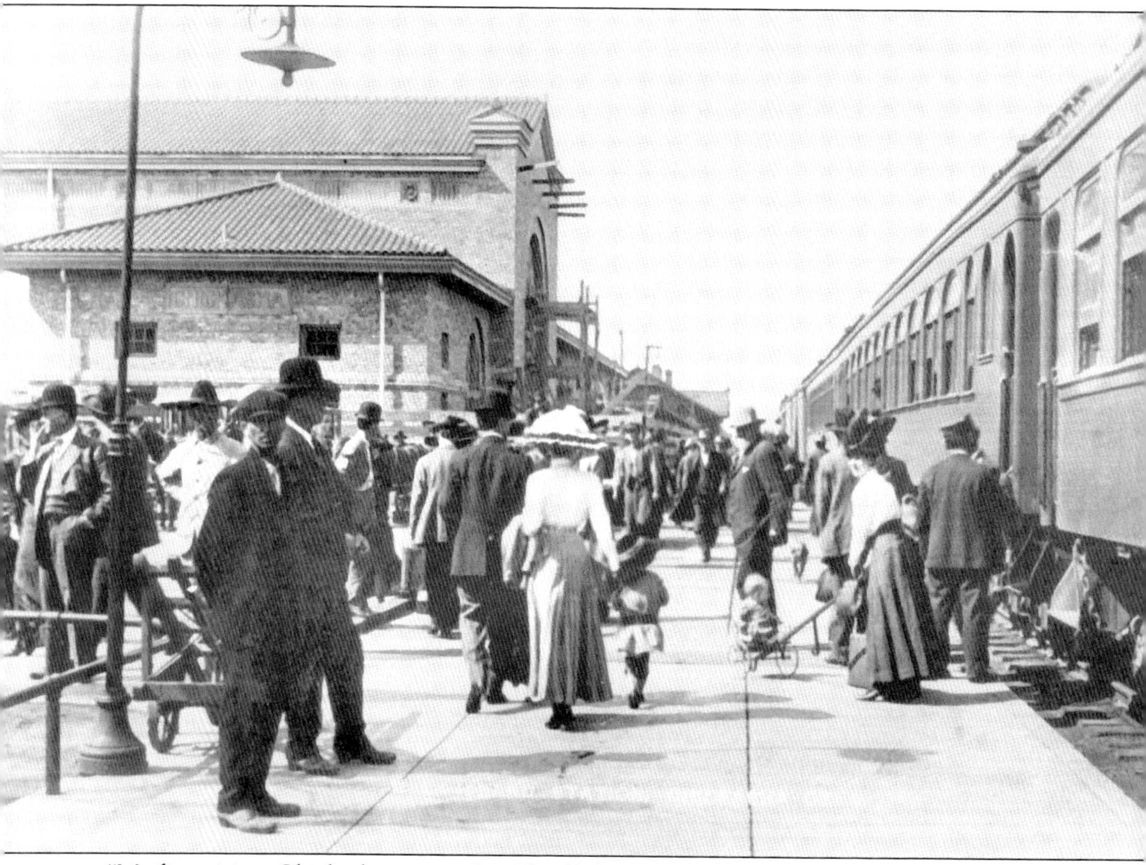

"My first visit to Chickasha was on the 4th of July, 1893. At that time, the town consisted of only one street . . . from the depot to about where Sixth Street is now. The buildings were all wooden shacks . . . One had to build a house or dig a dug-out. We built a hut and became residents of the future city of Chickasha," according to R.E.L. McClain. (Courtesy of the Grady County Historical Society.)

On the Cover: In 1911, Chickasha's main railway, the Chicago, Rock Island and Pacific Railroad (known as the Rock Island Railroad), opened its new train depot. The building was a brick structure covered in white stucco with a tiled roof, and it still stands in downtown Chickasha today. This is one of the earliest pictures of this depot, showing the building before the wooden supports were removed and the stucco was added. (Courtesy of the Grady Country Historical Society.)

IMAGES
of America

CHICKASHA

Dr. James Finck and Gennifer Majors
with the University of Science and Arts of Oklahoma
and Grady County Historical Society

ARCADIA
PUBLISHING

ISBN 978-0-7385-9179-7

Published by Arcadia Publishing
Charleston, South Carolina

Printed in the United States of America

Library of Congress Control Number: 2012932361

For all general information, please contact Arcadia Publishing:
Telephone 843-853-2070
Fax 843-853-0044
E-mail sales@arcadiapublishing.com
For customer service and orders:
Toll-Free 1-888-313-2665

Visit us on the Internet at www.arcadiapublishing.com

We would like to dedicate this book to the University of Science and Arts of Oklahoma for creating the type of learning environment that allows for professor-student collaboration. USAO is a special university with amazing students. We are all thankful to USAO for giving us a home, an education, a job, and memories we will keep for a lifetime.

Contents

Acknowledgments 6

Introduction 7

1. Transportation and Auxiliaries 9

2. Businesses 29

3. Culture 49

4. Religious Life 85

5. Education 95

6. The University of Arts and Sciences of Oklahoma 105

Bibliography 126

About the Organization 127

ACKNOWLEDGMENTS

The creation of this book would not be possible without the support of the Grady County Historical Society and the University of Science and Arts of Oklahoma, both of which opened up their photograph archives for our use. Special recognition is required for Pat Cunningham, director/curator of the Grady County Historical Society. She not only assisted in finding and prioritizing the photographs, but her knowledge of Chickasha's history was invaluable. We would also like to thank the Public Relations Department of USAO, headed by Randy Talley, and the staff at Nash Library for their assistance with pictures and information.

All research on the history of Chickasha begins with Irvin Munn. He deserves recognition for his books on Chickasha's history; they are the source of the majority of the information used in this book.

A very special thank-you to our acquisitions editor, Winnie Rodgers, for asking us to take on this project, for her assistance throughout, and mostly for her patience as we stumbled through the process.

I would also like to thank students Gennifer Majors and Megan Graumann. Megan helped gather the pictures and did some of the research, and Gennifer wrote a few of the chapters. Thank you for your help and timeless dedication. I have enjoyed having them in my class and working with them on this project. I know they will be successful in their future endeavors.

Unless otherwise noted, all images in chapters one through five are courtesy of the Grady County Historical Society. All images in chapter six are courtesy of the University of Science and Arts of Oklahoma.

Introduction

Chickasha, Oklahoma, is the perfect example of an all-American city. It is a quiet, peaceful town about 40 miles southwest of Oklahoma City. Yet for its size, Chickasha is a vibrant community full of extraordinary people and fantastic events that draw in visitors from not only around the state but the world. Being in Oklahoma, the land where Chickasha now sits was once part of Indian Territory and, in particular, under the control of the Chickasaw tribe. In the 1840s, the Chickasaw were one of the Five Civilized Tribes driven from their land in the American South and forced to live in the West. However, occupation solely by American Indians did not last long. During the days of the great cattle drives, the land was a favorite stopping point for drovers coming up from Texas to Kansas along the famous Chisholm Trail. The spring at what is now Shanoan Springs Park was a perfect watering hole for herds and cowboys. By the late 1870s, white settlers envious of the fertile land began encroaching upon Indian Territory, and some, known as intruders, slowly trickled in. By 1889, the government, bending to pressure, opened two million acres for settlement in Oklahoma, beginning the famous land rushes. By the late 19th century, the land where Chickasha now sits was owned by the Swing Ring, a cattle ranch operated by James L. Speed. What finally created the town of Chickasha was transportation, which is not only responsible for the creation of the town but has highly influenced its development over the years.

In 1892, the Rock Island Railroad halted construction to make land transactions, and while it waited, a boxcar was set up as headquarters for the temporary depot now called Chickasha. It did not take long for a tent city to spring up on the grounds. After the railroad continued its construction, Chickasha remained an important stop. Added to the importance of a depot, Chickasha had an abundance of open land, which brought opportunities for anyone needing a new start. Chickasha would continue to be an important hub for transportation. In later years, the St. Louis–San Francisco Railway (Frisco) as well as the Atchison, Topeka & Santa Fe Railway (Santa Fe) would pass through Chickasha. Today, not only rail traffic affects the town; several major highways crisscross through it, including US 81, 62, and 277, the H.E. Bailey Turnpike, and State Highways 9, 19, 39, and 92. Being in a strategic location with ample land, it did not take long for Chickasha to flourish. By 1902, the population had already reached over 6,000 residents, larger than the town of Tulsa. By 1909, with paved streets and brick buildings, the population soared to over 10,000. The town had a working water and sewer system and with its newly built hydroelectric dam, telephones and an electric streetcar were under construction. Chickasha was on its way.

Agriculturally, Chickasha was booming. By 1910, Grady County led the state in hog population, with more than 34,000. Chickasha led the region in cotton production, having 18 cotton mills, 200 cotton gins, and access to transportation. The town would soon add grain and flour mills and even an ironworks. With the open land, cattle grazed around Chickasha and, once again because of the railroad, the town made a logical location for stockyards where cattle would be held until being shipped around the nation. There have been setbacks to Chickasha's progress. Like all cities in the early 20th century, fires were a major concern. Chickasha was no exception, with many of its early buildings made of wood. Several fires threatened the city—and did a great bit of damage to different parts of town—in the years 1899, 1902, 1903, 1905,1908,1908, 1911, 1914, and 1924, but after each blaze Chickasha showed its determination to rebuild. Floods have also done severe damage to Chickasha, located on the Washita River. The most notable floods occurred in 1892, 1893, 1908, 1915, 1923, and finally 1927. Many of the records and pictures that could have been used in the creation of this book—including copies of the local newspaper, the *Chickasha Express*, and government records and pictures—were destroyed in these floods, especially the 1927 flood that damaged the courthouse.

One area that put Chickasha on the map was education. With statehood, the legislature chose Chickasha, because of its size, influence, and proximity to transportation, as a site for one of its schools of higher education. The legislators wanted to establish a school just for girls, one of the few of its kind in the nation. In 1908, the Oklahoma Industrial Institute and College for Girls was established, only to be renamed in 1916 to the Oklahoma College for Women. In 1965, the university opened its doors to include male students while changing its name to the Oklahoma College of Liberal Arts. Finally, the school changed its name to the current one, the University of Science and Arts of Oklahoma. The university is Oklahoma's only public liberal arts institution and has been ranked no. 1 in *US News & World Report* on its list of "Best Buys" for both cost and academics.

The town has continued to grow over the years due to its resources and location. The land allows for diverse crops and livestock, making it a perfect spot for agricultural development. Accessibility to natural gas and oil as well as a location on major shipping routes has created a perfect environment for industrial growth. Chickasha has prospered under these conditions. It is home to top medical facilities, including Grady Memorial Hospital, Five Oaks Medial Group, and Southern Plains Medical Center. Some of Chickasha's major industries are Gabriel Ride Control, a leader in producing shocks and struts; HIS Sensing; and Cimarron Trailers.

Yet, what Chickasha is probably most famous for today is its cultural events. Every year around Christmas, more than 250,000 visitors from around the state and even around the nation take a pilgrimage to Chickasha for the Festival of Light. More than 3.5 million lights sparkle in the 43-acre park. The Festival of Light is the biggest attraction, but not the only one. Two other major events are the Rock Island Arts Festival and the Spring Triad hosted by the university. In the fall, the Rock Island Arts Festival is full of music, arts and crafts, and food. In the spring, the Triad is composed of the largest academic meet in Oklahoma, the Montmartre Sidewalk Chalk Art Festival, and Droverstock, an outdoor music festival. Chickasha is also home to the county fair and numerous car shows.

People come to Chickasha because of the industry or festivals, but they stay and live in Chickasha because of the people and the old-fashioned, small-town feel. Chickasha is large enough to have all the modern amenities one could need, but still small enough to know one's neighbors and feel part of a community.

One

Transportation and Auxiliaries

Every community has services it provides for its citizens. Chickasha is no different. Some of the first services were provided by railroads. The city of Chickasha was created by the railroad companies known as the Santa Fe and Rock Island. The railroads still run through Chickasha, though they are not as big of an economic power as they once were. Chickasha was not only a stop on the Rock Island Railroad; during World War II, the town was home to a prisoner-of-war camp, US Army Borden General Hospital, and other services that helped the community over the years.

There were many other services in Chickasha that gave many people jobs and helped others who were sick. The city had the normal bureaucratic structures that every community needs, such as police, a fire department, and judges. The fire department not only had to put out fires but was, and still is, called upon to help pull people out of the rising waters of the Washita River when it floods.

Another service Chickasha had was the wonderful trolley system. Originally, the line just went to Shannon Springs Park, but eventually the line's route was altered to reach the Oklahoma College for Women.

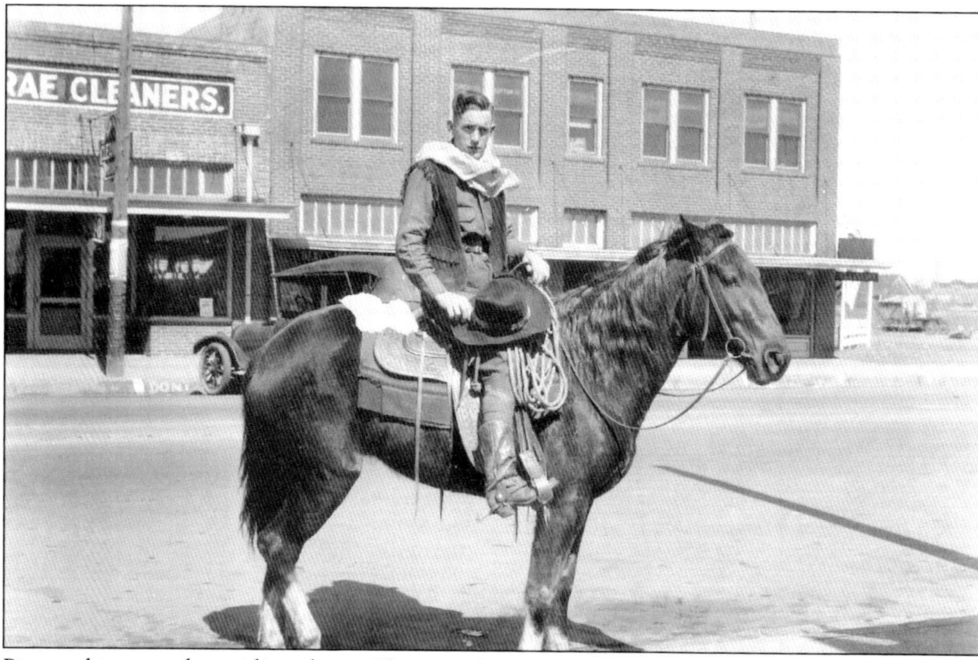

Pictured is a cowboy riding down Choctaw Avenue in the middle of downtown Chickasha. During the early years of Chickasha, agriculture was the major industry. It was not uncommon to see tractors alongside cars on the road, and there was still nothing weird about seeing a cowboy ride into town.

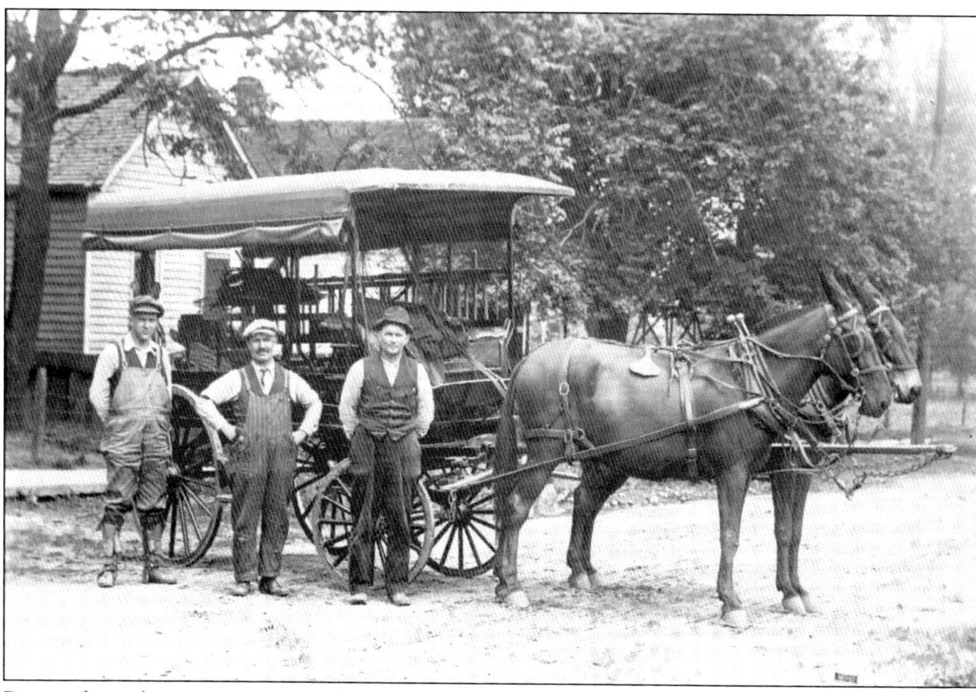

Pictured is a three-man crew working on paving Choctaw Avenue. Having the streets paved was a priority for the city. The downtown was described as a sea of mud after it rained. Chickasha was incorporated as a first-class city in 1902, and as such it needed some paved roads.

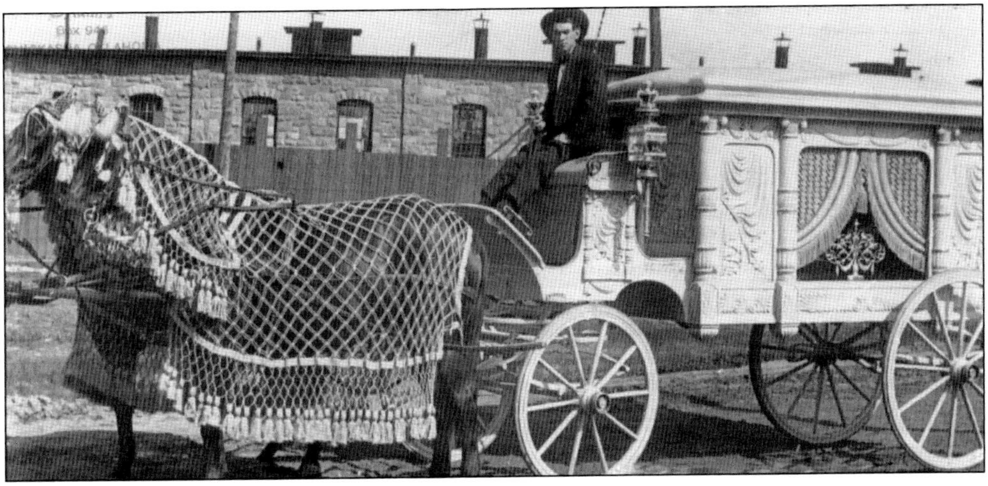

Here are two pictures of early horse-drawn hearses. A black shawl over the horse (below) meant that a man had died, while a white shawl (above) meant a women or child had passed. The bottom hearse belonged to O.M. Claycomb, probably the first funeral director in the city. Claycomb was listed as a furniture maker; it was very common in those days for the furniture maker and undertaker to be the same person. Caskets were made in the back of the shop, while funerals were held in local churches. Two other early funeral homes were the Chickasha Funeral Home, which in 1941 became the Sevier-Chickasha Funeral Home, and the Brown-Binyon Funeral Home, which opened in 1922 under the direction of Walter and Golda Brown.

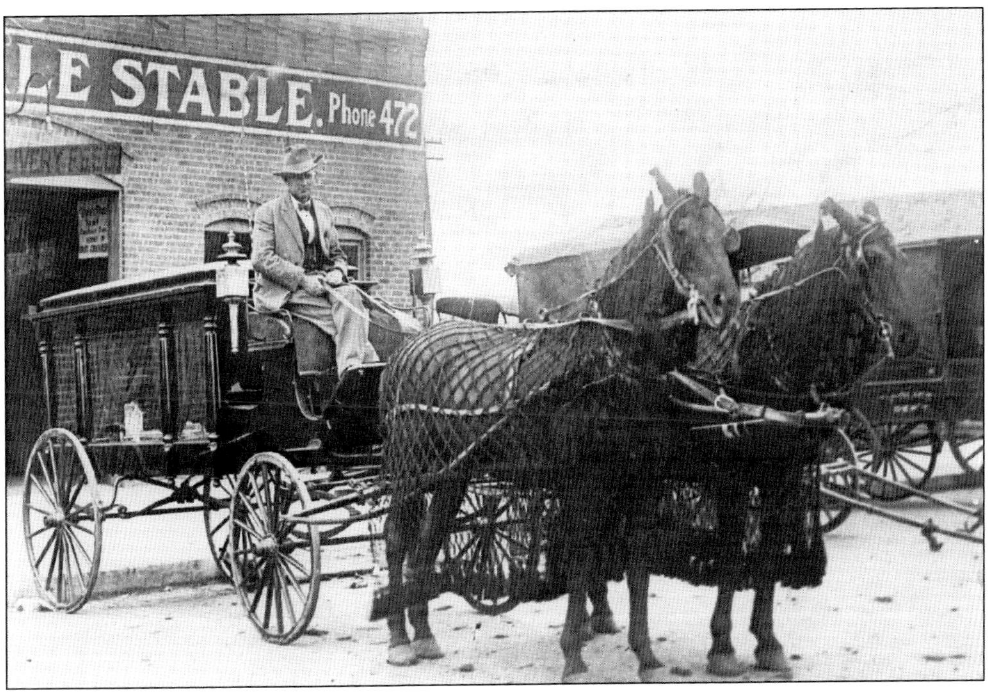

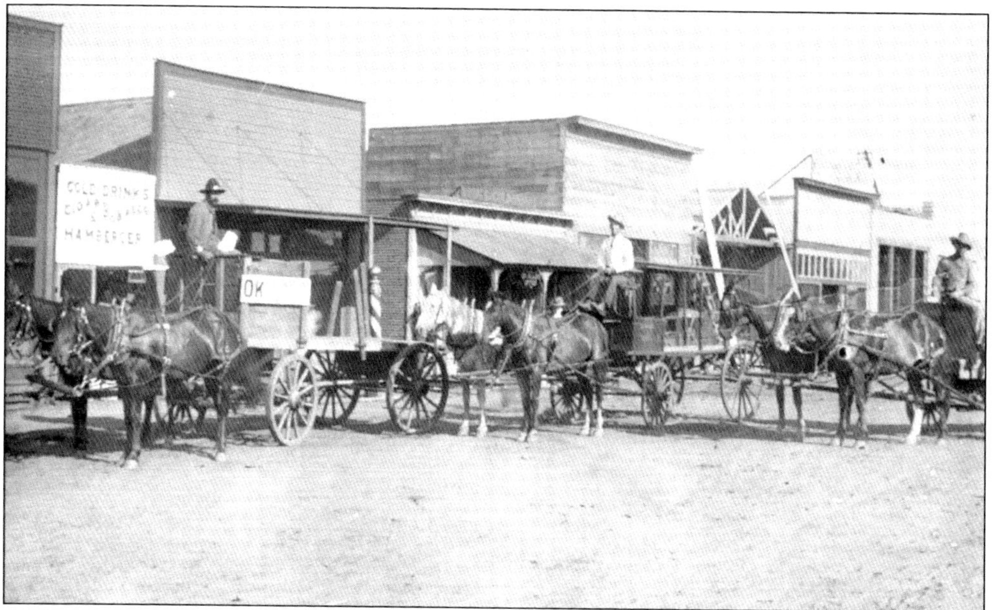

Traffic jams in downtown Chickasha as wagons are lining up to pick up their wares. The storefronts are all elevated high enough to avoid flood and mud in the days before the streets were paved. In the days before paved streets, when it rained, many large holes would form in the roadways, making them impossible to traverse.

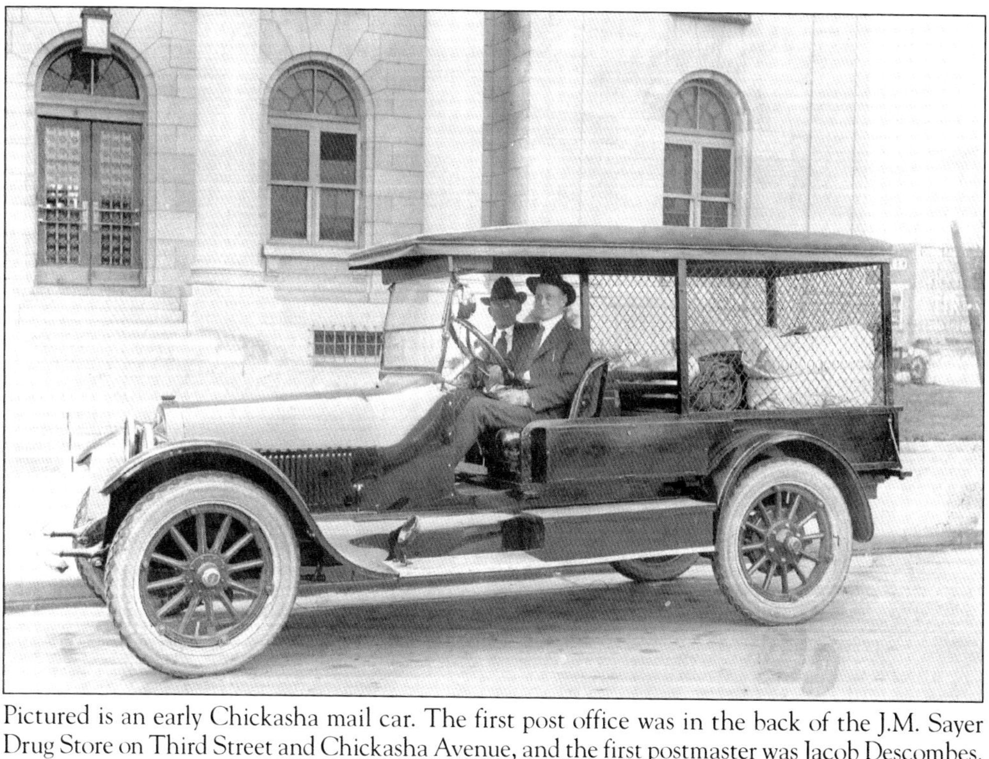

Pictured is an early Chickasha mail car. The first post office was in the back of the J.M. Sayer Drug Store on Third Street and Chickasha Avenue, and the first postmaster was Jacob Descombes. The second postmaster, Howard Miller, began in 1898. By August 1911, there were 41 working iron mailboxes around town to receive letters.

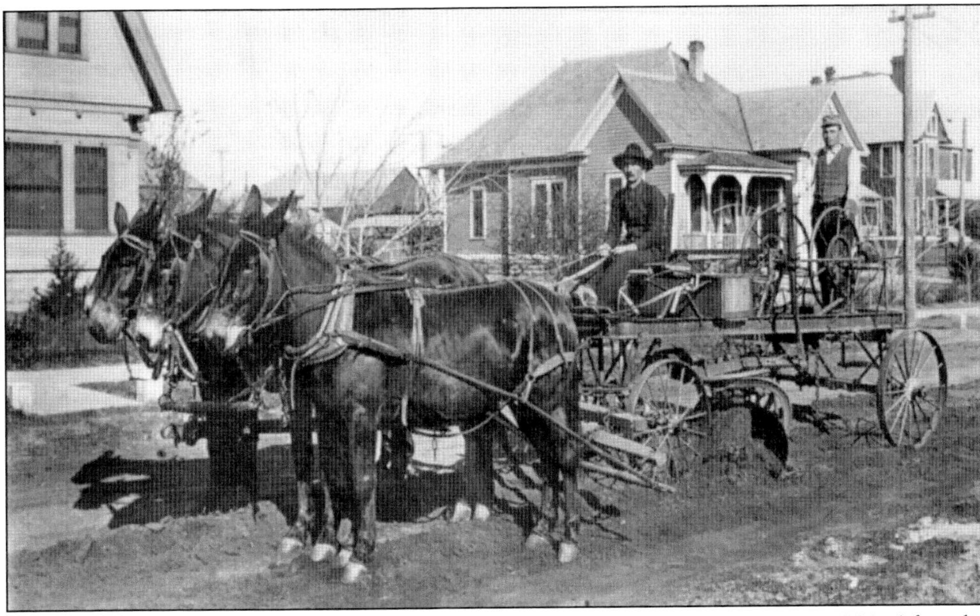

Chickasha Street Department workers are laying bricks on Choctaw Avenue in 1900. After the street was smoothed out, bricks were used at first, before tar-and-gravel or asphalt paving. Paving was completed on Chickasha Avenue to Sixth Street by 1906 and from Kansas Avenue to Sixth Street by 1901. Chickasha, Kansas, and Choctaw Avenues had sidewalks paved by 1908.

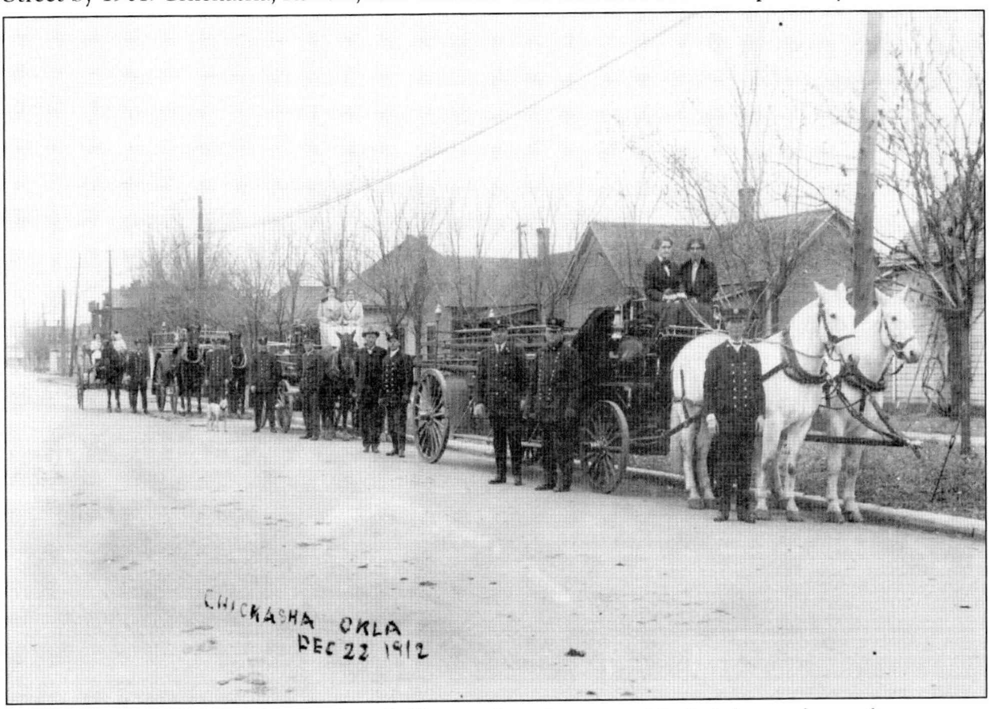

Here is an example of early paved roads. Pictured are firemen with their horse-drawn fire wagons. The fire department was important to Chickasha, as many fires did a great deal of damage to the city. The fire department began in 1900 with George Brown in charge. The first wagons had no horses; the livery owner had to agree to let the department use his horses to get to the fire.

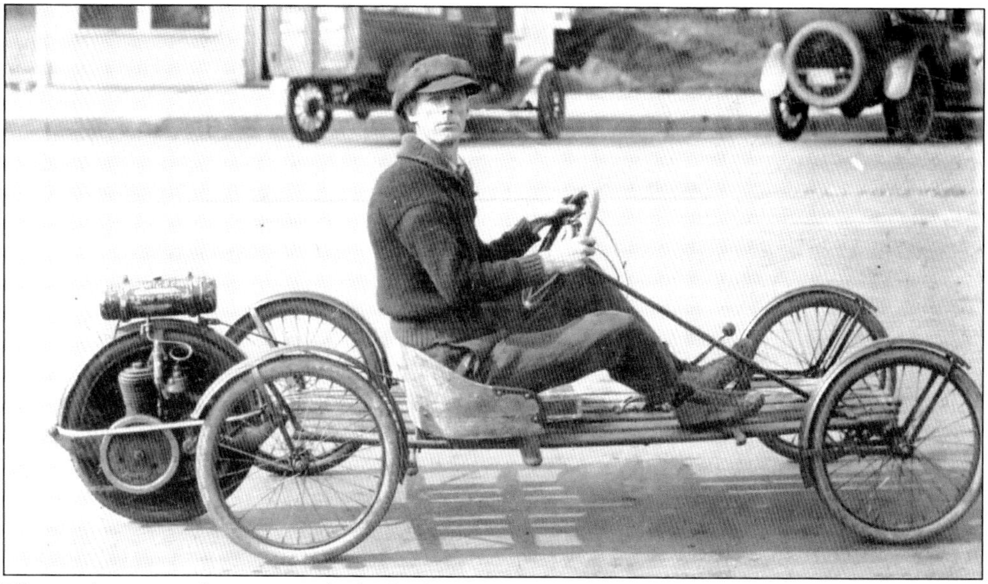

This early car on the streets of Chickasha was simple but got the driver where he wanted to go. Early cars were not welcomed by everyone in Chickasha; there were some that saw the new contraptions as a nuisance. They were seen as a problem for the teams of horses that spooked when the noisy vehicles drove by.

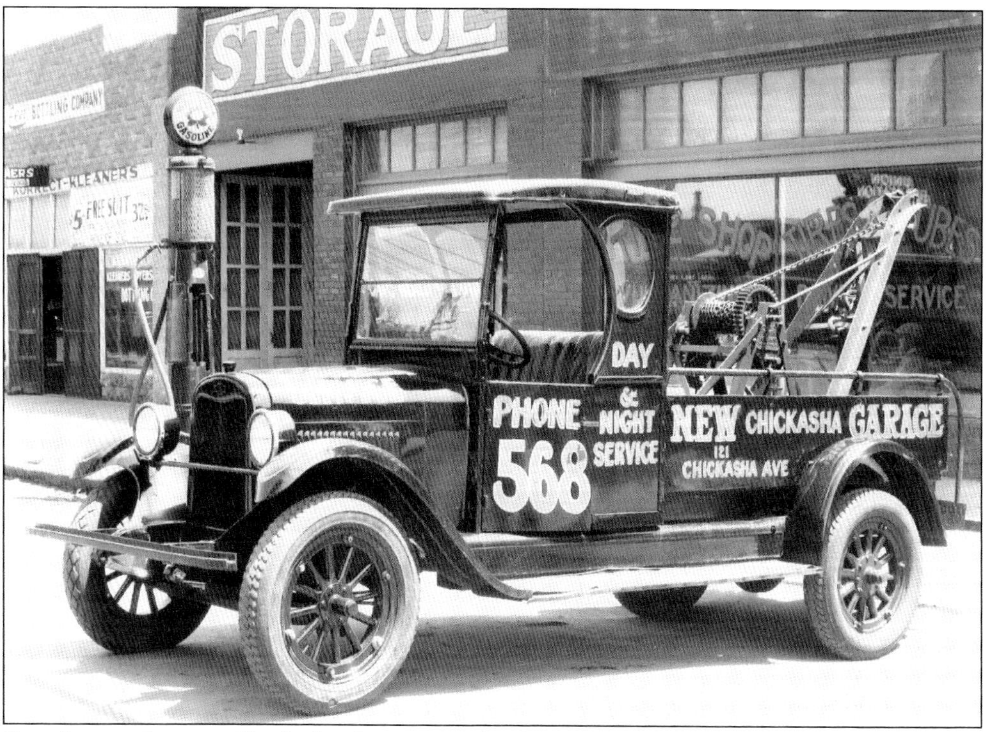

Seen here is the new Chickasha Garage wrecker located on 121 West Chickasha Avenue. As cars became more prominent in Chickasha, businesses were created to deal with the demand of cars breaking down. One of the earliest service stations belonged to Phil Heisier in 1927 and was located at Fourth Street and Kansas Avenue.

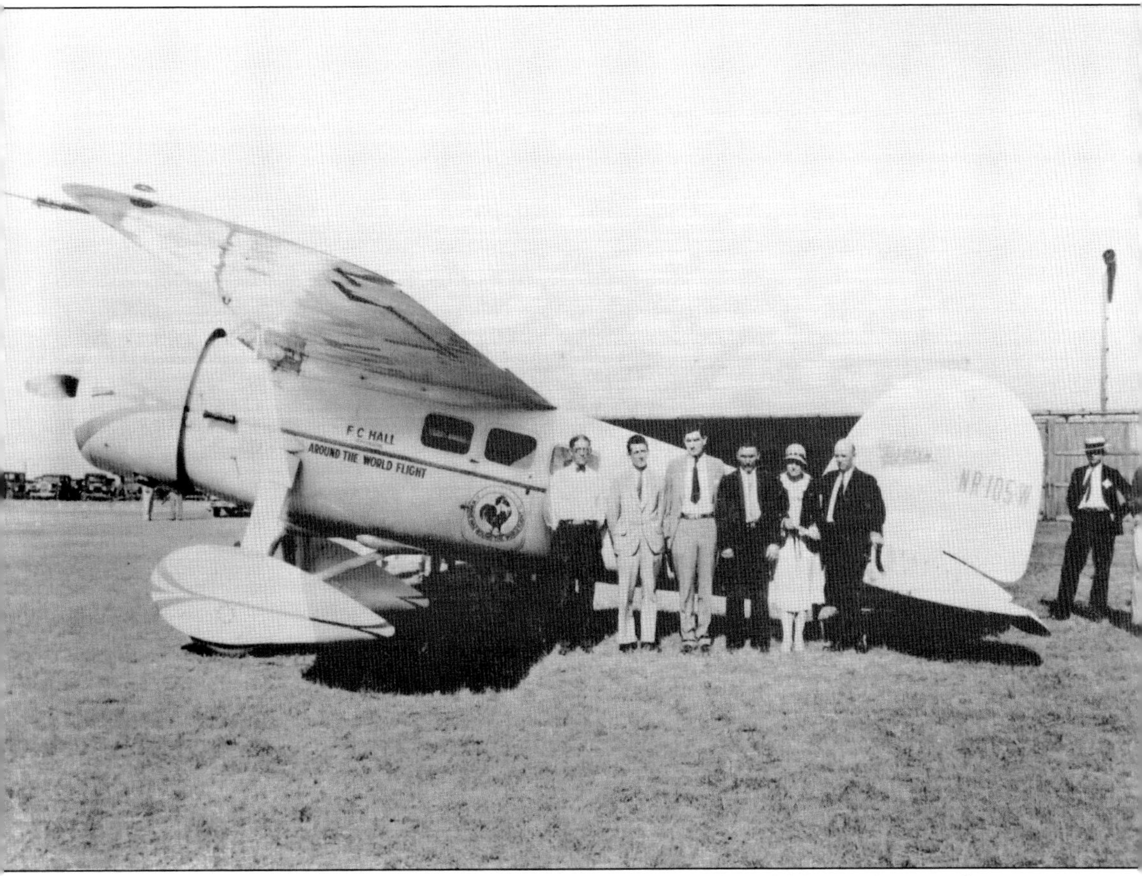

The *Winnie Mae* visits Chickasha. Pilot Wiley Post, from Maysville, Oklahoma, became famous for his flight around the globe in the *Winnie Mae* in 1931. His second trip in 1933 only took seven days, 18 hours, and 49 minutes. Wiley was sponsored by local Chickasha resident and oilman F.C. Hall, who purchased the *Winnie Mae* and named it after his daughter. This picture was taken on August 1, 1931, when Post stopped by Chickasha on his way home and was greeted by thousands. The people in the photograph are, from left to right, Dr. A.B. Leeds, Harrold Gatty, Post's navigator; Jess Larson, mayor; Wiley Post; B.B. Leeds; and F.C. Hall. In 1935, Post crashed over Alaska carrying his famous friend Will Rogers; both men died.

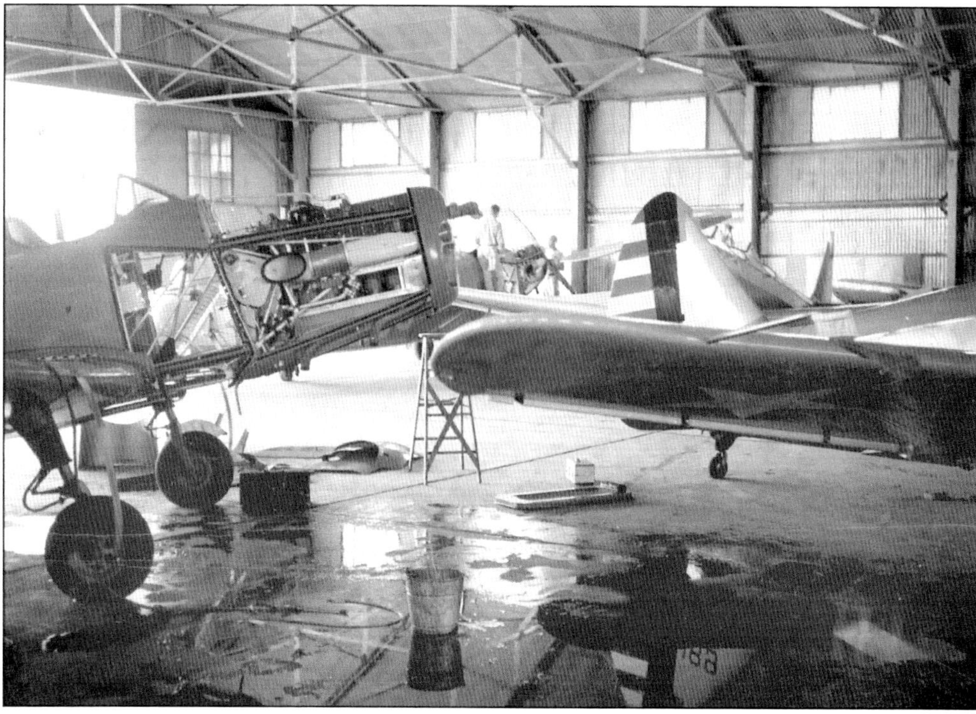

Aviation and Chickasha have gone together from the beginning. Oklahoma's first plane, the *Albatross*, was built by the Nicholas Brothers Bicycle Shop in Chickasha and tested by Lester Miller in 1911 in an airfield just north of town. That same year, M.S. Blackburn built the monoplane in Chickasha, the first all-steel plane constructed. In 1941, a school was built in town for training Army Air Corps pilots. In 1962, George Hector began the Hector Flying Service in Chickasha. Above is one of the hangers where the planes were repaired. Below is one of the planes from the W&B Flying School.

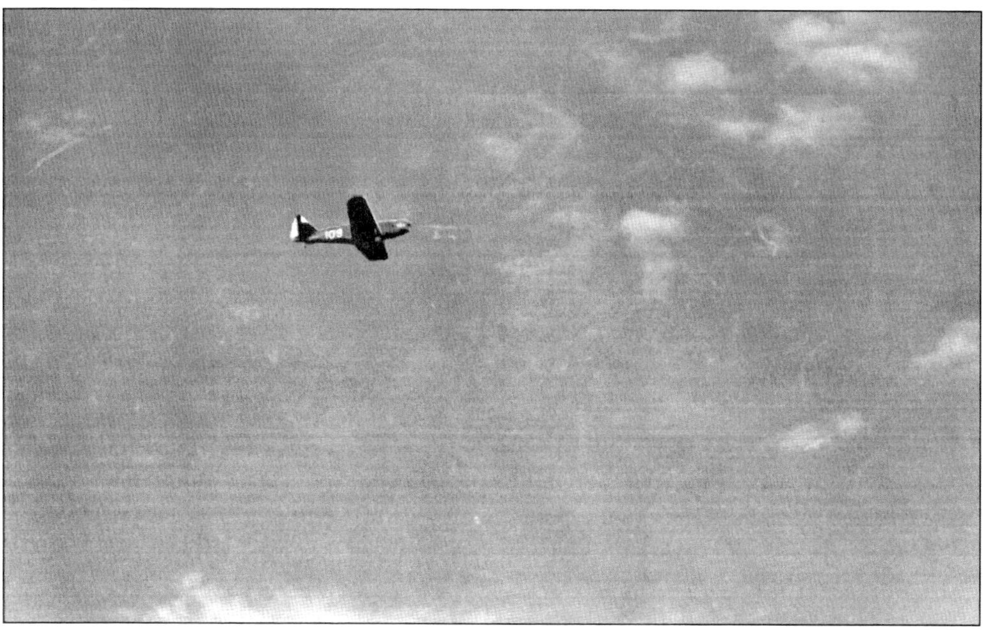

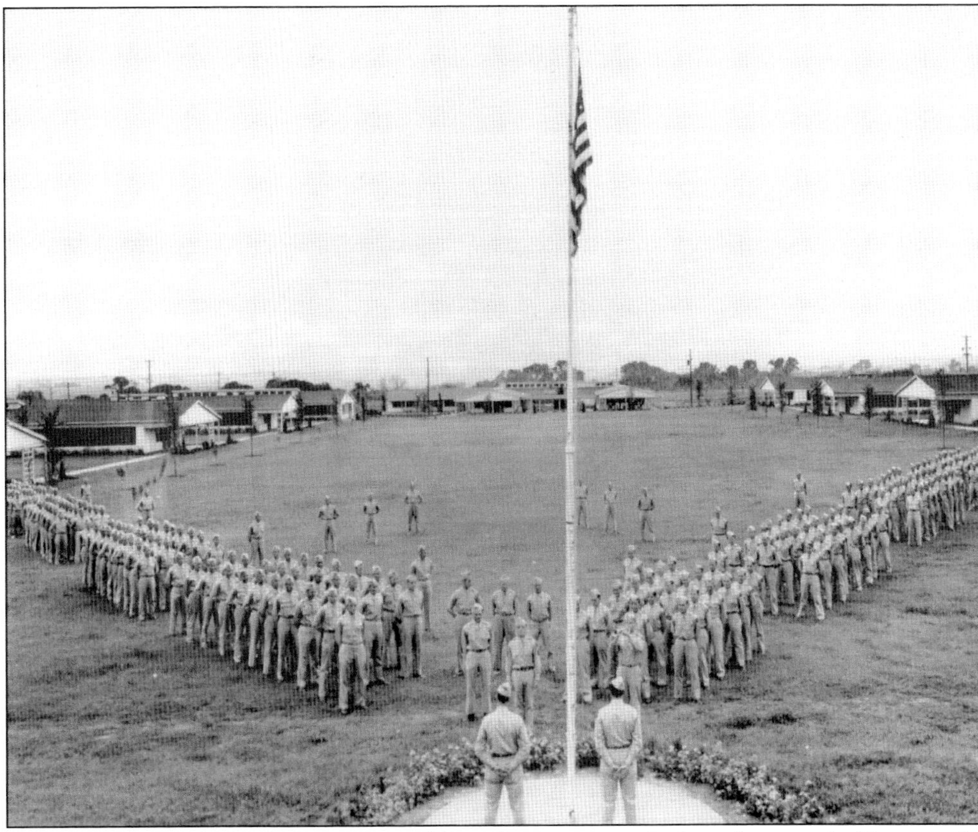

The area around Chickasha was open and free of mountains, which made it an ideal location for a flight school. In 1941, just prior to America's entrance into World War II, Chickasha approved of an $85,000 bond to fund the W&B Flying School in partnership with the federal government. Barracks were built, and during the war, over 8,000 cadets trained at the school. Ray Wilson and F.W. Bonfils organized the school, which was civilian-operated but supervised by the Army Air Corps. At the end of the war, the school was closed, and the property was given to the City of Chickasha. The above picture is of cadets on the drill field at the W&B Flying School. Below are men from the 316 Flying Training Detachment.

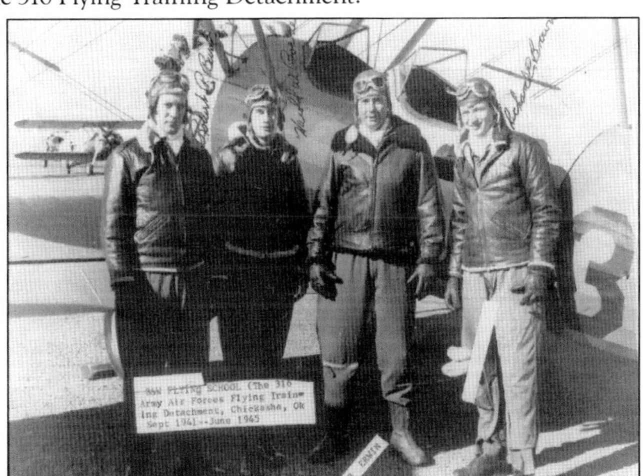

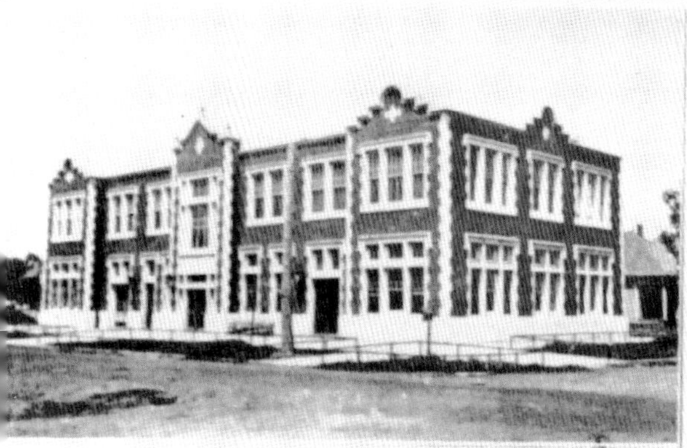

SANTA FE DEPOT AT CHICKASHA.

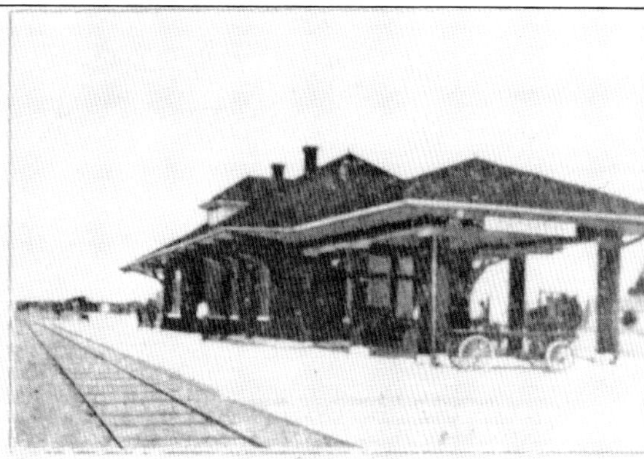

FRISCO DEPOT.

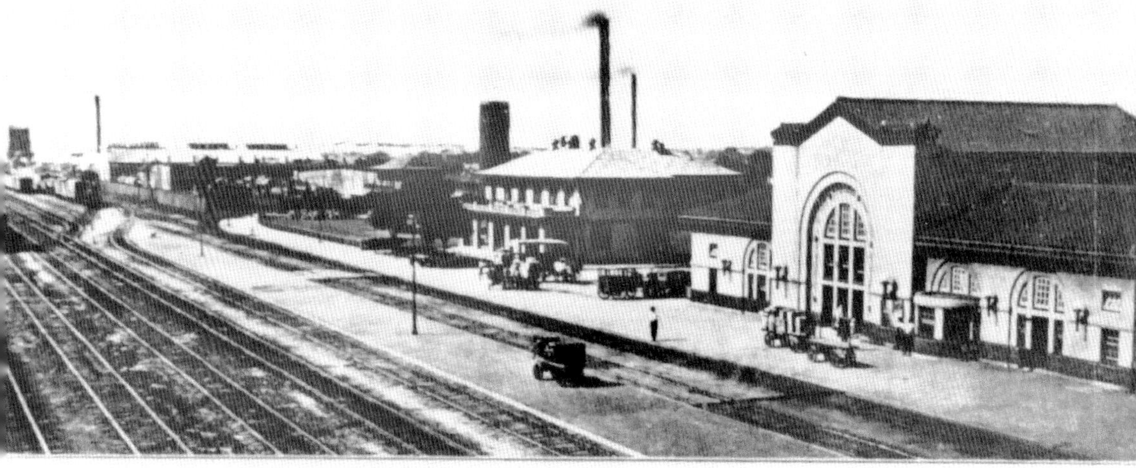

OCK ISLAND ROUND HOUSE AND YARDS, ALSO DEPOT AND GERONIMO HOTEL

The railroads are responsible for the location of Chickasha today. The town had its roots as a depot for the Rock Island Railroad (bottom). Later, the Frisco Railroad (top right) came to town in 1902, followed by the Oklahoma Central Railroad (top left). The Central Railroad, today known locally as the Santa Fe Railroad, had its origins in a Dutch company. It sent Gerritt Middleberg to Oklahoma to find land and later to supervise the construction of the line with his son Martin. Middleberg spent his time hunting around Chickasha; he enjoyed his hunt enough to recommend the area to his company. Middleburg, Oklahoma, was named in their honor— a corruption of the family name. When the line proved unsuccessful, it was later purchased by the Santa Fe Railway, which took over the depot. By 1945, the line continued to fail and was discontinued. Later, the depot was purchased by the *Chickasha Daily Express*.

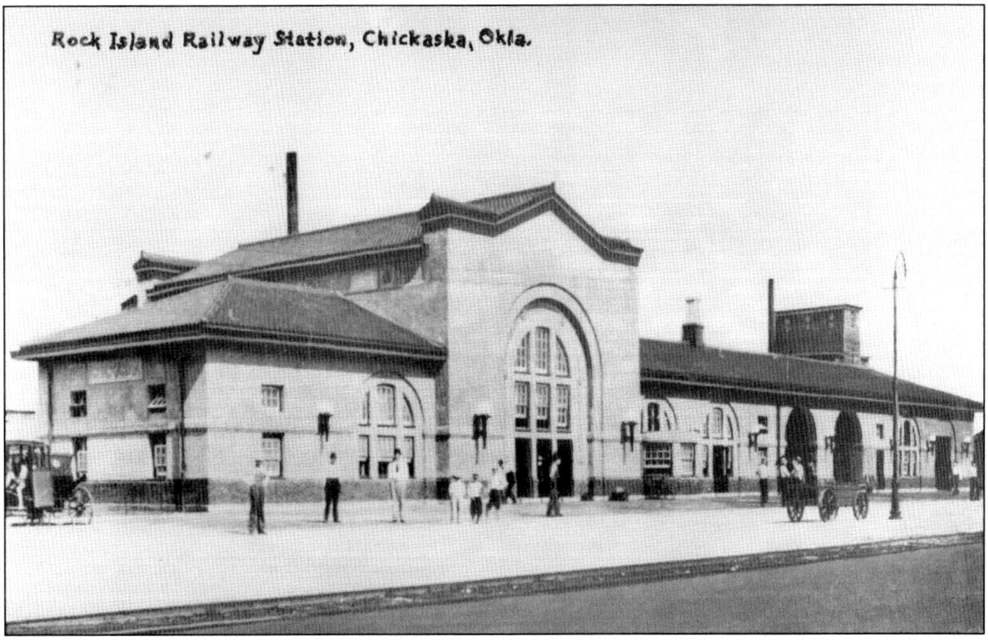

The first Rock Island Depot was a boxcar alongside the track. In 1911, construction began on the new brick-stucco building. In 1908, the Rock Island opened a fine dining restaurant, a rarity in this time. It also built a fancy hotel known as the Geronimo.

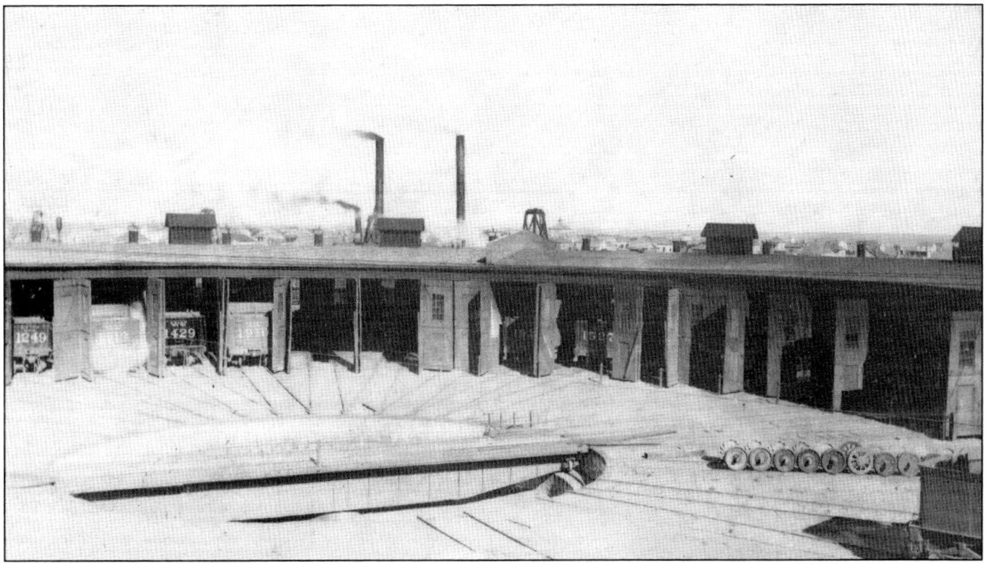

This 1905 picture shows the Rock Island roundhouse. When not carrying passengers or hauling freight, Rock Island engines were housed in the roundhouse. The center turntable of the roundhouse can be pivoted to provide access to each. Early steam engines were designed to travel forward with limited reverse movement; the roundhouse would turn the engine around.

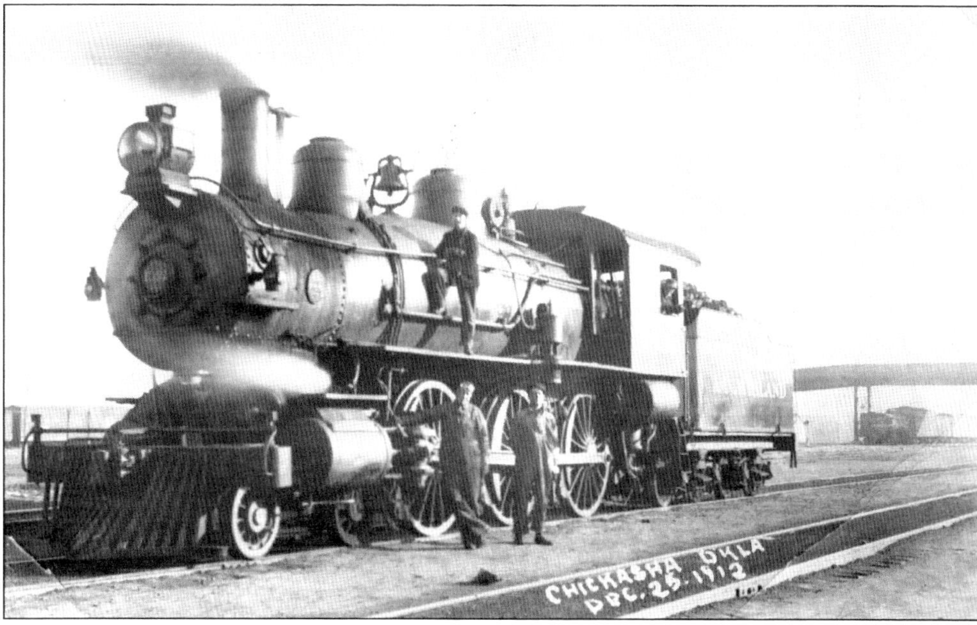

On Christmas Day, 1912, the Rock Island Railroad was still operating, so the employees spent their Christmas riding the rails.

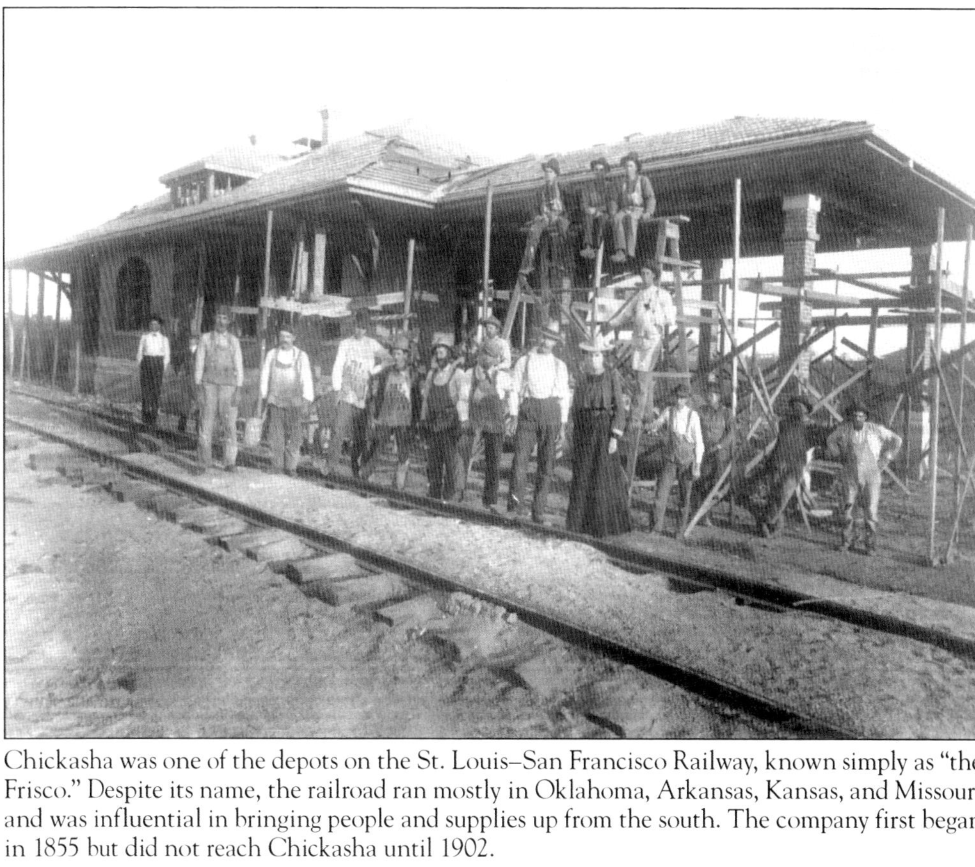

Chickasha was one of the depots on the St. Louis–San Francisco Railway, known simply as "the Frisco." Despite its name, the railroad ran mostly in Oklahoma, Arkansas, Kansas, and Missouri and was influential in bringing people and supplies up from the south. The company first began in 1855 but did not reach Chickasha until 1902.

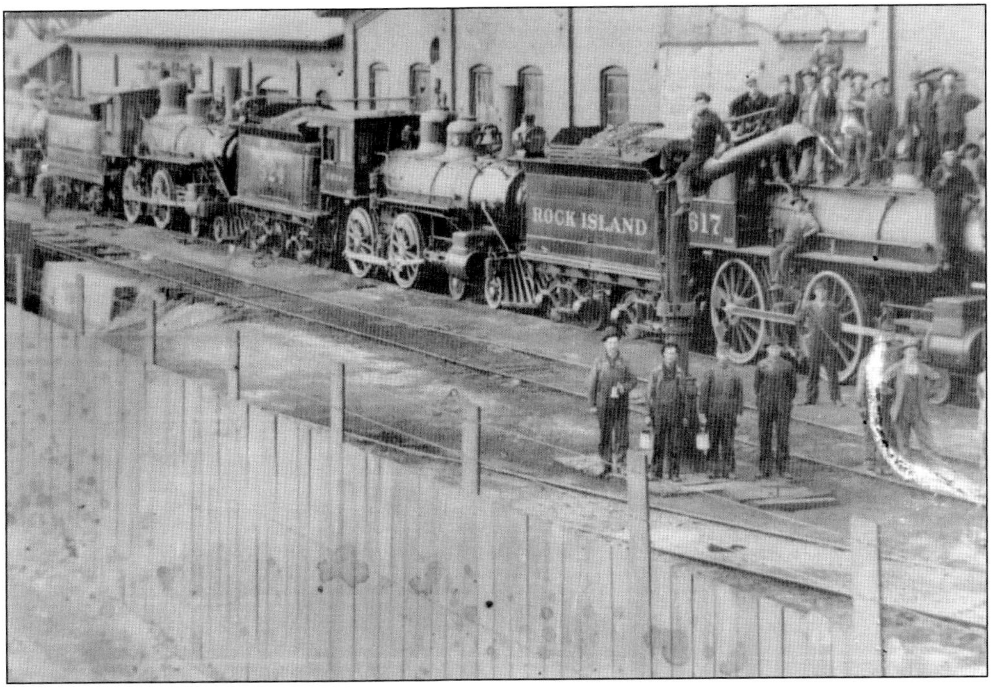

A group of men led by Al Jennings, an attorney, forced a railroad section gang to flag down a Rock Island train. Jennings and his men robbed the passengers and tried to blow up the safe. All were caught and charged with robbing the train—including the US mail, which as a federal crime carried a mandatory life sentence. In prison, Jennings used his legal skills. In an appeal, he was able to convince the courts that he had robbed the safe and the passengers but not the mail. Jennings was cleared and received a pardon from Pres. Theodore Roosevelt. Jennings returned to Oklahoma, where he ran for state offices and wrote his autobiography.

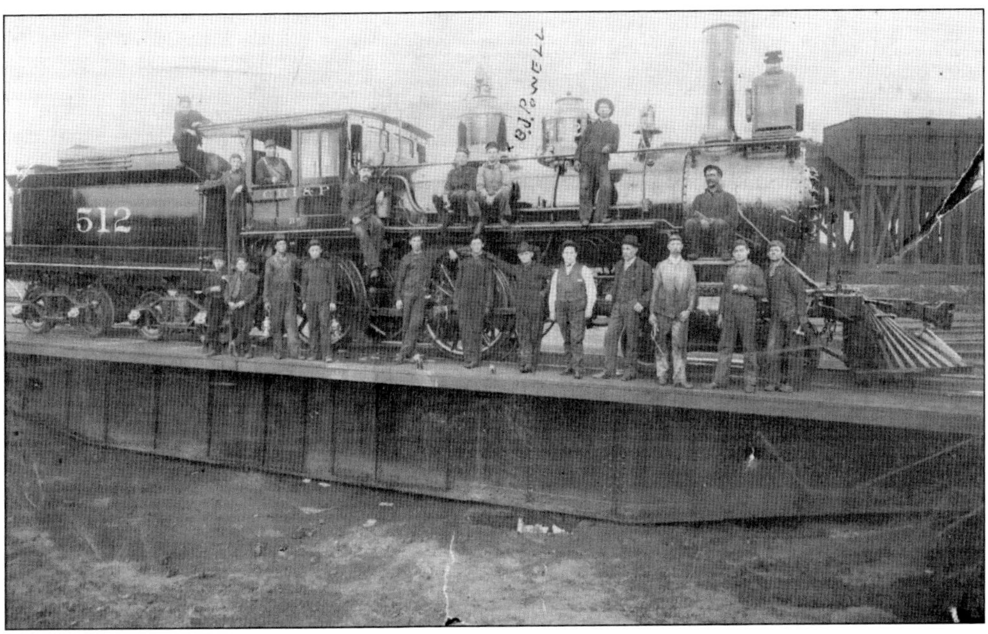

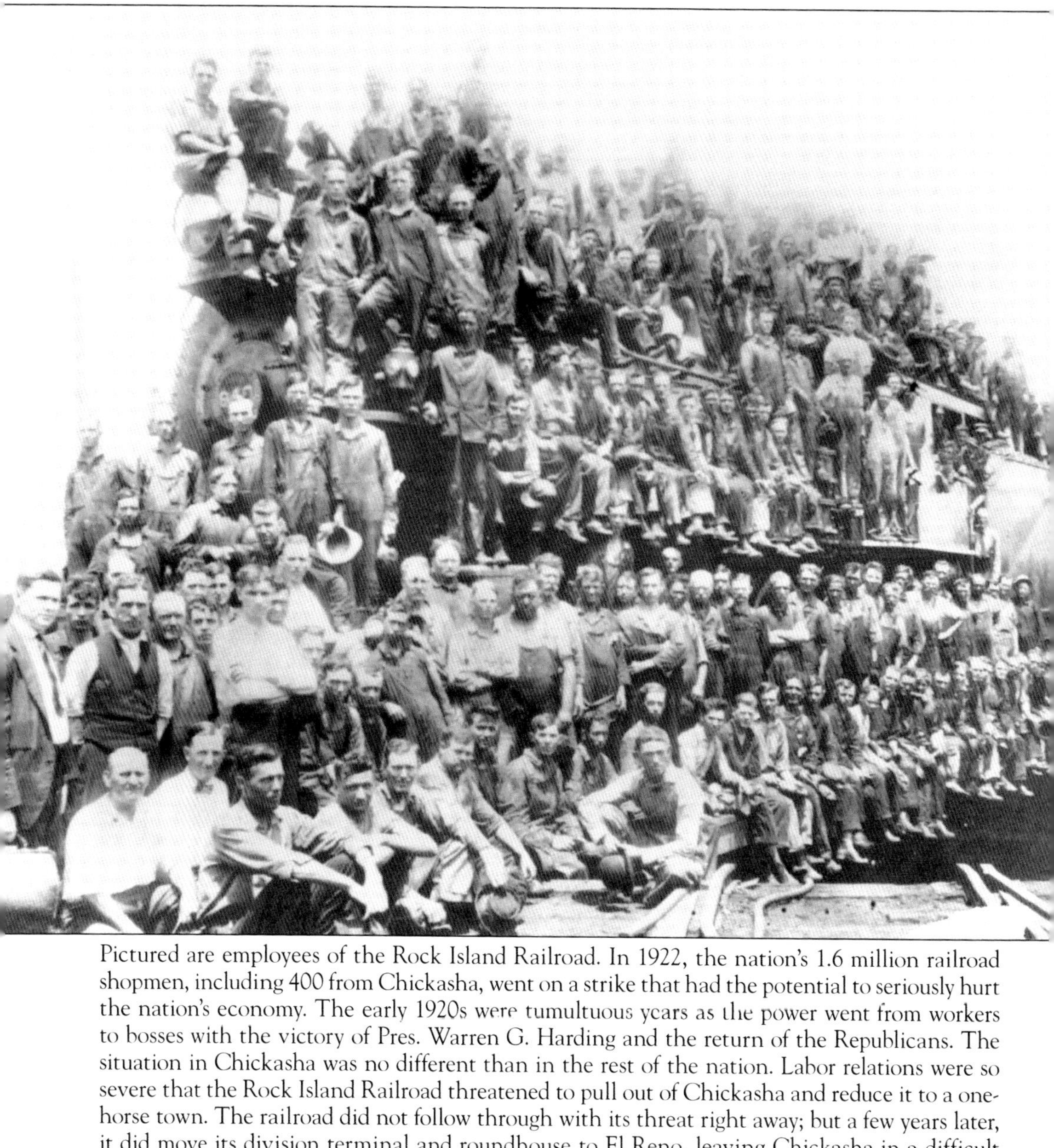

Pictured are employees of the Rock Island Railroad. In 1922, the nation's 1.6 million railroad shopmen, including 400 from Chickasha, went on a strike that had the potential to seriously hurt the nation's economy. The early 1920s were tumultuous years as the power went from workers to bosses with the victory of Pres. Warren G. Harding and the return of the Republicans. The situation in Chickasha was no different than in the rest of the nation. Labor relations were so severe that the Rock Island Railroad threatened to pull out of Chickasha and reduce it to a one-horse town. The railroad did not follow through with its threat right away; but a few years later, it did move its division terminal and roundhouse to El Reno, leaving Chickasha in a difficult position as men scrambled to find work.

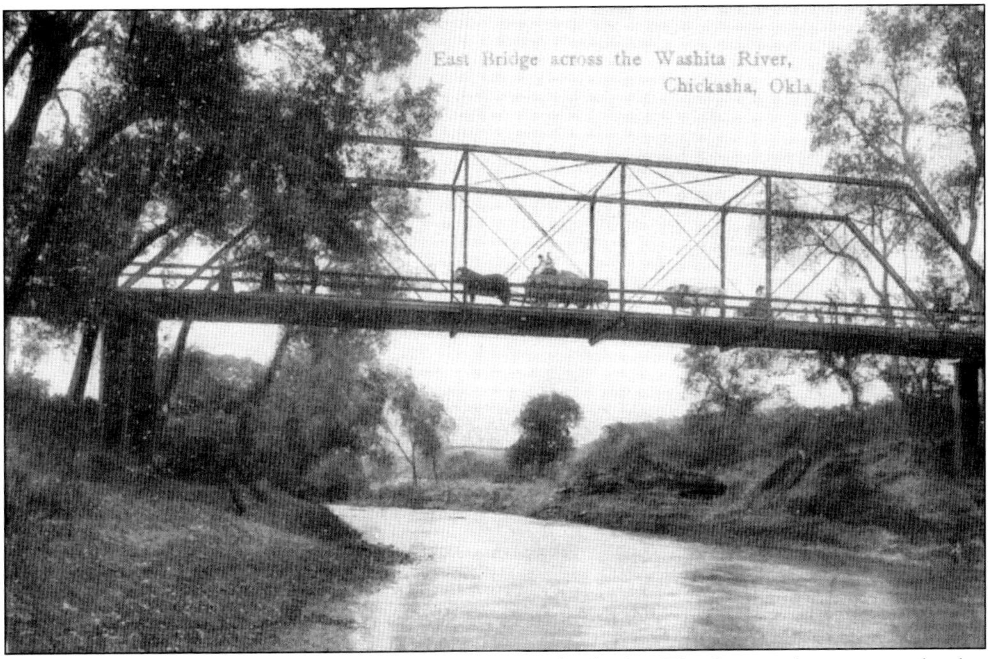

Pictured is the East Bridge over the Washita River in Chickasha. The first steel suspension bridge was built in 1894 and looked similar to the East Bridge. The first bridge was free-of-charge for any American Indians, but a toll was charged for everyone else. The bridge was 26 feet high and 250 feet long.

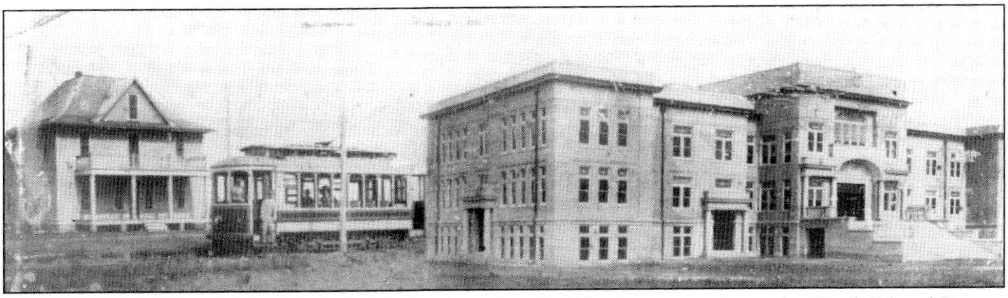

Chickasha's streetcar expanded over 6.5 miles of track. The line went from the Rock Island Depot along Chickasha Avenue all the way to the Oklahoma College for Women. Later, a spur was added to the baseball park. This picture is the station at the Women's College. From the angle of the picture, it looks as if the streetcar is as large as the three-story administration building.

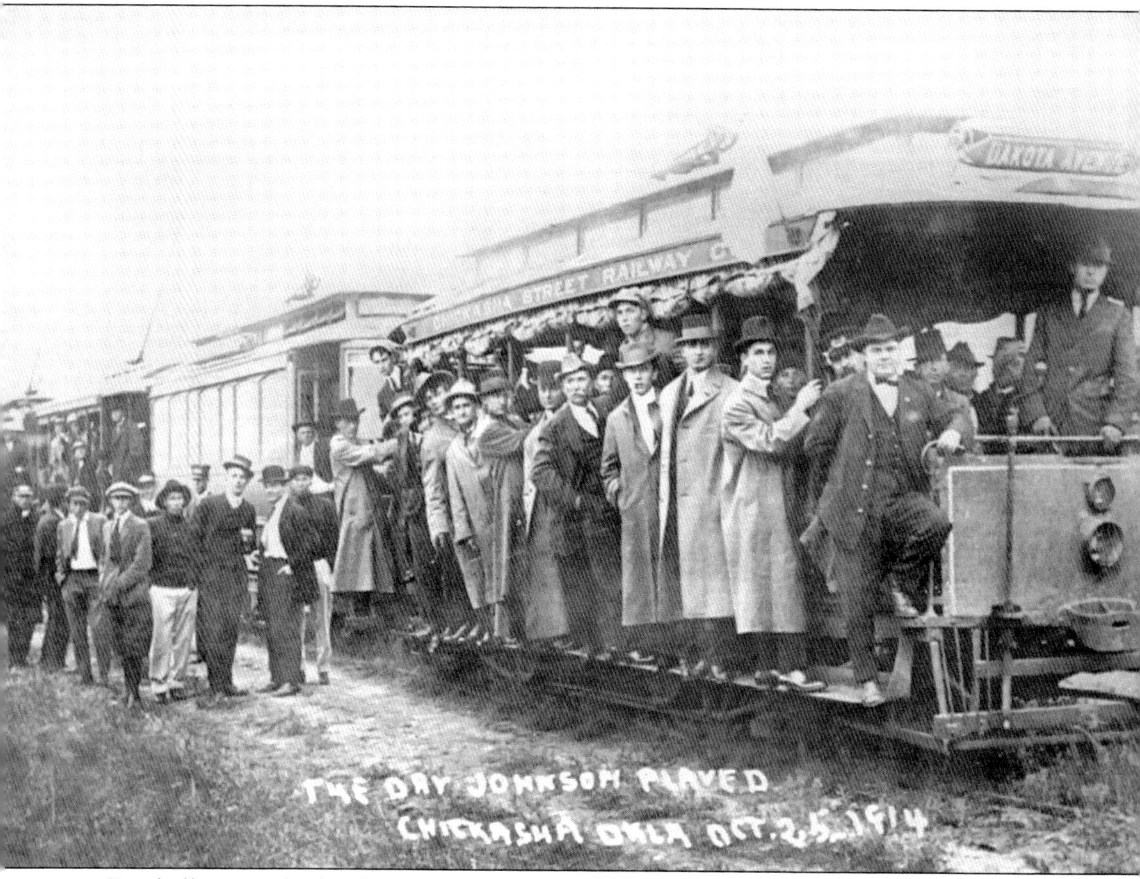

Baseball was truly the American pastime in Oklahoma, and small-town professional teams were all that the state had. In 1914, the towns of Minco and Geary both claimed the mantle of state champion. It was decided they would play a game at the ballpark in Chickasha. Wealthy men from Minco hired—for a few hundred dollars—"The Big Train" Walter Johnson, from the Washington Senators, to pitch for their team. As seen in the picture, fans from all over came to Chickasha to see the game, piling in the streetcars to get to the field. Johnson was known as one of the greatest pitchers of his time, he had thrown an American League record 416 winning games and pitched 113 shutouts. That day, in front of a crowd of over a 1,000 people, he won the game for Minco 6-0.

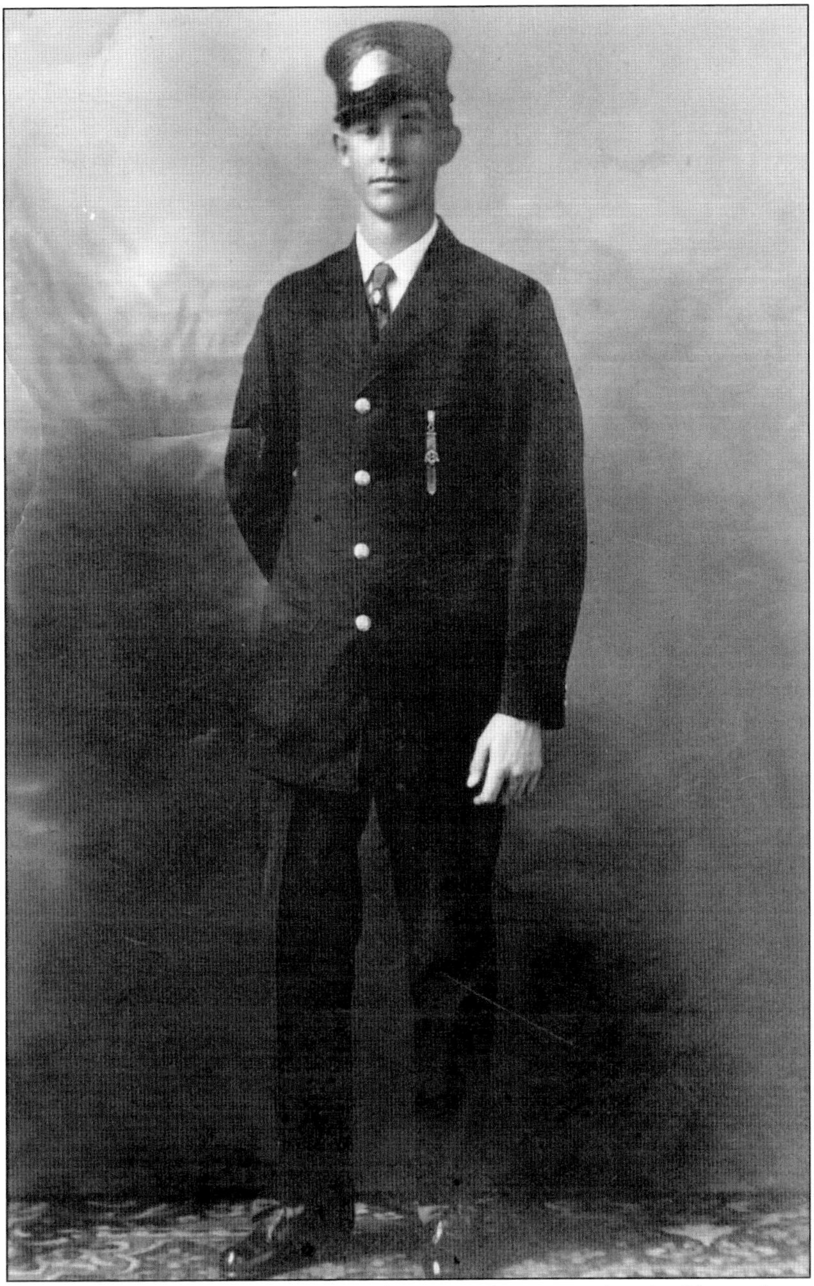

By 1910, Chickasha had a population of around 15,000—large enough to build a modern streetcar, known as the Chickasha Street Railway. It was opened in July 1910, with 1,615 fares on the first day, which brought in over $20,000. The 6.5-mile track had seven cars, both open and closed models. In the early years, the streetcar was very successful; in years before automobiles, the rail was very convenient. However, with the influx of cars, the rail lost much of its popularity. By the 1920s, the demand for the streetcars was gone. In a town the size of Chickasha, there was not a large need for public transportation; most things could be reached by walking, so in 1927, the streetcar was shut down. Afterwards, the tracks were torn out, guaranteeing it would not be brought back.

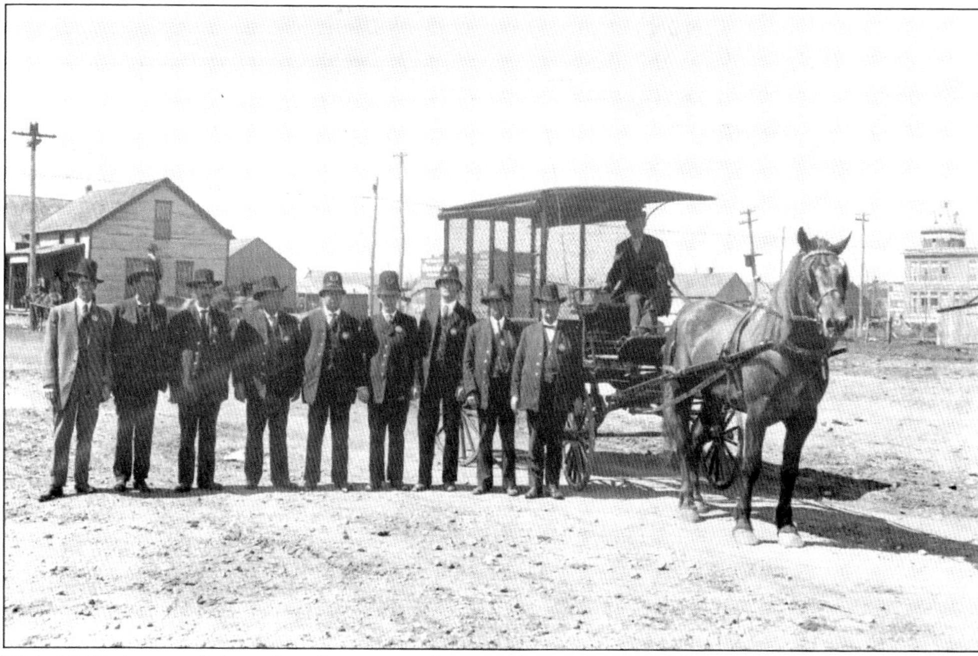

This 1909 picture of the police force was taken on the corner of Fifth Street and Choctaw Avenue in front of city hall. The first police department began in 1899 with the first elections for chief of police. John Hartman was the first chief, but with no real city ordinances to enforce, his job was minimal.

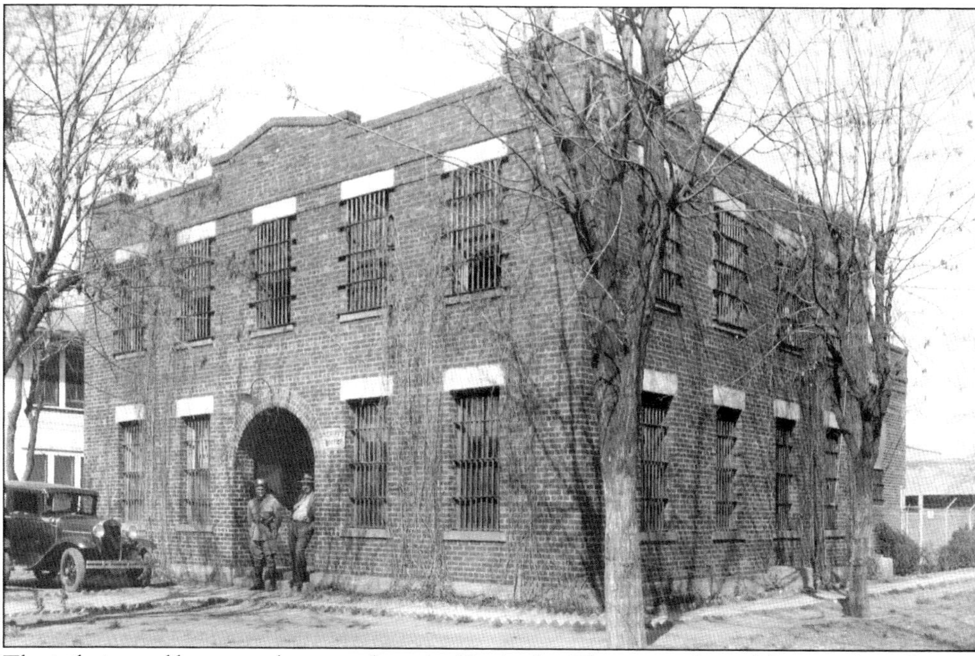

The jail pictured here was the second one in Chickasha. The original wood frame jail was located north of the courthouse but was later moved to Shanoan Springs Park. The 1982 *Chickasha Daily Express* described one of the jail's more violent earlier moments when a mob tried to break into the prison to remove and hang an inmate who was accused of rape.

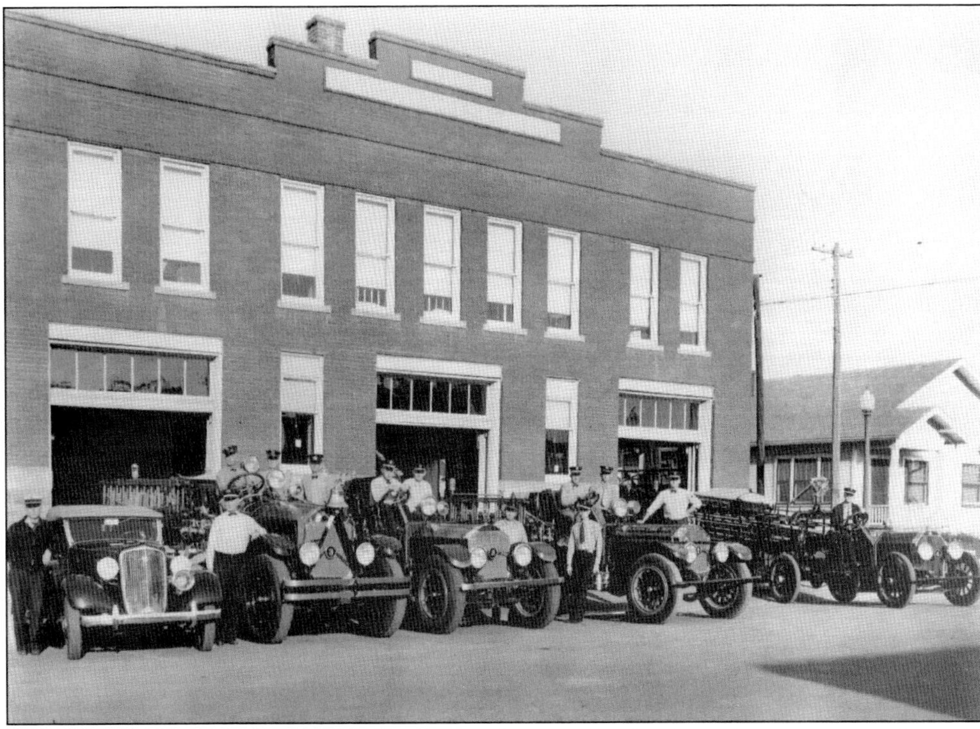

By reading this book, it should become obvious how much of a threat fires were not only to the early years, but to all of Chickasha's history. Several of the structures shown in these pages have been burned down. The first Chickasha fire department was nothing more than a volunteer bucket brigade. In 1900, the first official fire department was organized and housed in a small building on Forth Street and Kansas Avenue. At first, the engines were pulled by men, until the city bought them horses. This 1916 picture below shows one of the first fire vehicles, which grew, by 1934, to the fleet shown above.

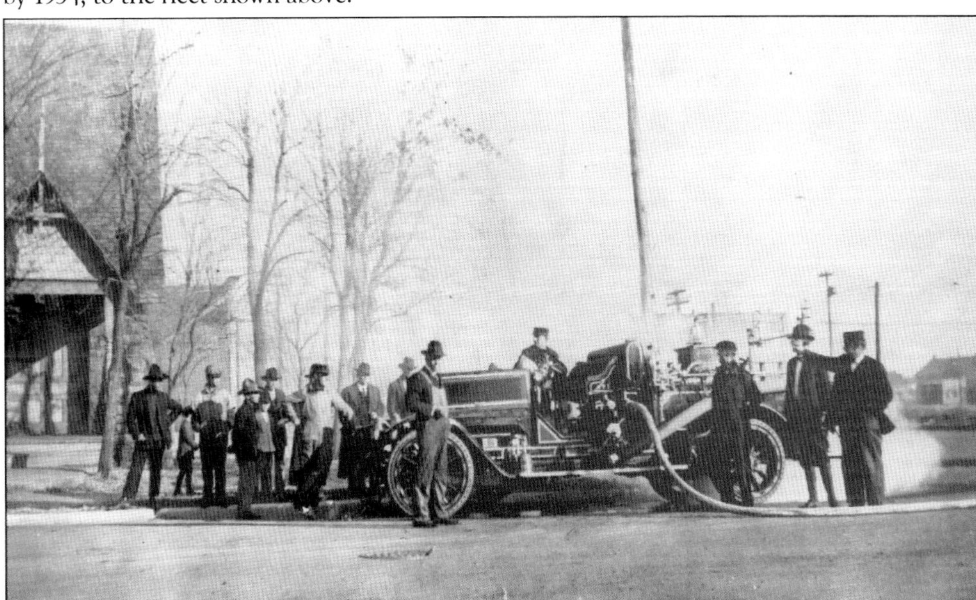

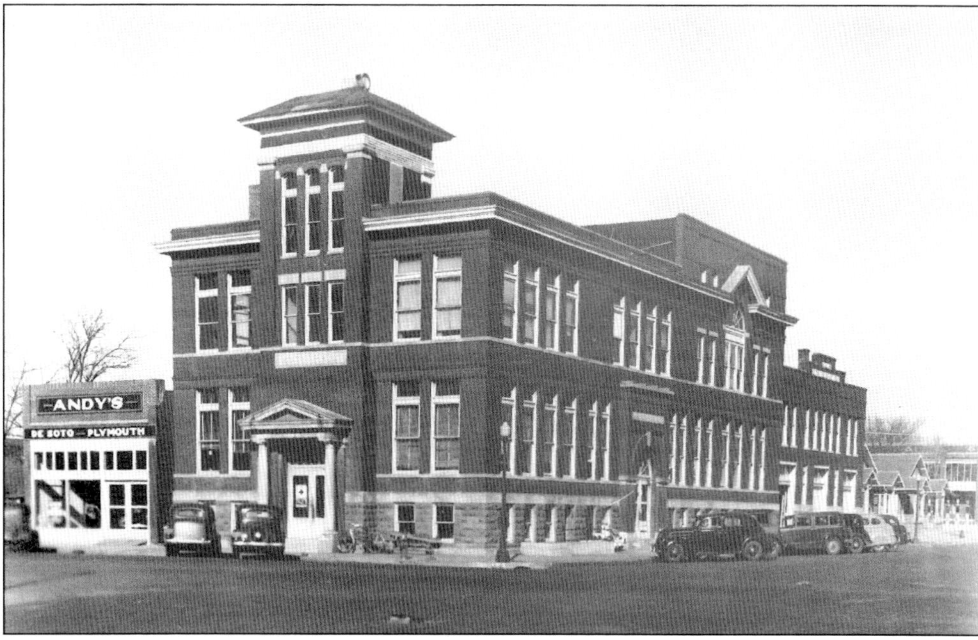

Shown in the above photograph, Chickasha's first city hall was built in 1909 at Sixth Street and Chickasha Avenue. Warning locals of floods, tornadoes, and other disasters, an emergency siren was perched on top of the building. The structure housed the city offices, police headquarters, and the fire station, complete with its horse-drawn fire truck. This original city hall was demolished in 1930, and a modern building (below) was constructed in its place; it was one of the first poured cement buildings. Today, the new building houses only Chickasha's police department, and the city hall is located in the town's old federal building at 117 North Fourth Street.

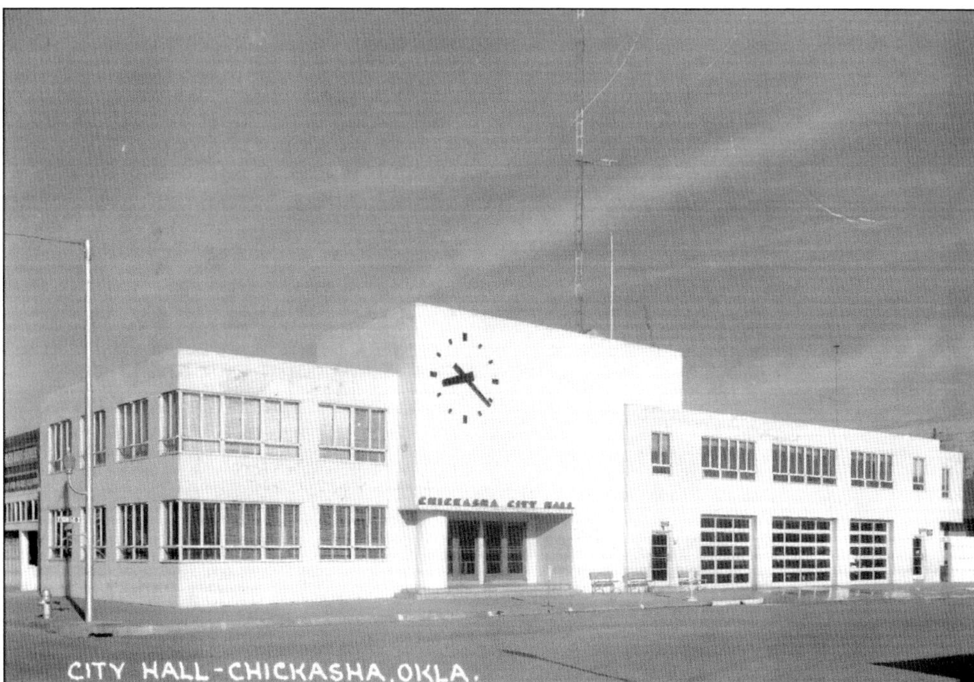

Two

Businesses

Chickasha has a rich economic history, from the Cowboy Saloon opening in the 1800s to Rue 21 opening in 2011. Chickasha has been home to businesses ranging from The Dixie clothing and home goods store to flower shops. One particular flower shop was owned by the Dews family, a prominent family in Chickasha for many years who provided the flower arrangements for many local weddings and funerals, as well as the ever-popular dozen roses to get the wayward husband out of trouble. Having come through the Depression, Chickasha has seen some tough economic times. Residents not only had access to clothing stores, but there were several grocery stores. Dunn's is one such grocery store that has stood the test of time. Shopping is only one business the citizens of this lovely city enjoy. There were many theaters, such as the Rialto, that provided a nice evening out for some.

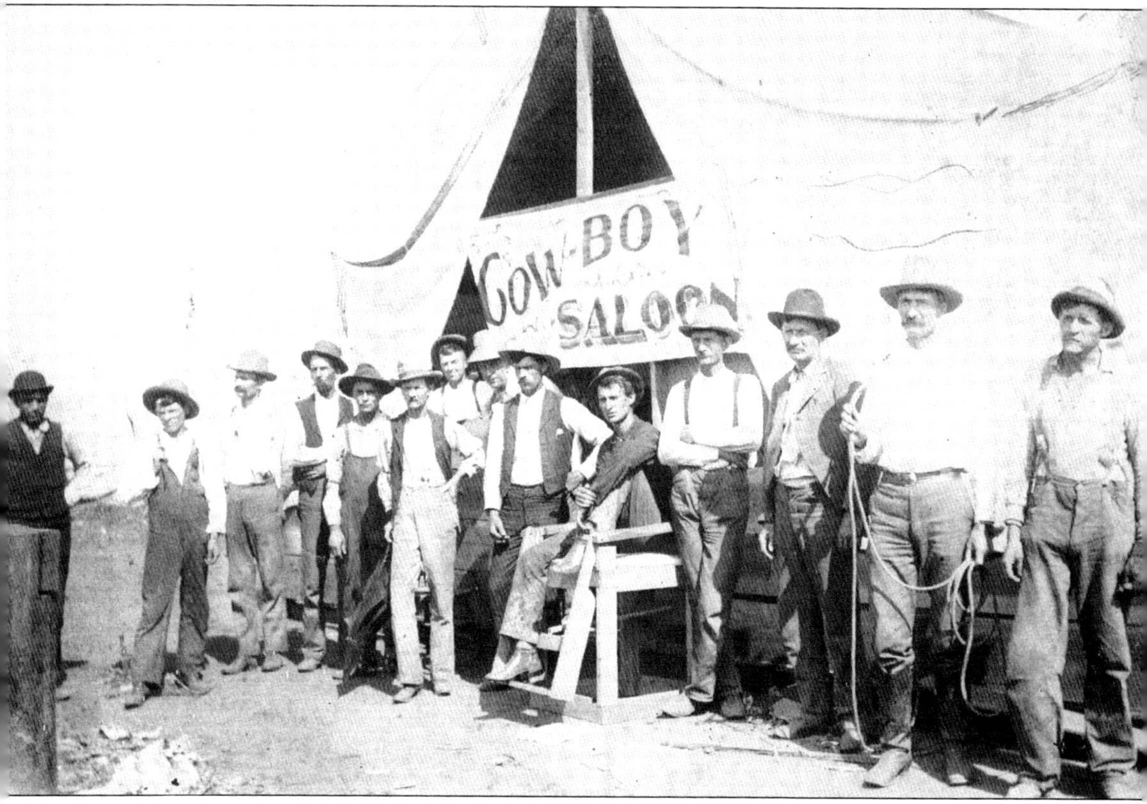

In many ways, Chickasha was a Western boomtown. It began as a tent city, but it did not take long for the population to rapidly expand. There was money to be made, so many looking for opportunity began to arrive. With a rowdy bunch of railroad men, saloons were some of the first businesses established. This picture is of the first known business in Chickasha, the Cowboy Saloon, which was nothing more than a tent. Before long, other bars and saloons, known as "Territorial Thirst Parlors" and including the Headlight and Tuxedo Club, appeared along the streets of Chickasha. Many drinking establishments were in the basements of large buildings, such as the Chickasha National Bank. A number of these businesses were also known gambling houses. Gambling was legal and acceptable in the early years, but with the Progressive Era, the federal and state government cracked down on such vice in 1916 and outlawed gambling. Of course, gambling never went away, and today's legalized gambling is a major source of revenue for Oklahoma.

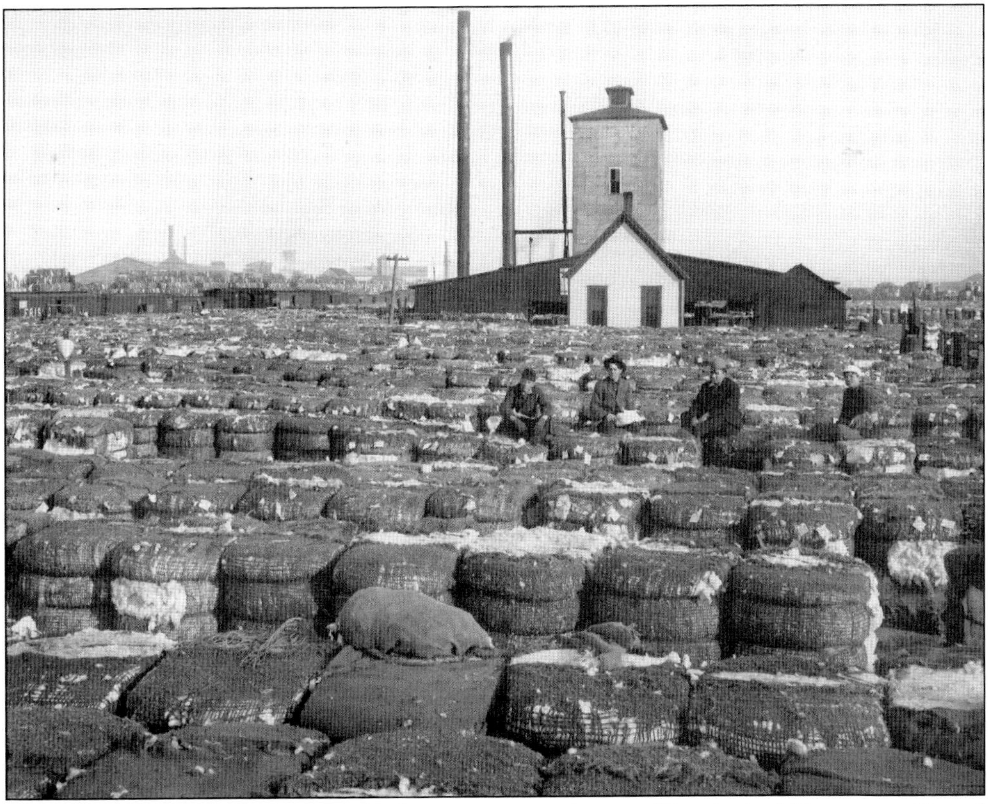

In the early years, Chickasha was a leader in cotton production. The city had 18 cotton mills and dozens of cotton gins. Cotton was slow to come to Chickasha and to Oklahoma. The Indians did not grow cotton, so it took until after the land opened to white settlers to know if cotton would even grow. In the early 20th century, cotton production was beginning in the state, and farmers soon saw the economic benefit. Cotton did so well in Oklahoma that by 1922, it was the most valuable crop in the state, and Oklahoma ranked fourth nationally in cotton production. In 1899, the Chickasha Cotton Oil Company formed; it incorporated in 1919. It sold cottonseed oil, cotton lint, baled cotton, felt, cottonseed meal, cottonseed cake, and feed. The company had the ability to separate over a million bales of cotton each season.

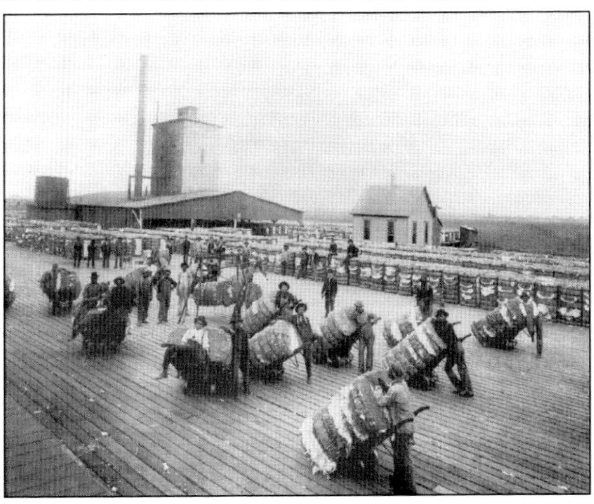

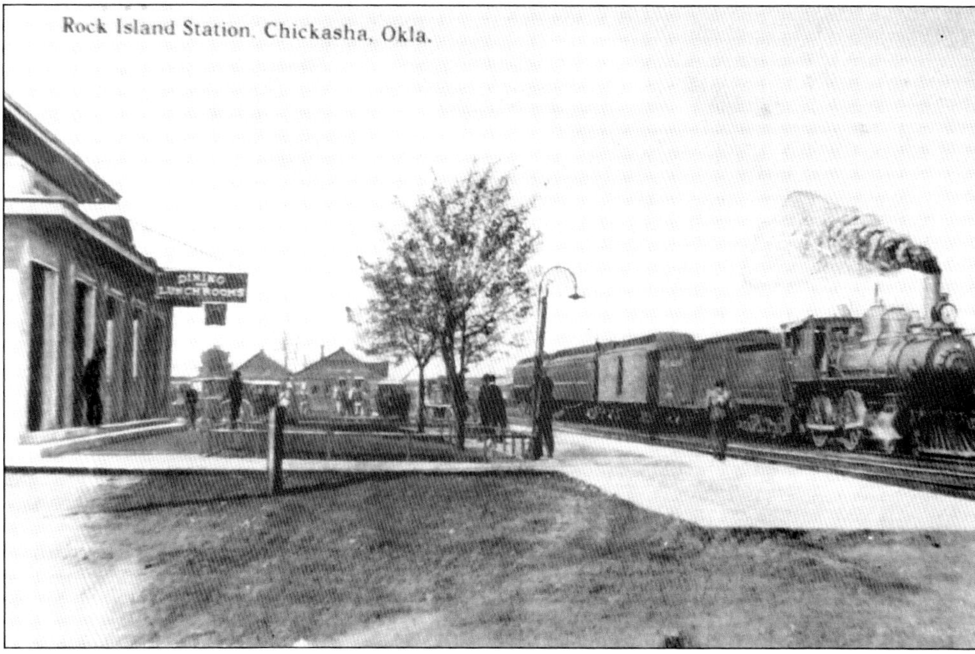

The Rock Island Railroad depot began as a boxcar in 1892, but as Chickasha became a more important stop, it had to make improvements. At the beginning of the 20th century, dining cars were not yet on trains, so passengers had to get off the train and eat at the stations. In 1908, the Rock Island Depot added a fancy dining room as well as a hotel, named the Geronimo (above), and a barbershop (below). The Geronimo was considered state-of-the-art at the time. People took the train just to stay and eat at the hotel. The barbershop took up an entire bottom floor and had six chairs. J.E. Holloway and D. Lee Holloway are pictured giving a shave and a cut.

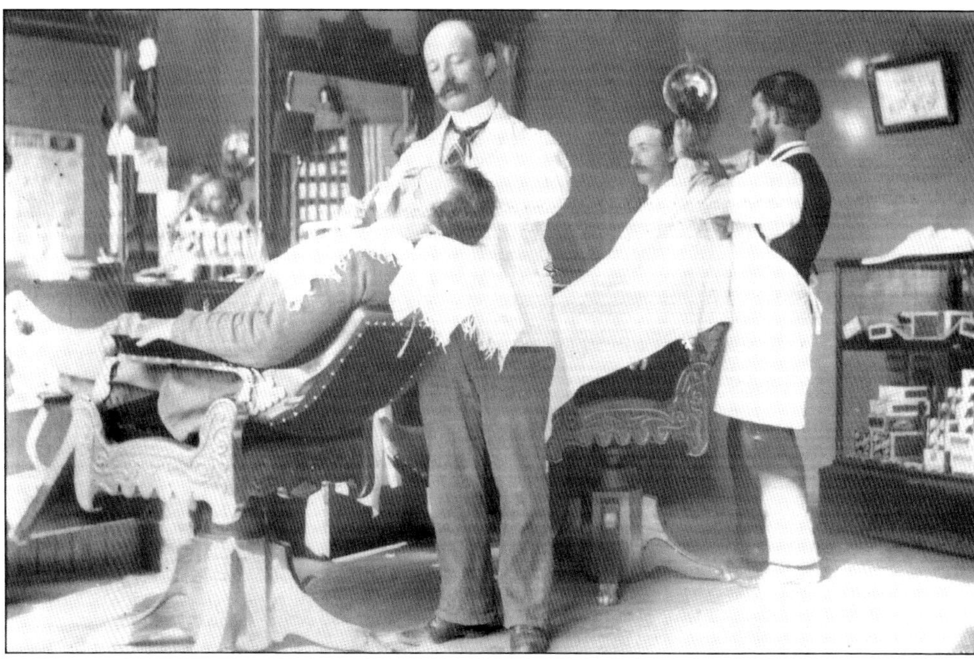

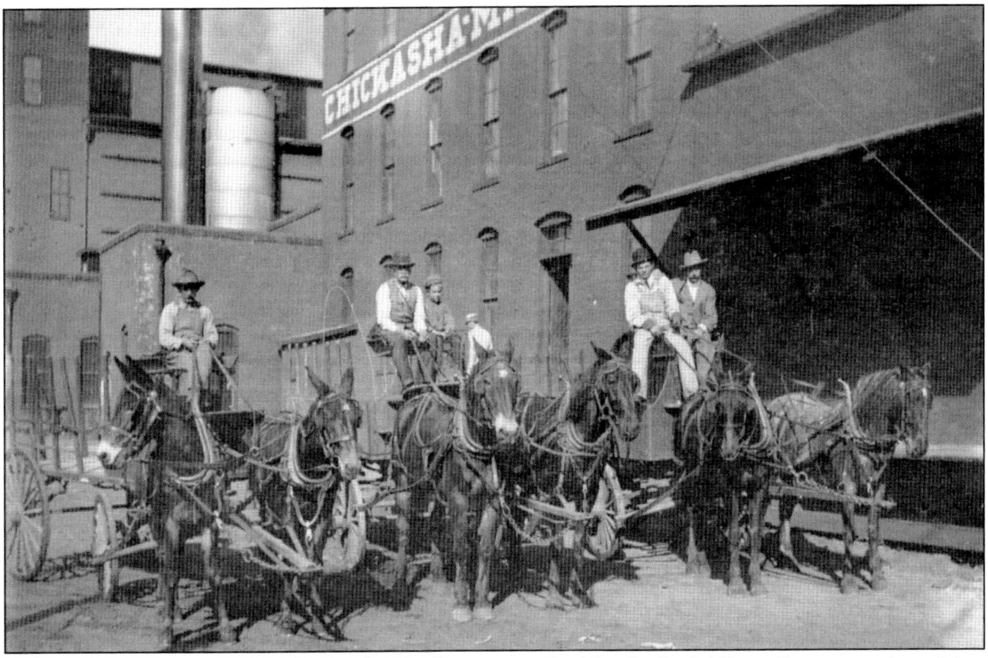

The July 27, 1901, edition of the *Modern Miller* praises the Chickasha Milling Company: describing it as a three-story structure having the latest machinery in good order. There is a large corncrib on the property and a fine track scale in connection to the elevator. The office is detached from the mill to avoid dust. The milling company was established in 1899 on the corner of Chickasha and Choctaw Avenues. It produced the Full Cream and Searchlight labels, made from hard wheat flour; and the Bouquet and Queen of Dixie brands, made from soft wheat flour. Above are some of the deliverymen set to move their products. Pictured below is the grain elevator. Today, the elevator still towers over downtown Chickasha and is a major landmark.

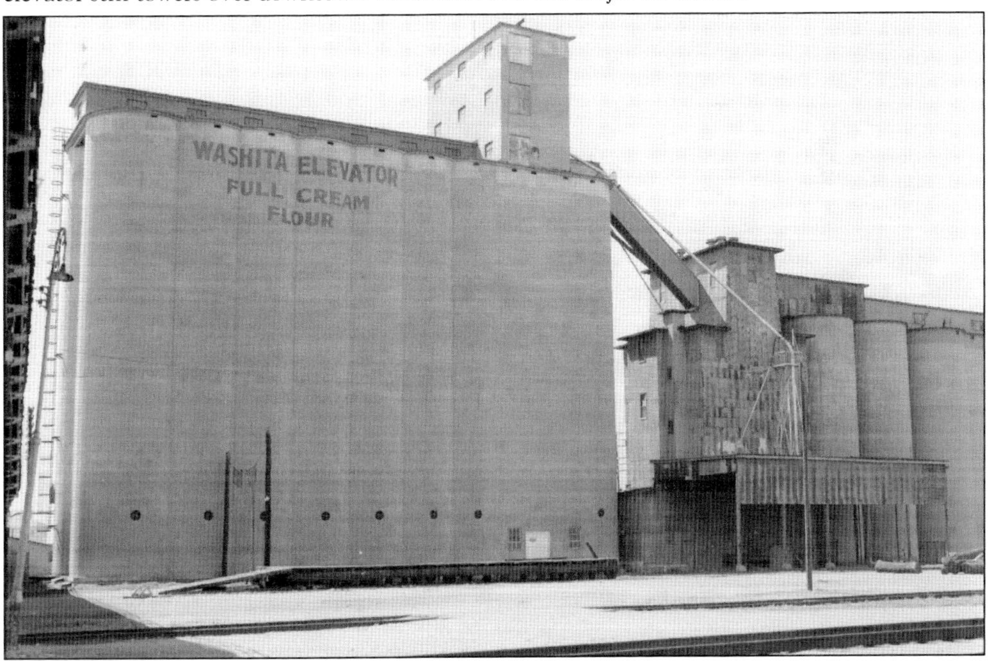

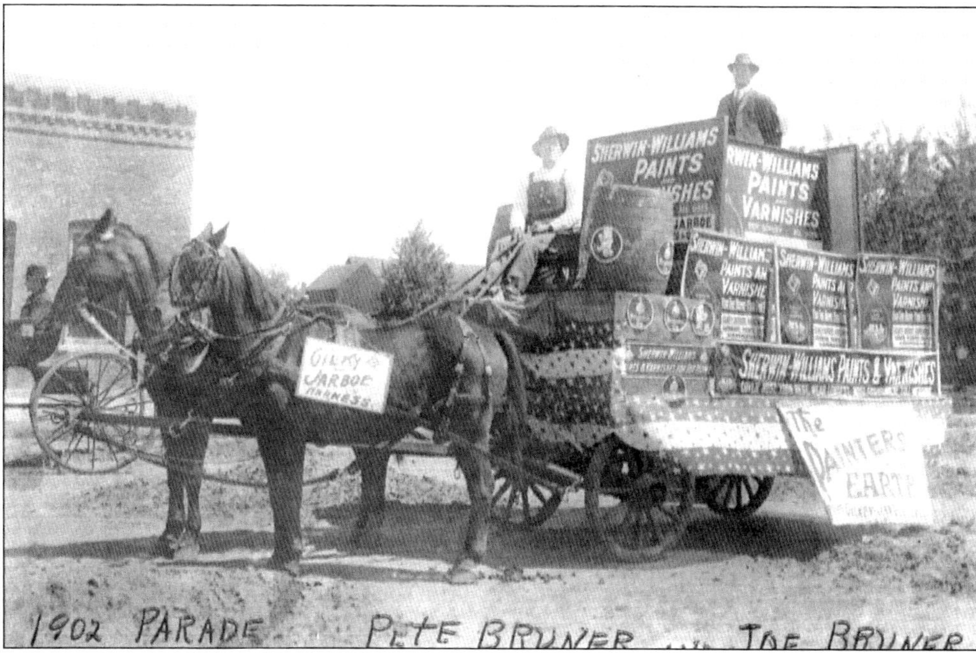

In this 1902 parade picture, Pete and Joe Bruner are advertising the new Sherman-Williams products from Gilkey and Jarboe Hardware. Henry Sherman and Edward Williams began their paint company in 1866 in Cleveland, Ohio. With so much that needed painting, the first Sherman-Williams representative arrived in Oklahoma the same week that it was opened to white settlement.

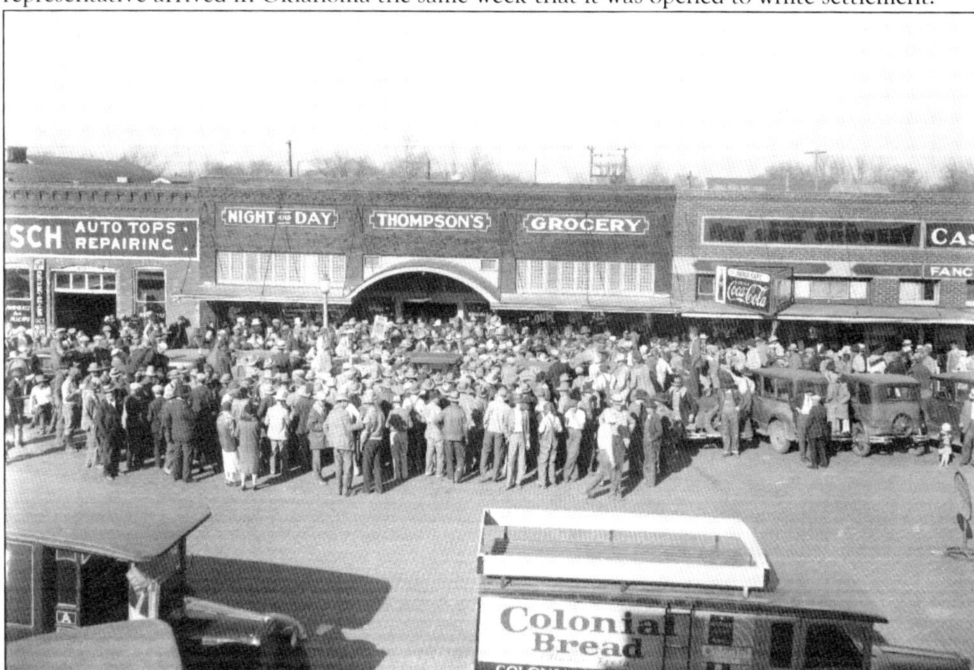

This photograph shows a crowd gathered outside of Thompson's Grocery for a giveaway. The picture was taken during the Great Depression, when anything free was a blessing. The little café to the right was called Nickel Café because it only cost a nickel to buy a hamburger and coffee.

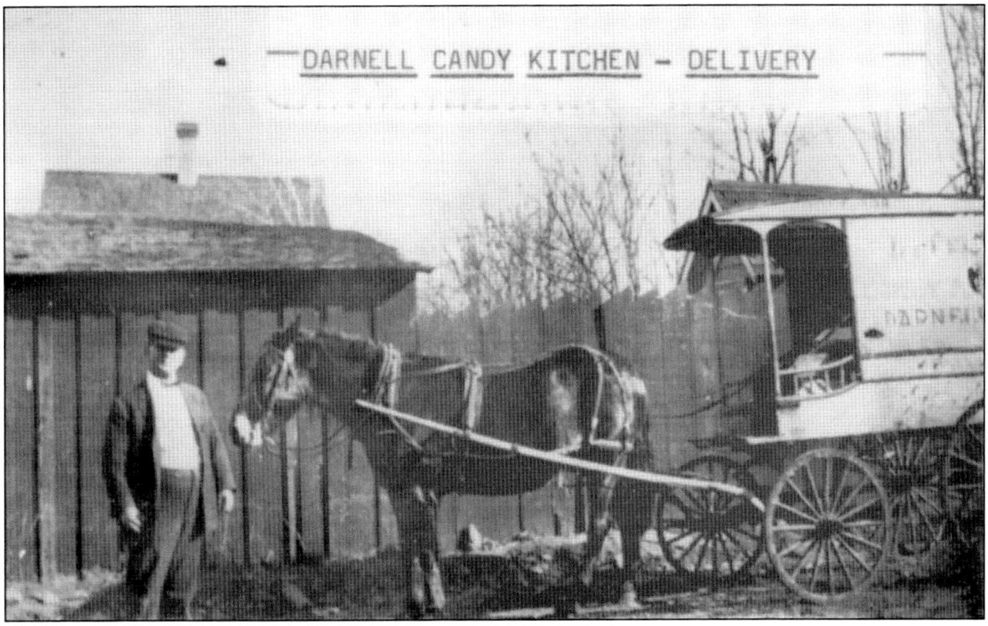

A popular attraction for adults and youth alike was Darnell's Confectionery. Y.W. Darnell arrived in Chickasha in 1903 and began tempting Chickasha citizens with his tasty treats. Darnell sold hand-pulled taffy and stick candy year-round, and also pecan, coconut, and peanut brittle. He was also famous for his fudge. His wife had her own shop, where she would make hand-dipped chocolates. Darnell kept his supplies of coconut, syrup, and chocolate in the back, where the candy could be made in copper kettles (below). As well as candy, the shop sold cigars, cigarettes, and fountain drinks. He also offered homemade ice cream that he would deliver (above).

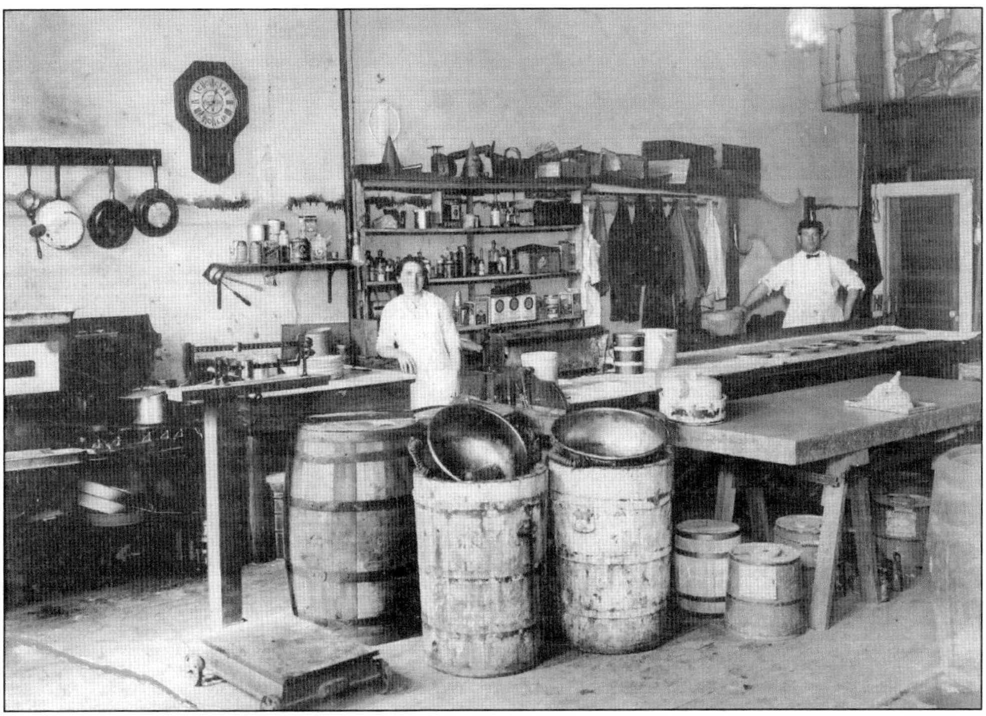

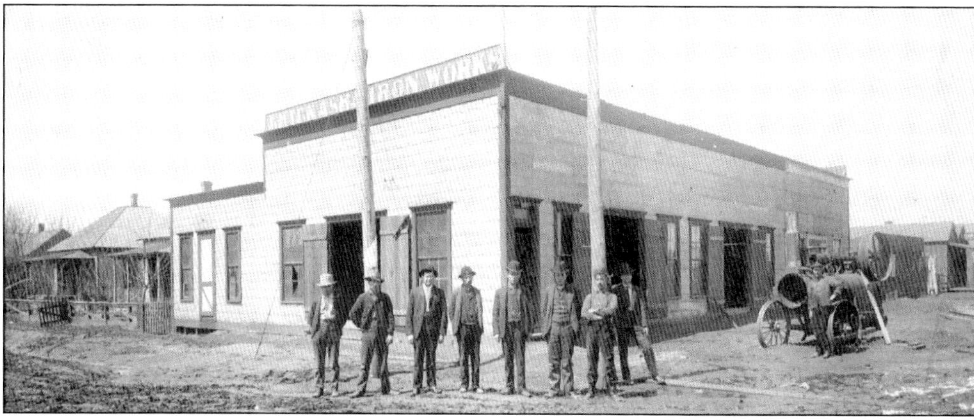

Here is an early picture of the employees of the Chickasha Iron Works. Started in 1898 by G.P. Rogers, the Chickasha Iron Works was one of the largest foundries and machine shops in Oklahoma. In 1904, it was bought by the Conrad brothers. The brothers were expert machinists employed by the Rock Island Railroad.

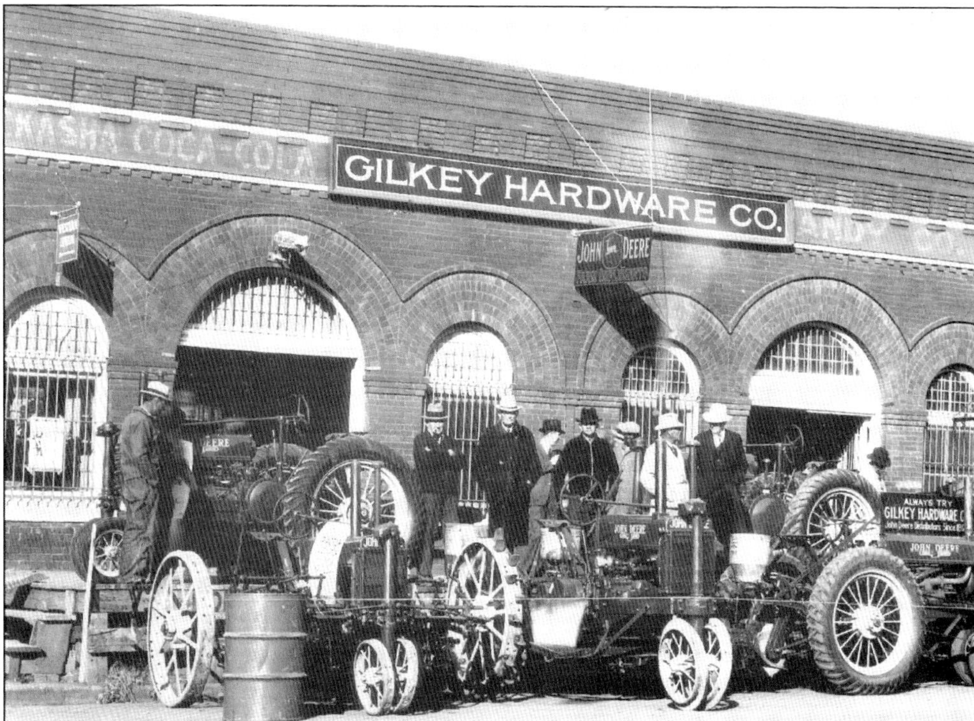

This is a 1930s photograph of the Gilkey Hardware Company. The street in front of Gilkey's is a perfect example of a street paved with bricks. Gilkey was advertising the new John Deere tractors. Agriculture was an important part of Chickasha's economy. Deere & Company acquired the manufacturer of Waterloo Boy tractors in 1918, and its tractors carried that name until 1923, when the John Deere name first appeared on tractors.

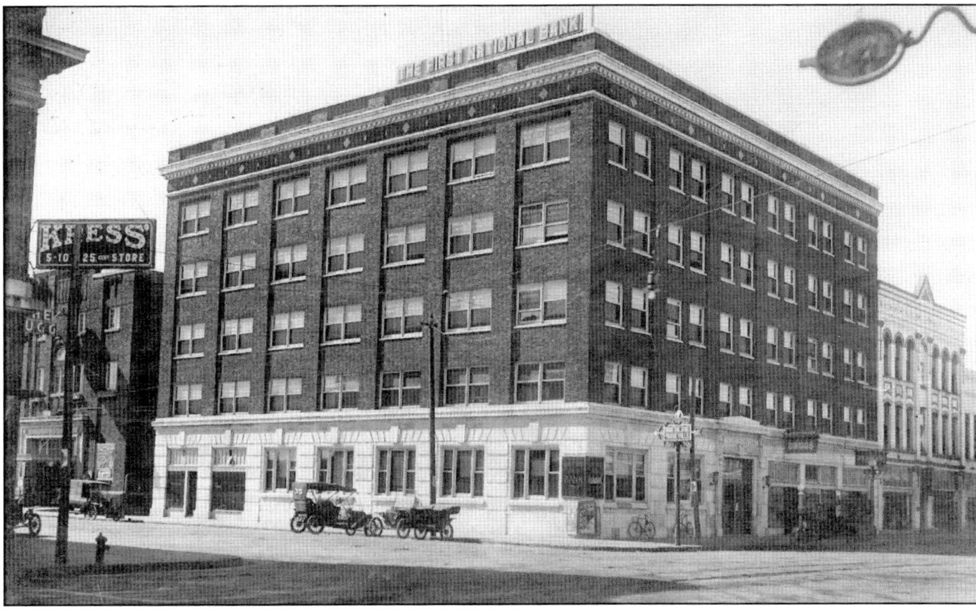

With the founding of Chickasha, the Citizens Bank was also created. This bank was simply a tent with armed guards. Quickly, other banks formed with more permanent structures. The Bank of Chickasha opened in 1894, and the First National Bank of Chickasha opened in 1900. Pictured here, the First National Bank building was constructed in 1913 by J.D. Sugg, who also operated the Sugg Theatre.

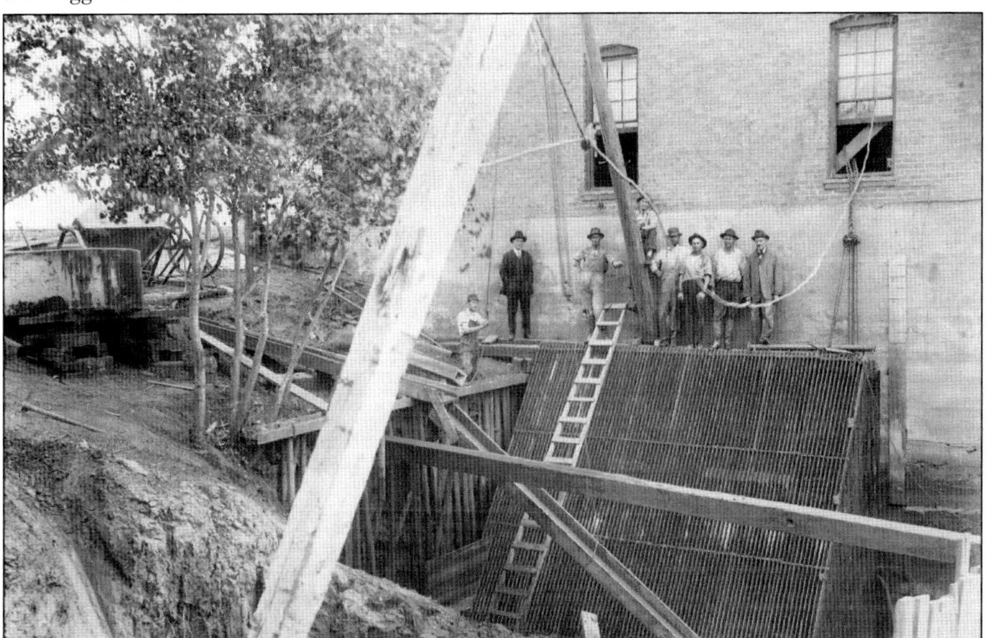

This picture shows the electric waterpower dam that was built by the Chickasha Electric Company in 1909. The dam was built along the Washita River, where it failed to serve the ulterior purpose of blocking the water when the river would rise and flood Chickasha. The electric company was opened around the early 1900s, and in 1902, it was located at First Street and Colorado Avenue.

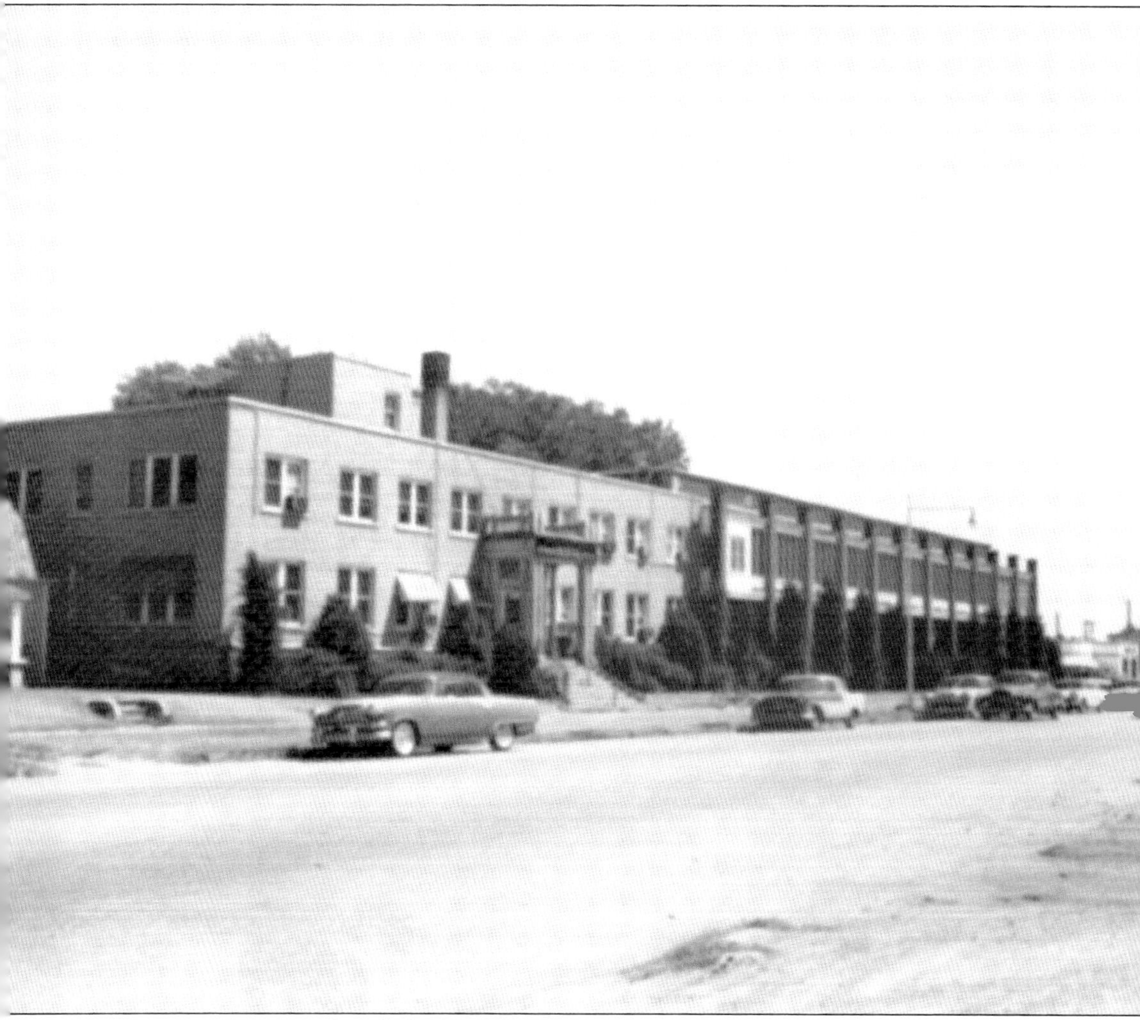

On January 19, 1978 the *Chickasha Daily Express* wrote about early medical care, stating that "the snakes on Hermes's staff, the symbol of physicians, were probably rattlesnakes in early Chickasha." The city's first doctor arrived in 1892 to treat the new community's ills. About 10 years later, in 1904, Dr. W.L Peters arrived and built the city's first hospital, which only had five beds and was actually part of his home. In 1910, Dr. Walter Henry Livermore moved to town and built an updated hospital over the Dugan Department Store. Two years later—with the help of his new partner, Dr. D.S. Downey—Dr. Livermore moved the hospital to the newer building over the First National Bank. Finally, in 1915, the two men purchased the apartment building shown here and turned it into a hospital. The Livermores lived in one part of the building. They also let some the nurses who were training live in the hospital.

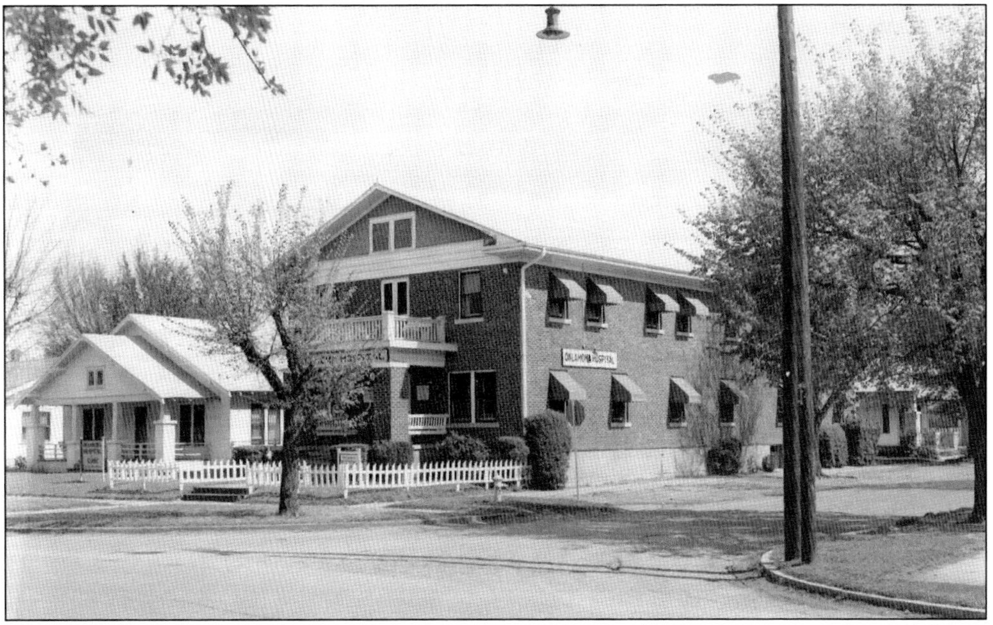

The Cottage Hospital was started in 1923 by Dr. L.E. Emanuel. The Great Depression hit Oklahoma hard. Families did not have the income to spend on basic health-care needs. One consequence of the economic times was the closure of medical facilities. The Cottage Hospital was one such institution. Later, Dr. Charles Ohl bought the hospital and reopened it as the Women's and Children's Hospital.

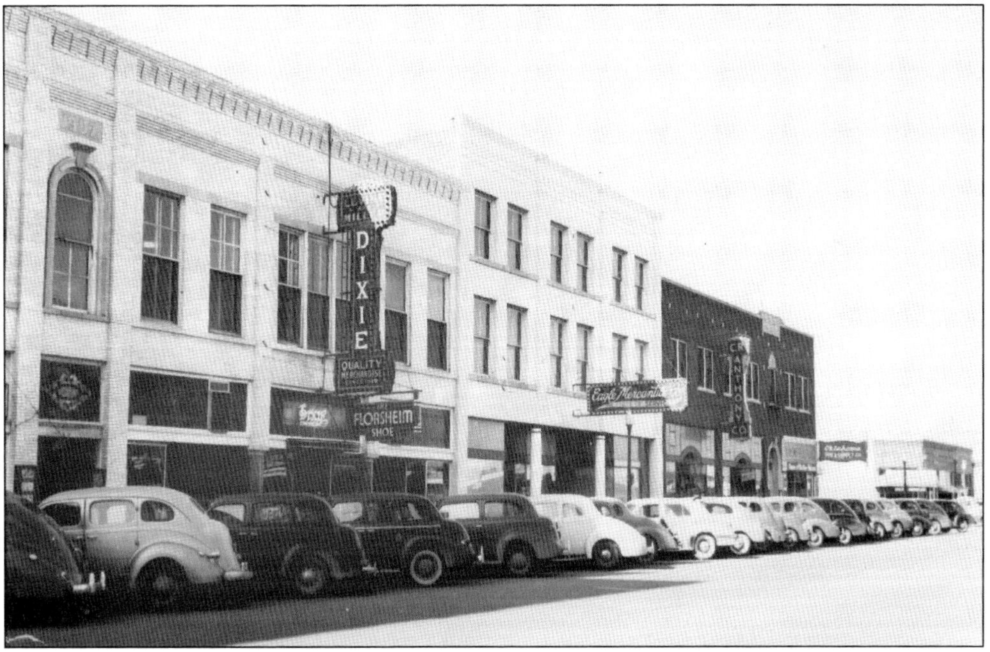

The new Dixie department store opened its doors on March 8, 1919, and promised its customers that no large city store would have more up-to-date clothes or other "nifty stuff." Ben Levine and Charles Miller were the original owners of the two-story building, and Miller was still part of the operations 41 years later. Today, the Dixie houses the Grady County Historical Society.

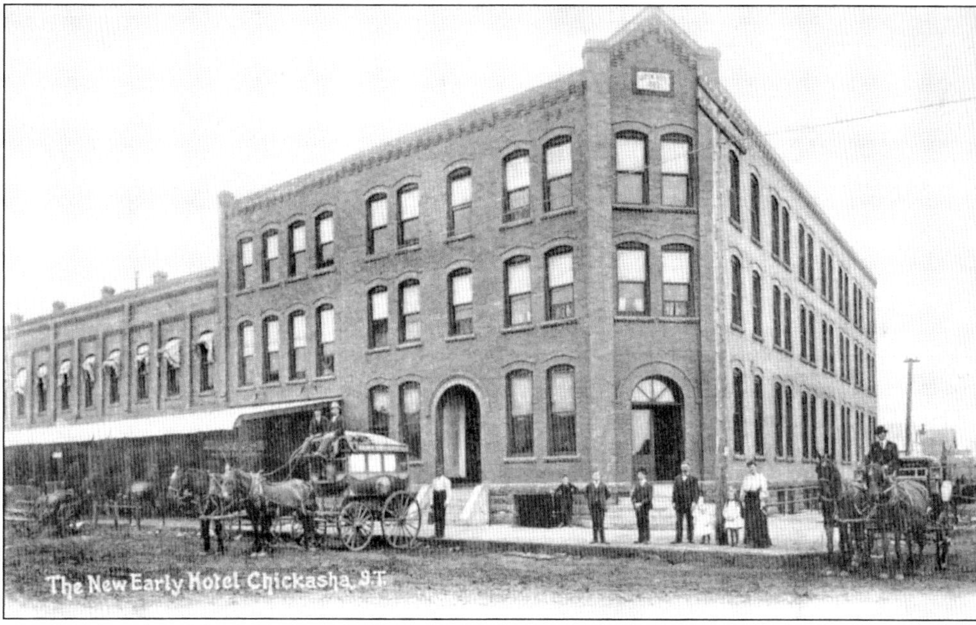

The first hotel in Chickasha was built in 1892 and was called the Western. The next year, James H. Griffin built the Grand Avenue Hotel. With a raised floor and pigs living under it, it was far from a fancy establishment. In 1901, the Grand burned down along with the whole block, but Griffin built the New Early Hotel in 1903 that took up the entire block.

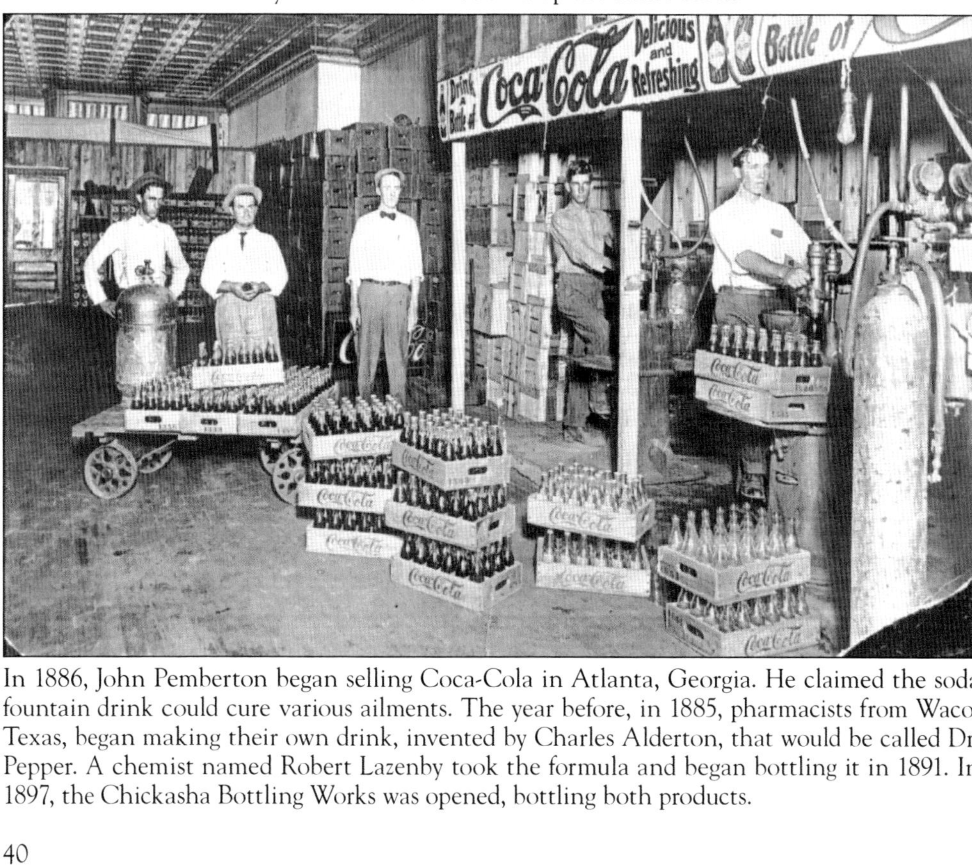

In 1886, John Pemberton began selling Coca-Cola in Atlanta, Georgia. He claimed the soda fountain drink could cure various ailments. The year before, in 1885, pharmacists from Waco, Texas, began making their own drink, invented by Charles Alderton, that would be called Dr. Pepper. A chemist named Robert Lazenby took the formula and began bottling it in 1891. In 1897, the Chickasha Bottling Works was opened, bottling both products.

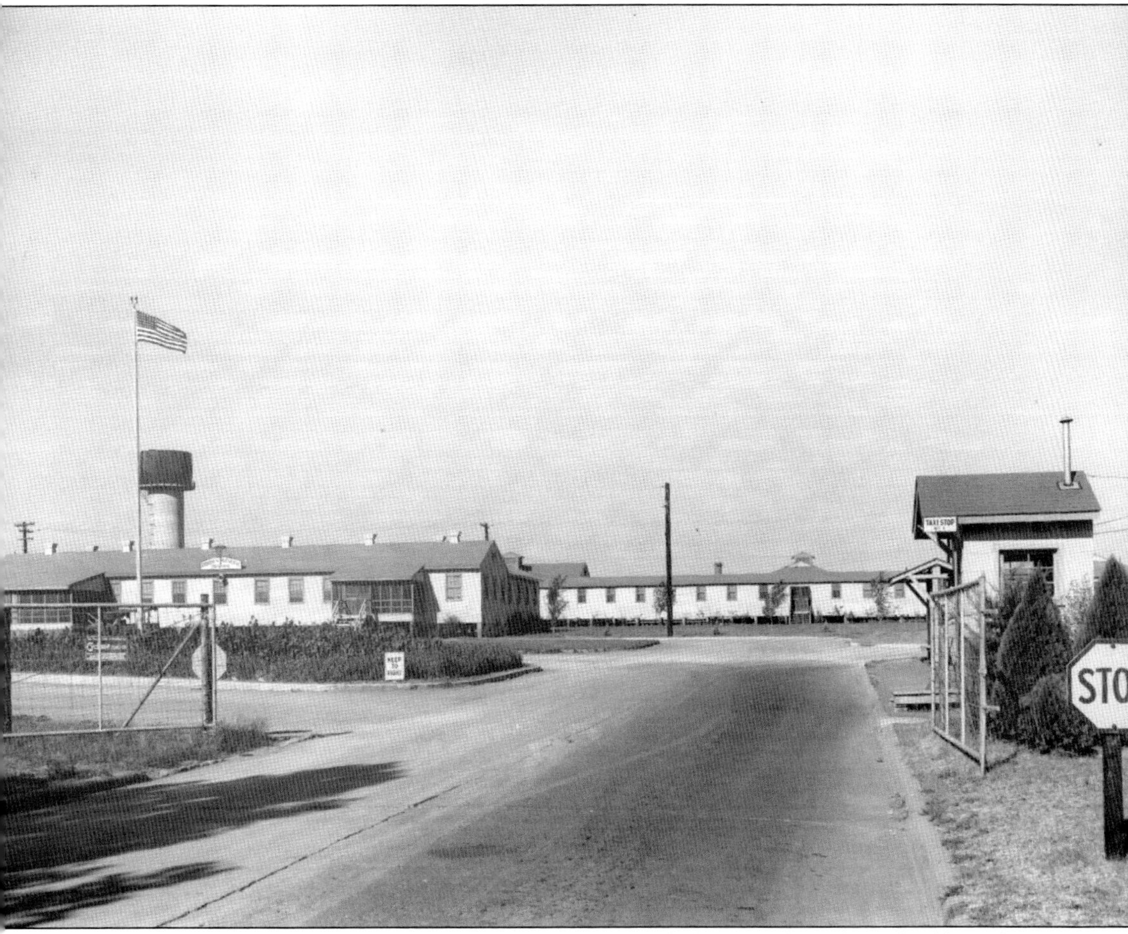

In 1942, during World War II, Chickasha lobbied the Army and obtained the rights to build Borden General Hospital. The hospital was under the direction of the 49th Medical Unit. Some of the work done at the hospital was performed by German prisoners of war housed at the fairgrounds. The first American troops started arriving at the Frisco Railroad Station in 1943 after fighting in the Pacific. The hospital was designed to hold 1,000 beds, but beginning in 1944, it had to make more room. From December 1944 through January 1945, American troops in Europe engaged in what became known as the Battle of the Bulge. American causalities (dead, wounded, and missing) were over 89,000, and many wounded soldiers made their way to Chickasha. Today, the site where Borden Hospital sat contains the Grady Memorial Hospital. In 1956, a bond was passed to raise the $930,000 necessary to construct a modern facility, and that hospital opened its doors in 1959. A county health clinic was also built.

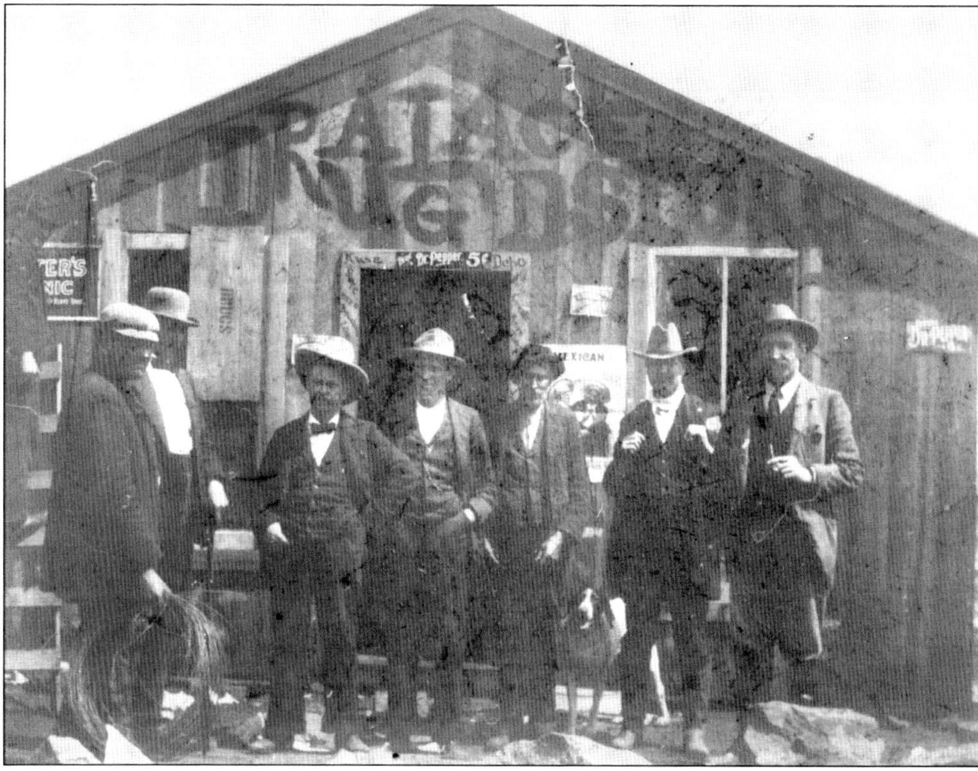

The Palace Drug was a drugstore owned by James Pettyjohn in 1892. It was originally a small wooden building located at 203 Chickasha Avenue when the area was still Indian Territory. Afterwards, the Palace Drug moved into and out of several different locations in town, even having two stores open at once. In the Palace Drug's newer building (interior pictured below), there was a mezzanine where Dr. D.M. Johnston kept his office for his doctor's practice at one time. Dr. Johnston was one of Chickasha's first doctors, moving into the area in 1892, soon before an outbreak of illnesses like typhoid fever, malaria, and smallpox.

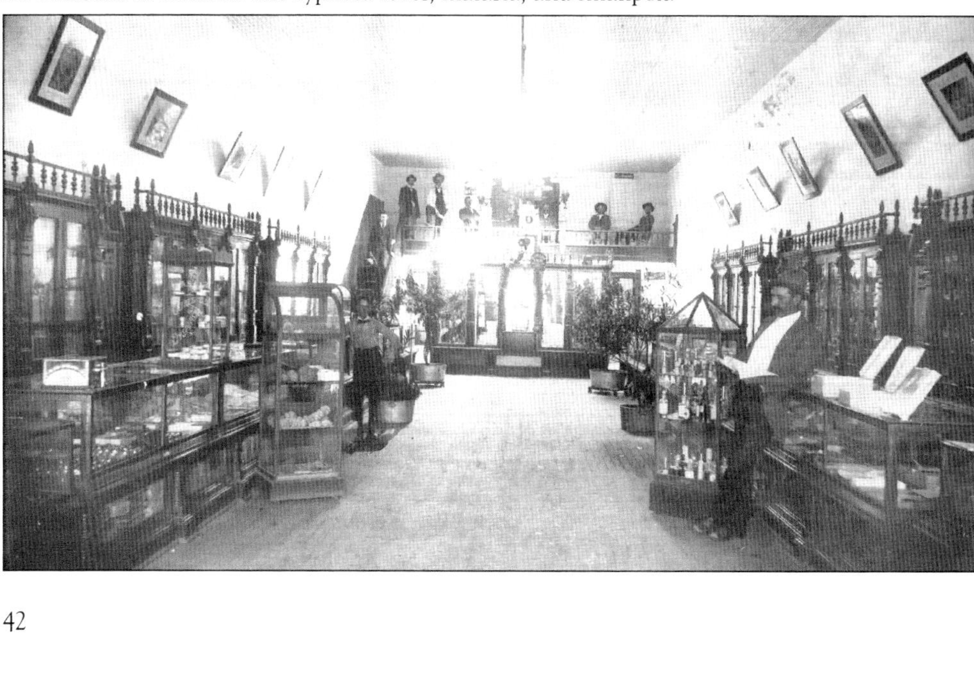

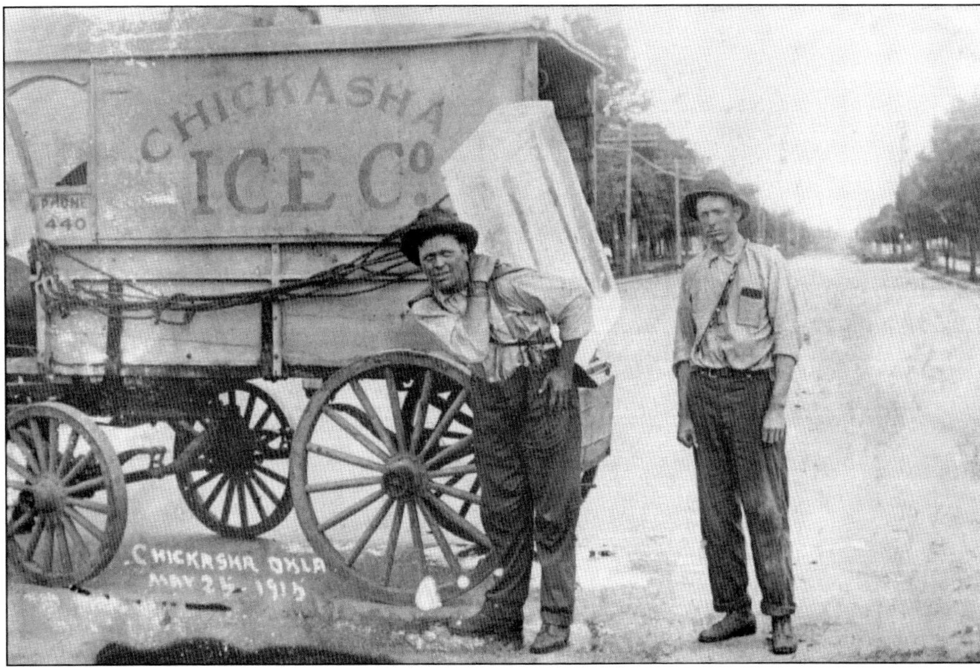

Before the discovery of electricity and the invention of refrigerators, ice was necessary to keep food cold and unspoiled. The Chickasha Ice Plant was built in 1915 at the corner of Sixth Street and Frisco Avenue. An ammonia solution was pushed through pipes immersed in saltwater to make blocks of ice in metal containers. This picture shoes Andrew and Jim Farley delivering ice for the company.

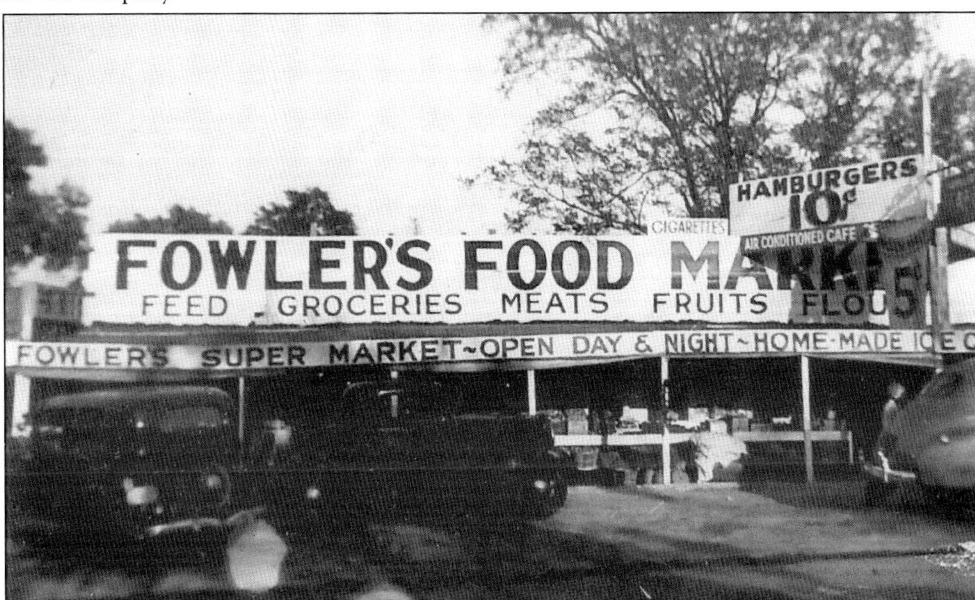

Fowler's Food Mart was an example of early business in Chickasha and the city's first supermarket. Olin Fowler had an oddity at the business that made it famous: he built his store around a tree that continued to grow in his shop. Fowler sold groceries as well as damaged freight items. He later added a café.

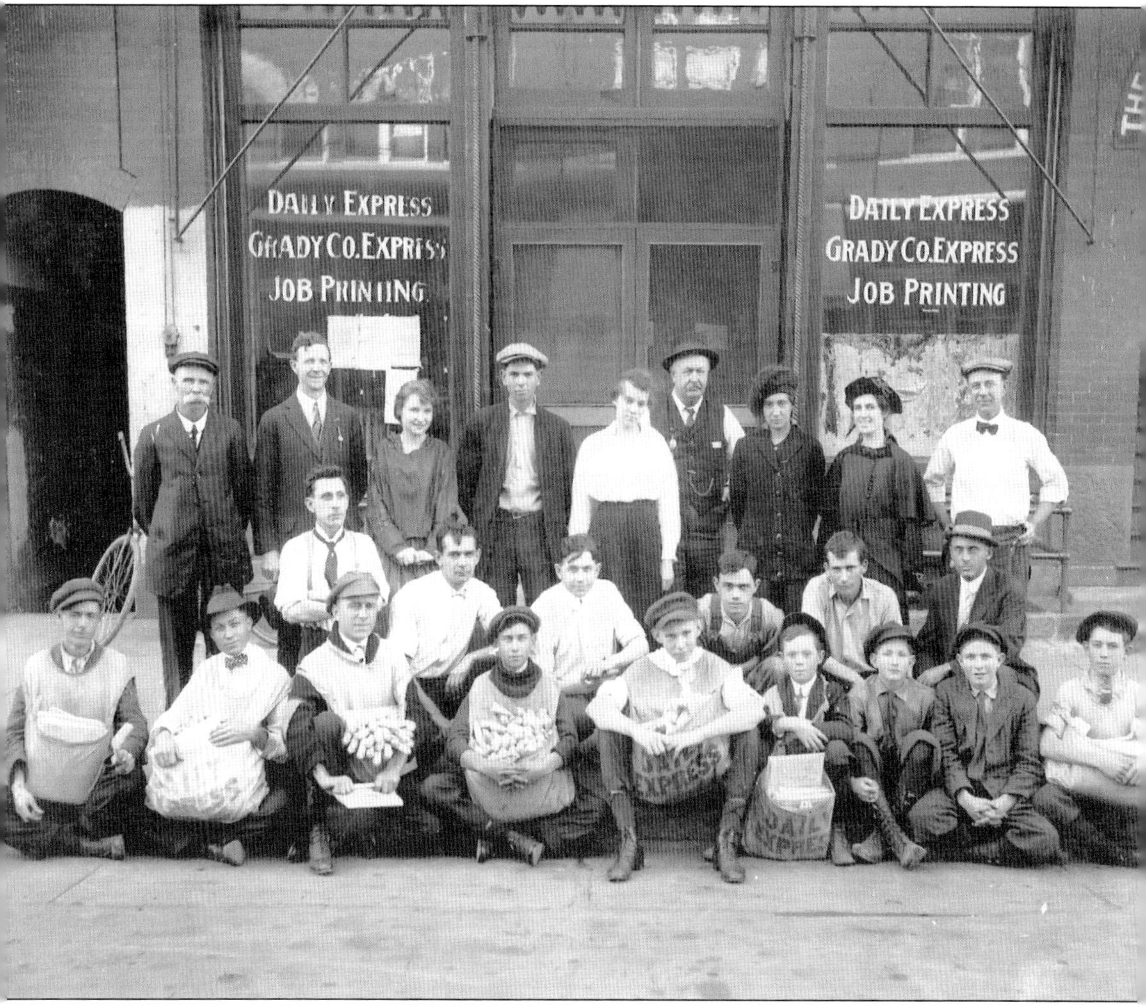

This picture is of the newsies for the *Weekly Express*. The paper, founded by W.R. Orme, was the first newspaper in Chickasha and began publishing a weekly addition in the year the town was founded. By 1899, the *Weekly Express* had begun to publish a daily addition. In 1903, George Evans and William Granlee became coeditors of the paper. By 1915, Evans had become sole owner, and under his direction, the *Weekly Express* prospered. A second paper, under the direction of L.L. Beavers and George Loman, began in 1892 and was known as the *Record* but later was renamed to the *Telegram*. A third paper began after 1908, when J.W. and Grace Kayser were married and took over publishing the *Chickasha Star*. It began as a daily, but later became a weekly. Mr. Kayser did the reporting, while Mrs. Kayser ran the society page and a recipe section. Later, her recipes were bound together in a popular book.

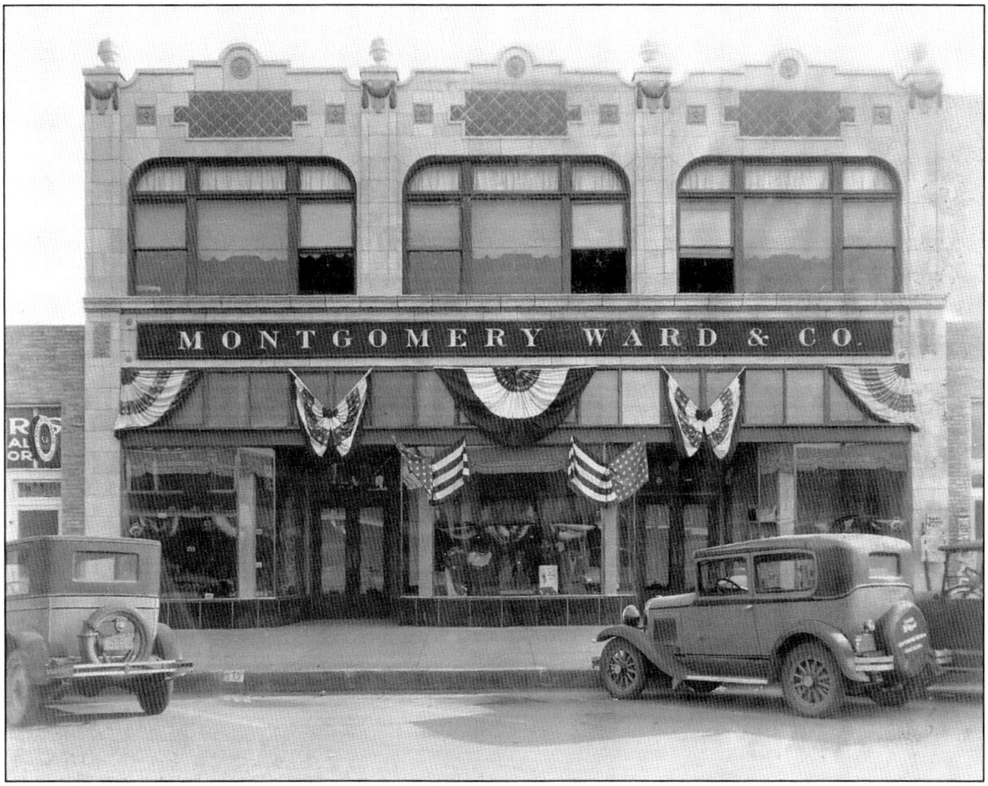

In 1872, Montgomery Ward issued his first catalog for mail-order goods that he thought rural costumers might like. His wish book grew from a few pages to hundreds within a few short years. In 1913, Ward began building retail stores to sell his wares. This location for Montgomery Ward was built in 1927 as a two-story terra-cotta brick building on 519 West Chickasha Avenue.

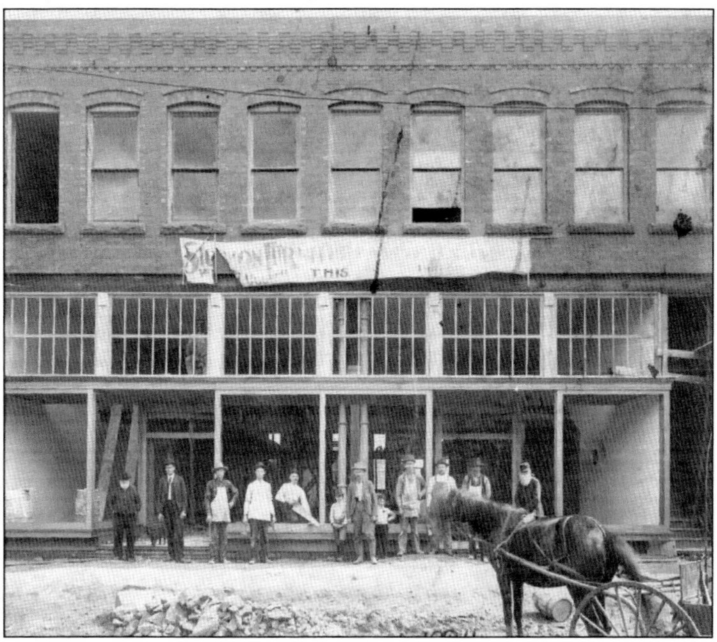

The Sigmon Furniture and Carpet Company was opened by Chickasha's Sigmon family as a shop for wholesale and retail carpet, mantels, mattresses, and, naturally, furniture. It was opened at 319-321 Chickasha Avenue before 1905. The Sigmons also ran a factory where they produced some of what they sold in their store. It was located on Frisco Avenue near the Rock Island tracks before being relocated to Oklahoma City.

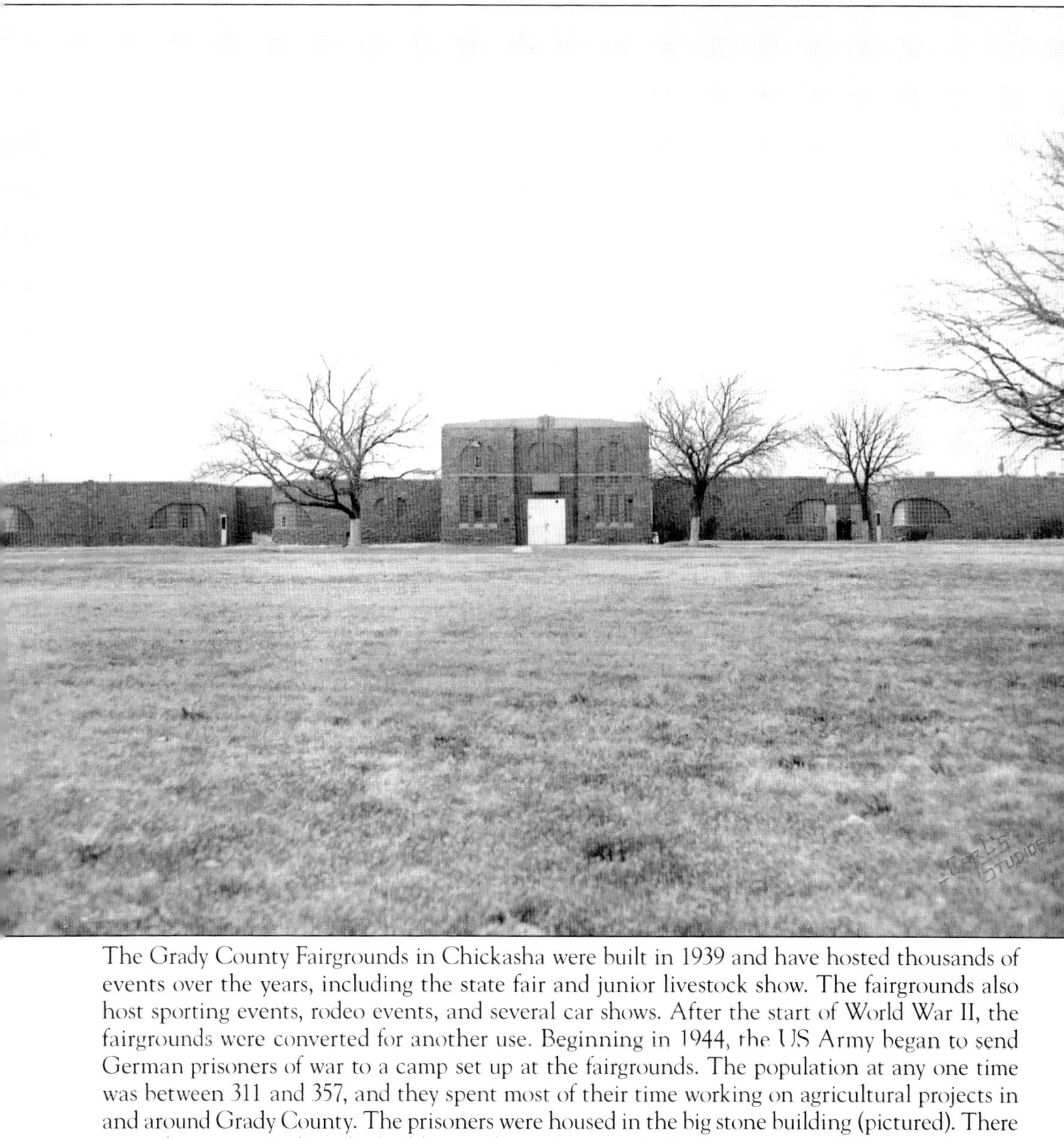

The Grady County Fairgrounds in Chickasha were built in 1939 and have hosted thousands of events over the years, including the state fair and junior livestock show. The fairgrounds also host sporting events, rodeo events, and several car shows. After the start of World War II, the fairgrounds were converted for another use. Beginning in 1944, the US Army began to send German prisoners of war to a camp set up at the fairgrounds. The population at any one time was between 311 and 357, and they spent most of their time working on agricultural projects in and around Grady County. The prisoners were housed in the big stone building (pictured). There was a fence surrounding the building and guard towers in the corners.

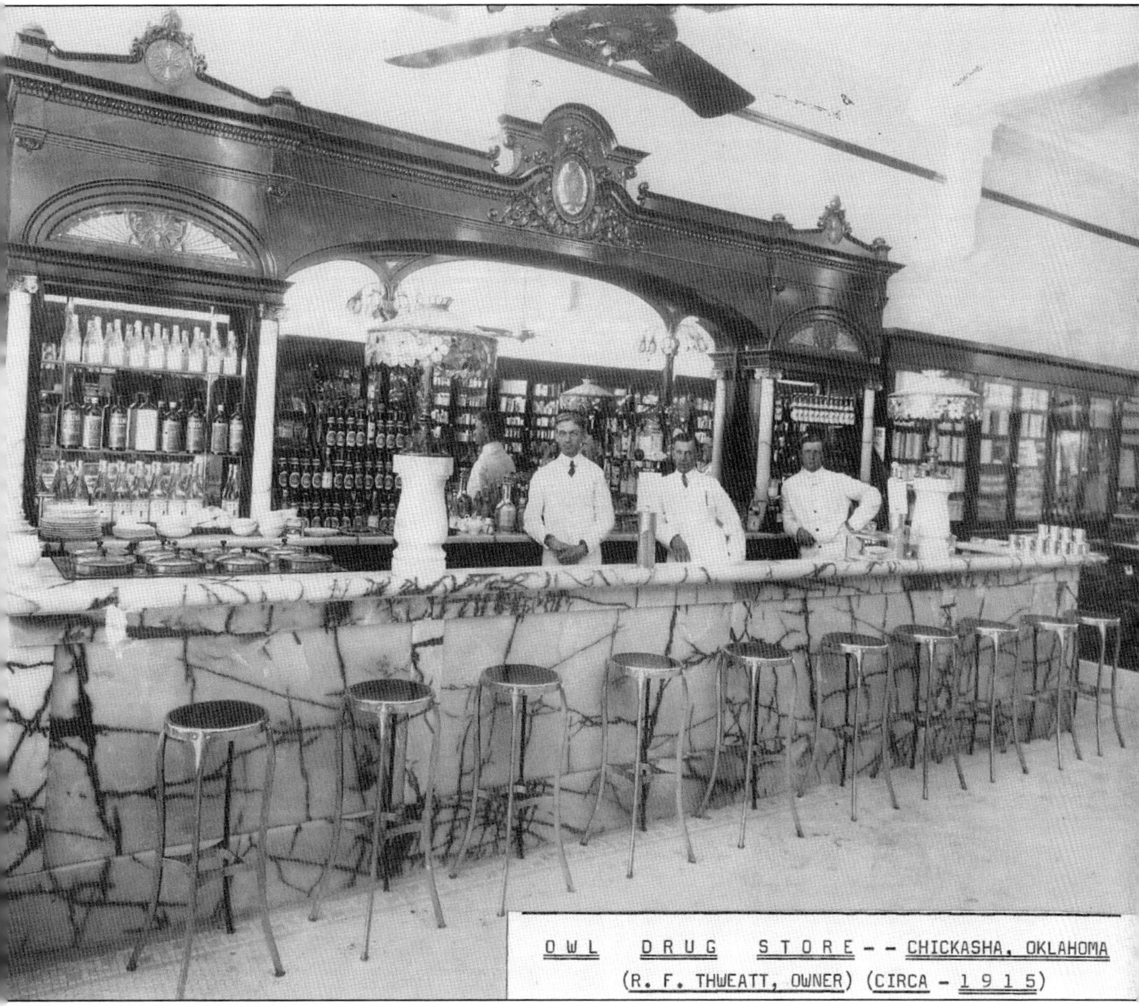

This c. 1915 picture was taken was taken inside Owl Drug Store, when it was located at 226 Chickasha Avenue and owned by R.F. Thweatt. Later, it was purchased by Carl McCormick after he returned from World War II, and he owned it until 1959. What set the Owl Drug Store apart from other establishments in Chickasha was its marble counter.

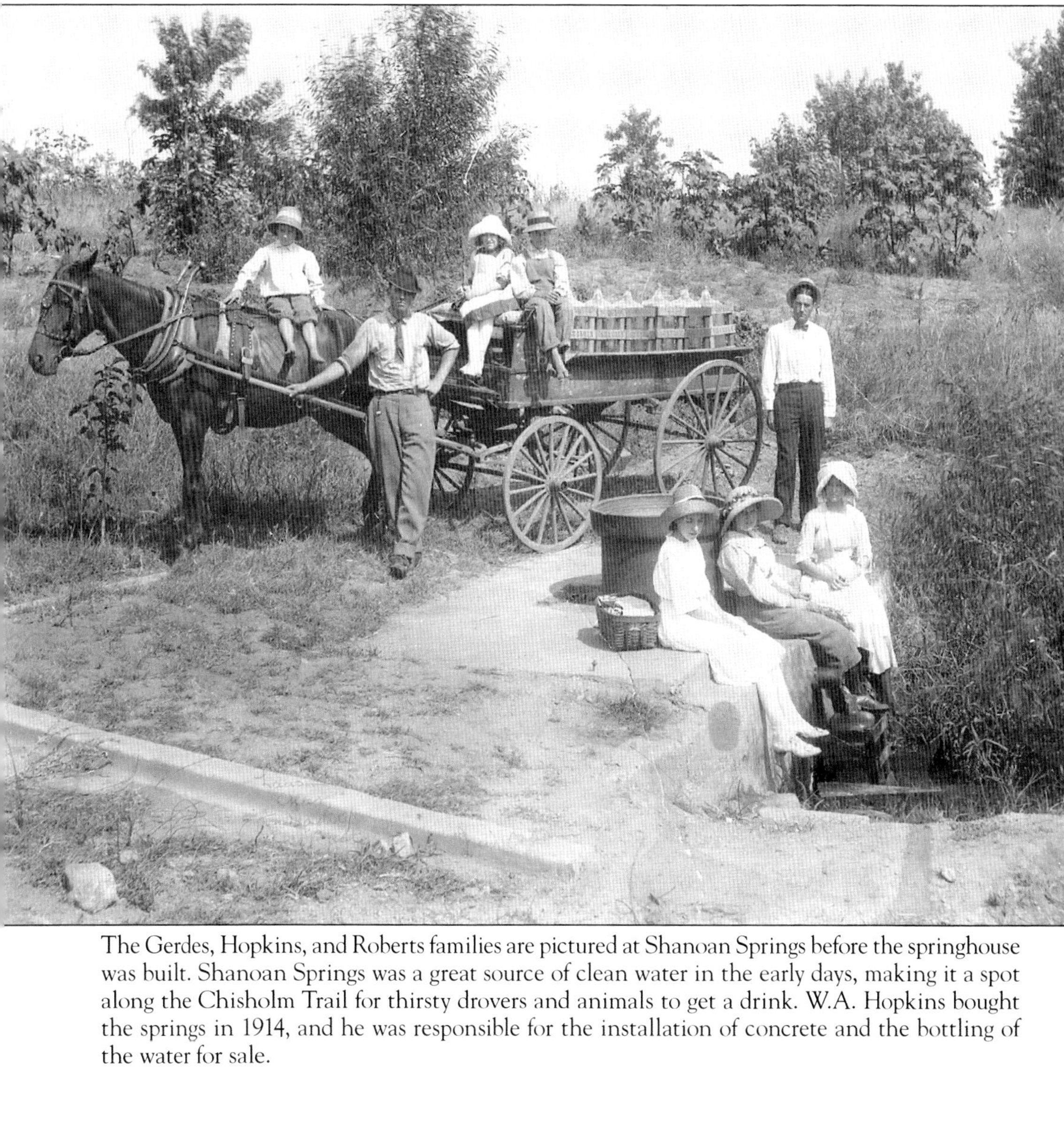

The Gerdes, Hopkins, and Roberts families are pictured at Shanoan Springs before the springhouse was built. Shanoan Springs was a great source of clean water in the early days, making it a spot along the Chisholm Trail for thirsty drovers and animals to get a drink. W.A. Hopkins bought the springs in 1914, and he was responsible for the installation of concrete and the bottling of the water for sale.

Three

CULTURE

Chickasha has an incredibly rich cultural history. The town featured quite a few theaters along its main street, including the Sugg and the Wagner Opera House. Dozens of parades marched past those theaters over the decades, bringing out the entire community in celebration. The year 1902 saw the first carnival, with a town queen who paraded through town. Many of these social happenings heavily involved the local business owners who formed a facet of Chickasha's culture all their own. These prominent citizens built businesses and homes that are still landmarks in the town today. And there were a number of social clubs and organizations, dating to the earliest days of the town.

The Sorosis Study Club was one of Chickasha's earliest organizations, founded in 1896. Clubs like the American Association of University Women promoted the higher education and community involvement of women. Chickasha also had Lions, Rotary, Junior Social Workers, and other clubs that promoted the town's well-being. There was a large number of secret society lodges for both men and women, too, and the Chickasha Commercial Club was a crucial organization that developed as an early chamber of commerce in 1902.

Chickasha's black community hosted many organizations like the Flower Lovers and Tuesday Evening Thimble clubs. Their lodges existed when the land was Indian Territory and included the United Order of Friendship and Odd Fellows. Women had secret societies like the Household of Ruth. Both the men's and women's lodges marched behind the Lincoln High School band in an annual parade down First Street. There was also the Negro Chamber of Commerce, an association that promoted the health and social growth of the community.

Shannon Springs Park is perhaps one of the most lasting cultural attributes in Chickasha. Featuring natural springs, a lake, and an enormous swimming pool over the years, it has existed for much of the town's history. The fish-filled lake is still there today, and every Christmas season the park is sensationally decorated with lights and ornaments.

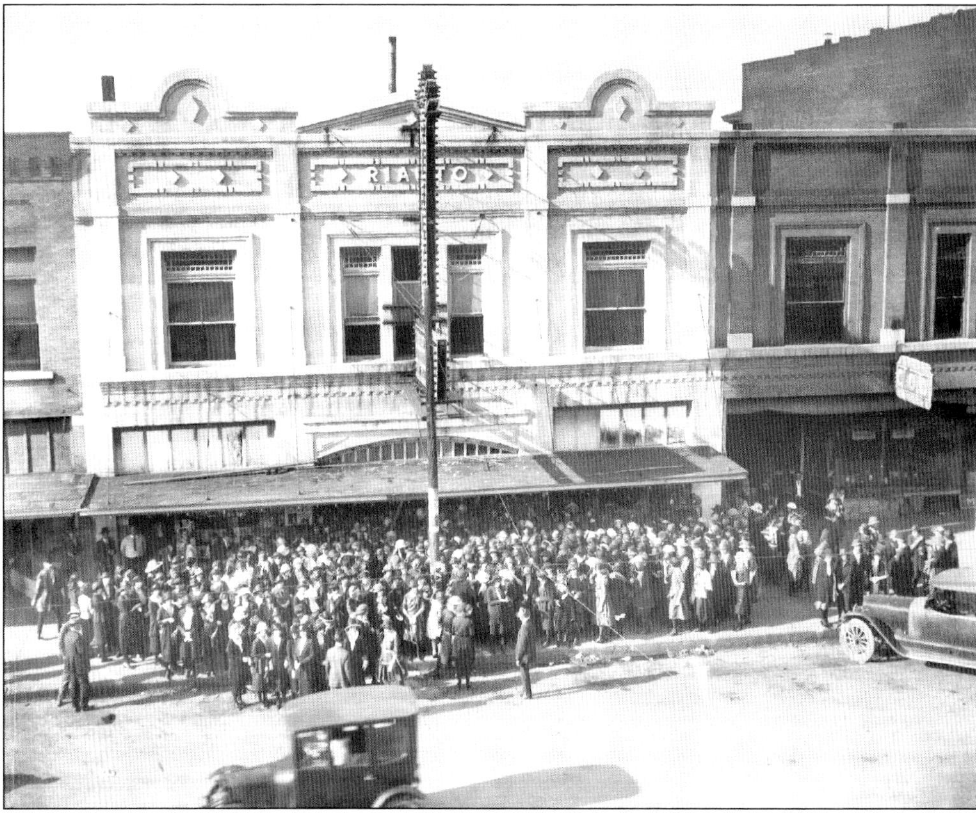

The Rialto Theatre was one of a surprisingly large number of Chickasha theaters in the early 1900s. The building was located at 420 Chickasha Avenue, placing the theater in the heart of historic Chickasha's entertainment and shopping area. The Rialto gave theatergoers a chance to watch some of the earliest talking picture shows, including its showing of *The Jazz Singer* in 1929. Local theaters were also incredibly popular thanks to their air-conditioning. Like Chickasha's Sugg and Kozy Theatres, the Rialto was part of the Publix Theatres chain, which later became part of Paramount Pictures.

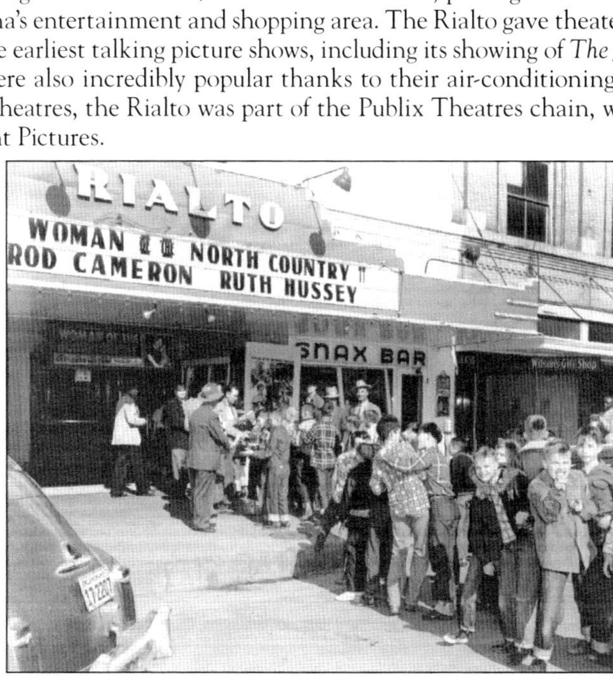

Around 1930, Chickasha's Sugg Theatre was converted into the Washita Theatre. By the time the theater had been renamed the Washita, patrons came in to view anything from operas to vaudeville to movies. The theater kept its reclining seats and box seats that had been part of the Sugg. Sadly, the building burned down soon afterwards; and the property, located on Fourth Street, was sold to Bernie Rothbaum in 1939. The pictures here show the new Washita, which was built down the street from where the old theater had burned down. Today, it is used as a Chickasha community theater.

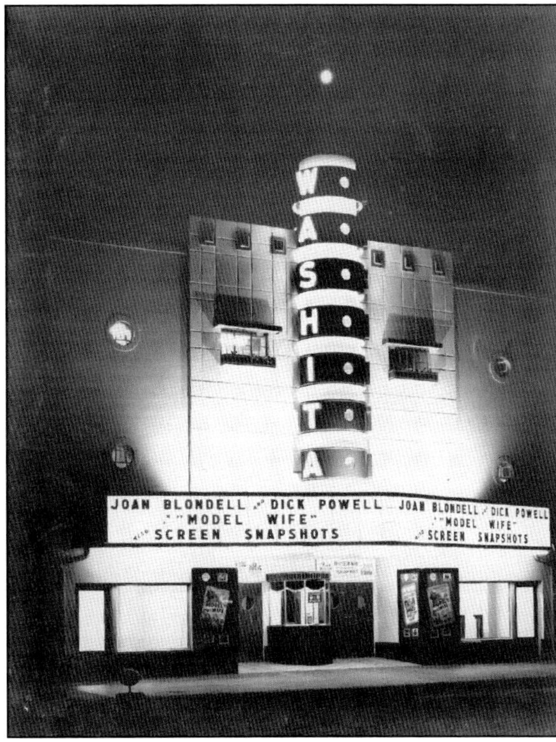

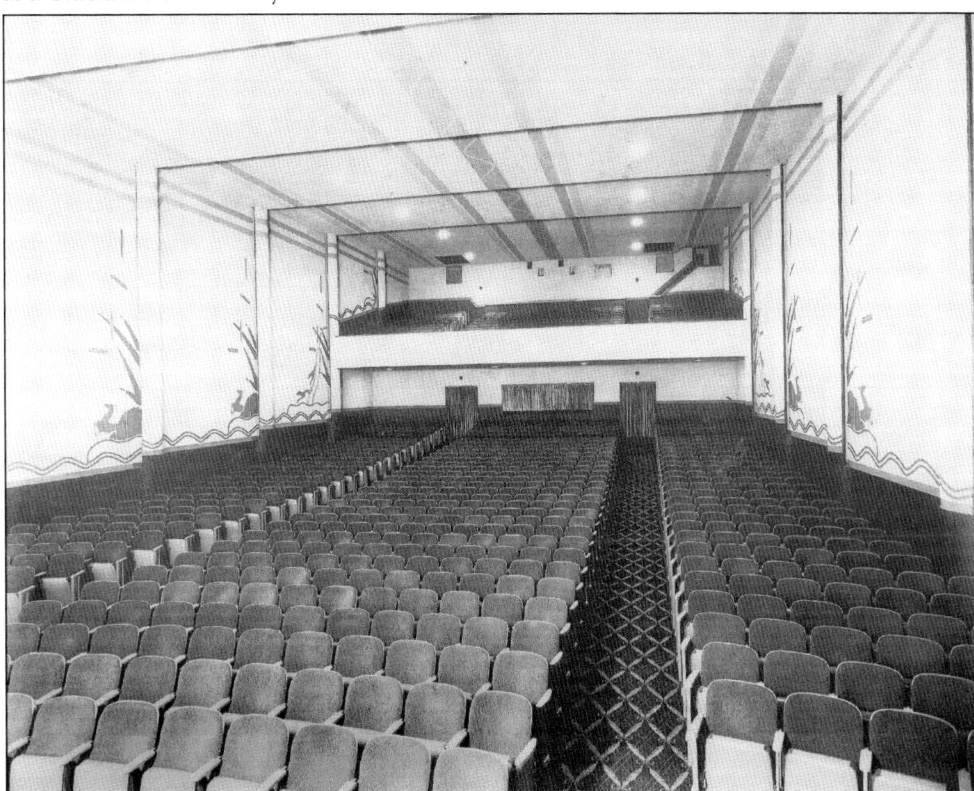

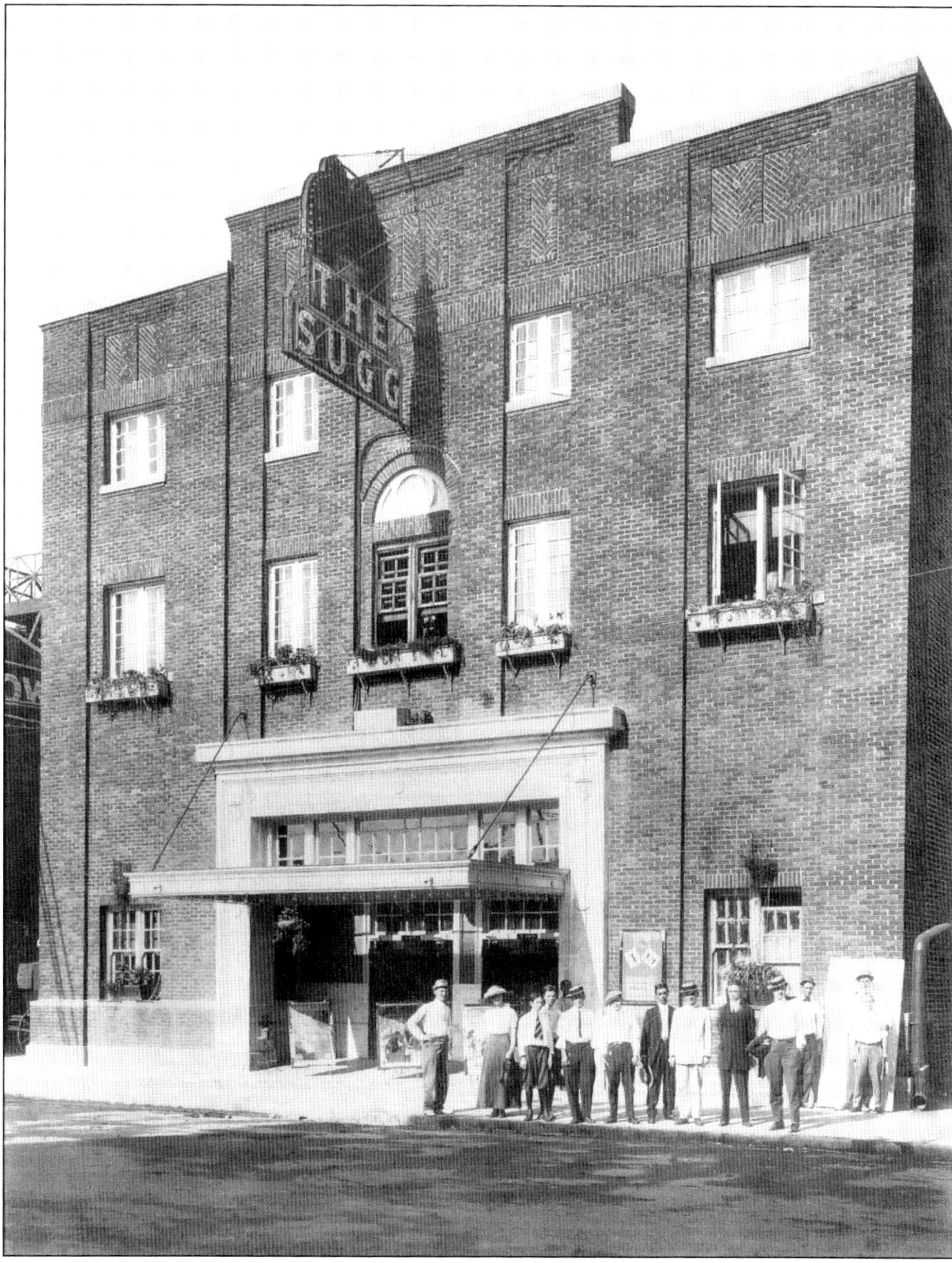

Opened between 1910 and 1920, the Sugg was one of Chickasha's oldest theaters. The Sugg Theatre was built by rancher and president of Chickasha's First National Bank, J.D. Sugg. Redbrick and white concrete embellishments made up the outside, and inside there were plush reclining seats, where patrons could view stock companies performing different programs every night for up to a week at a time. There were even upstairs boxes for the wealthier theatergoers. After Sugg's death in 1925 the theater was renamed the Washita Theatre. The building unfortunately burned down, and Bernie Rothbaum bought the property in 1939.

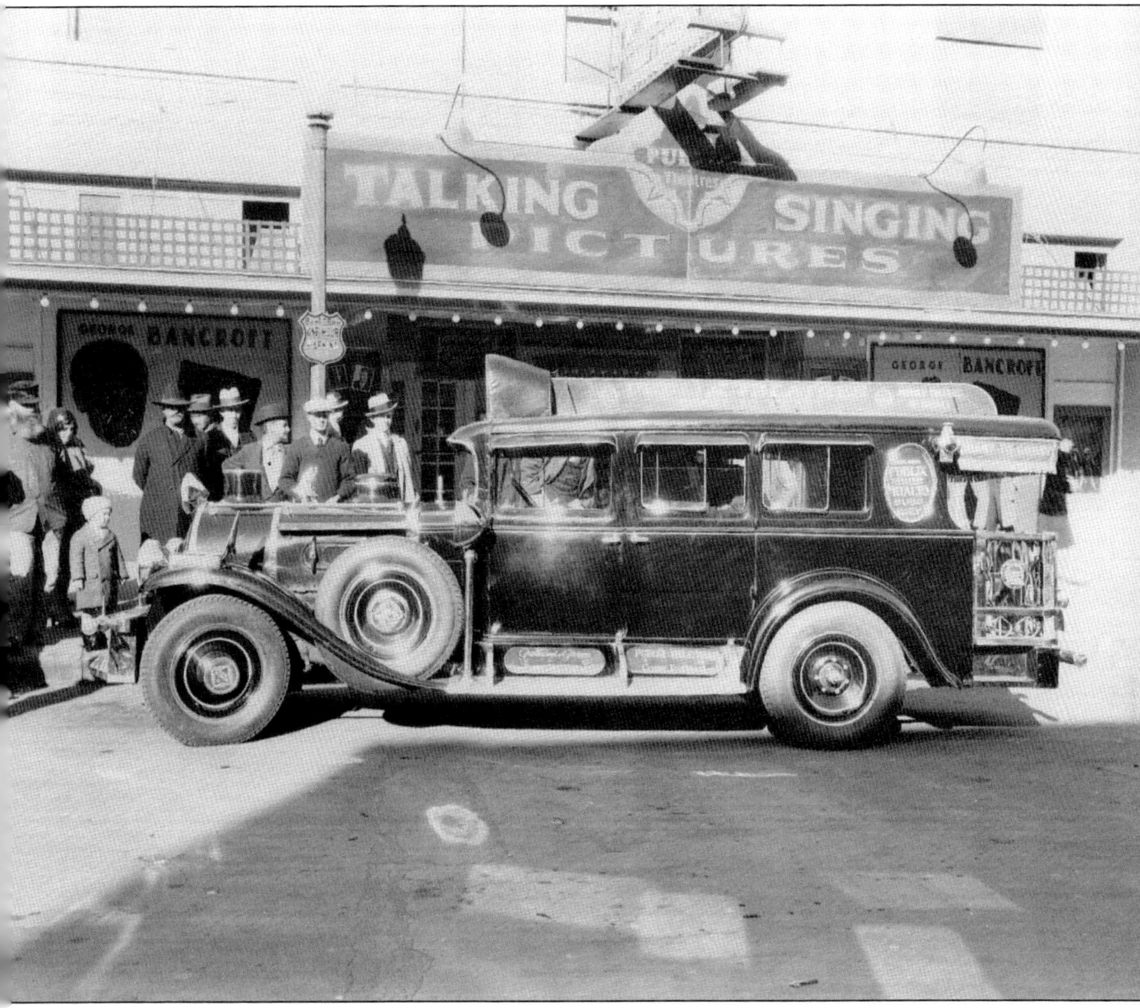

In the early 1930s, Publix Theatres sent this vehicle as a mobile advertisement to its chain theaters across the country. Publix Theatres was film-house division of Paramount Pictures in the early 1900s. The advertisement car stopped for a while in front of Chickasha's Rialto, Kozy, and Sugg theaters, which were all owned by Publix. In this picture, the car is surrounded by spectators in front of the Rialto Theatre. The car had a headlight and brass bell on its hood, window drapes, and hubcaps marked "Publix." It also had a water bag attached to its front bumper for its trips across the American deserts.

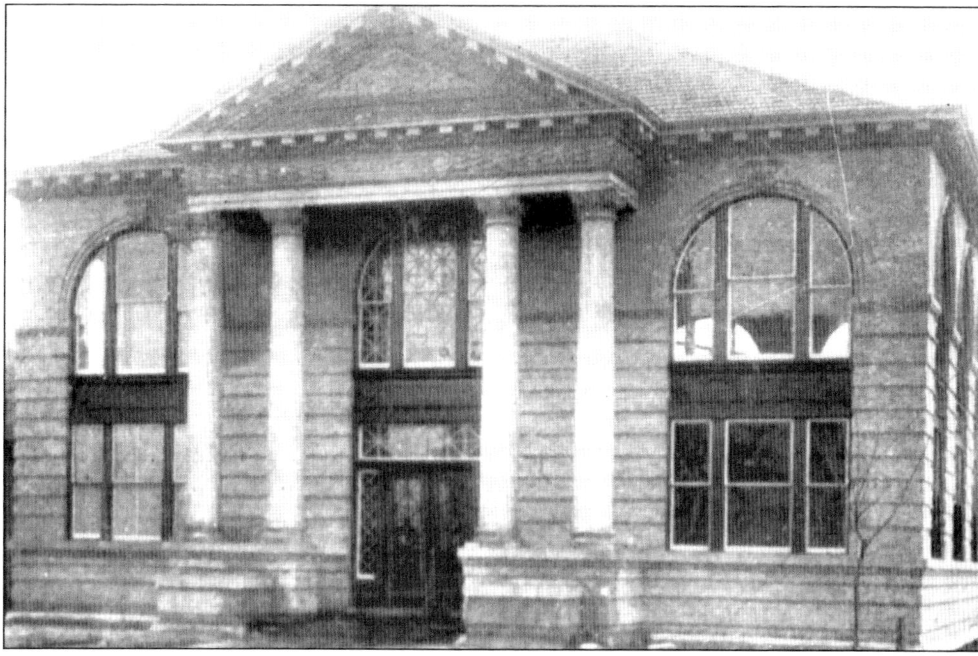

The Carnegie library opened in 1906 with $10,000 from philanthropist Andrew Carnegie. It was the first free public library built in what was Indian Territory. It had two stories in light-colored brick with white concrete decorations and an auditorium inside. The first books were purchased with money donated by local business owners and schoolchildren. It was demolished in 1961, and a modern library now stands in its place.

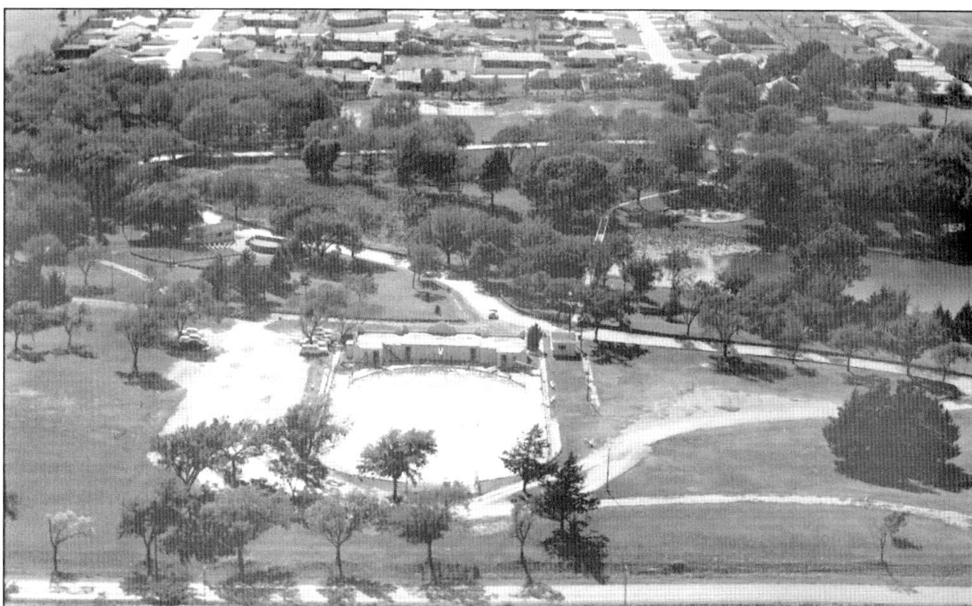

Shannon Springs Park began as a small water source in the 1880s. Soon, it became a more entertaining destination. It once had a bowling alley and a streetcar stop. Chickasha bought the land in 1922, and built a lake, bathhouses, and concession stand. The large pool in the picture was added in 1936. Today, Shannon Springs is famous for its annual Festival of Lights.

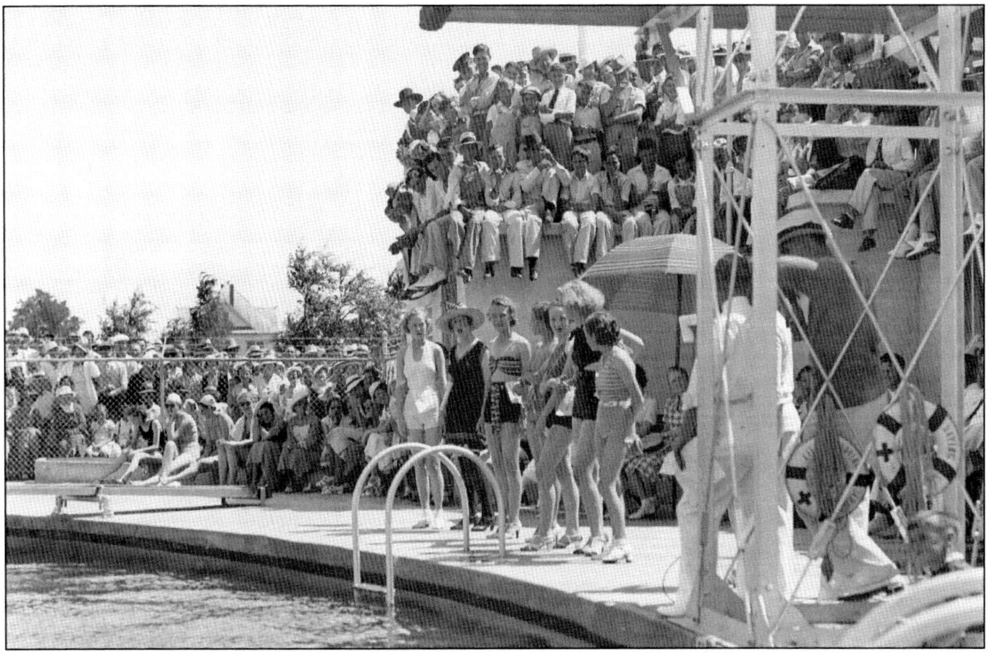

The pool at Shannon Springs Park was opened on June 23, 1936. This picture shows a beauty contest that, along with a diving contest, was part of the opening ceremony. The pool was 100 by 200 feet, large enough to hold 400 visitors. On July 19, 1936, the temperature reached 115 degrees, hot enough that two tons of ice were ordered and dumped into the pool.

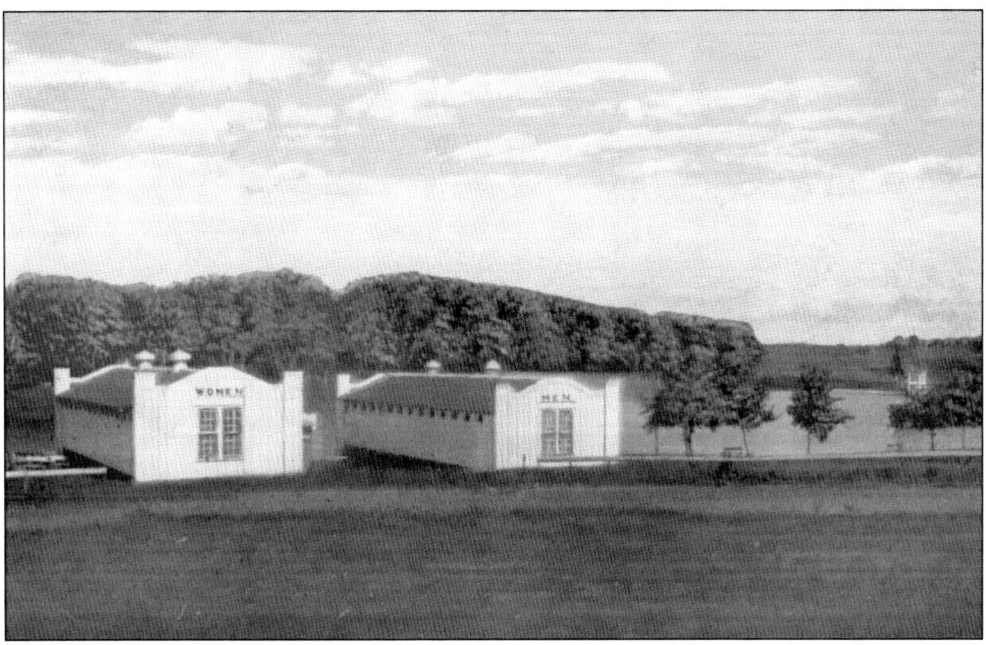

These bathhouses were built at Shannon Springs Park in 1922. They sat on the edge of the lake, which was a popular swimming spot for Chickasha residents. Visitors could also come to the park to picnic or fish for the crappie and bass that stocked the lake. The bathhouses were torn down approximately when the swimming pool was built in 1936.

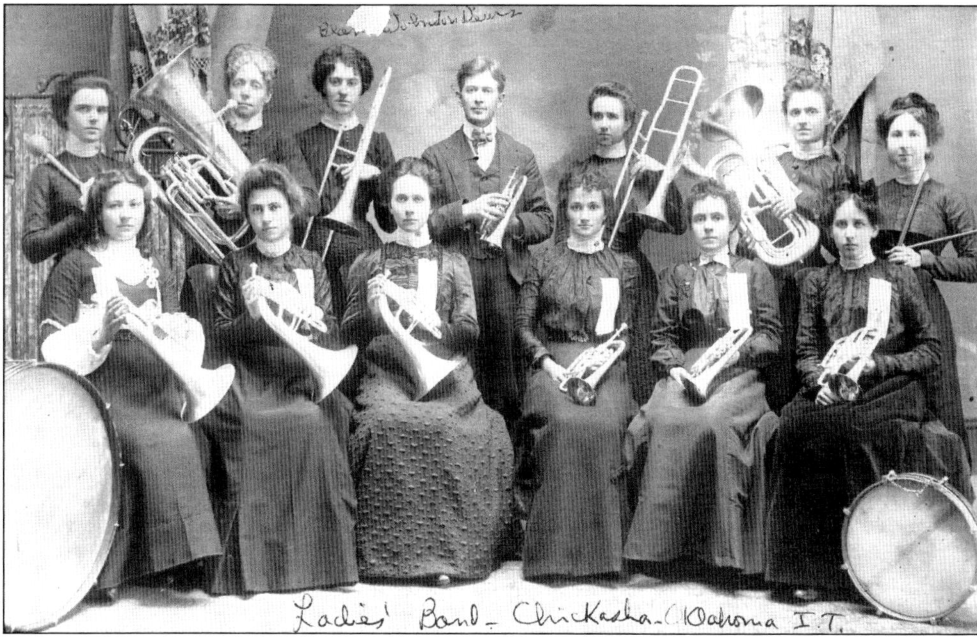

The Ladies Band was organized by George Fox in 1900. The group consisted of 12 young ladies, including Clara Miller,? Shipley, Blanche Jonston Dews, ? Fox, Mrs. Hubert Utt, Nettie Munsell, Mrs. Jim Terrell, Burch Scoffern, Mr. and Mrs. George Fox, and Rose Auten. The band performed at Chickasha's first Fourth of July celebration in 1896.

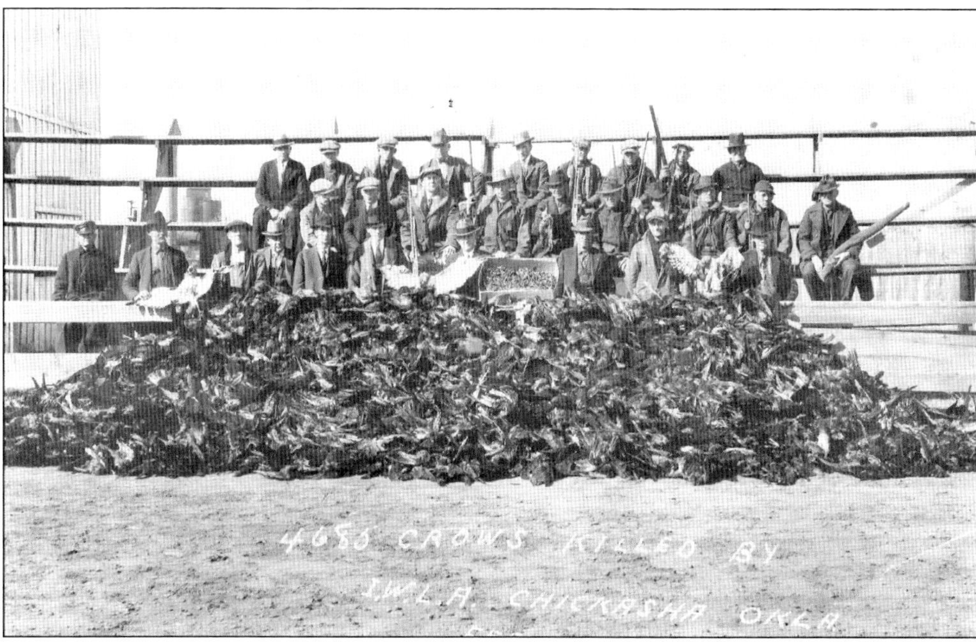

In 1925, Chickasha was plagued with a dangerous number of crows. Members of the local Izaak Walton League of America chapter grabbed their guns and addressed the problem. The IWLA is a national organization that was formed in 1922 to protect American wildlife and wilderness. On February 9, 1925, the Chickasha IWLA eliminated 4,685 crows, preserving the area's natural habitat and putting the minds of locals at ease.

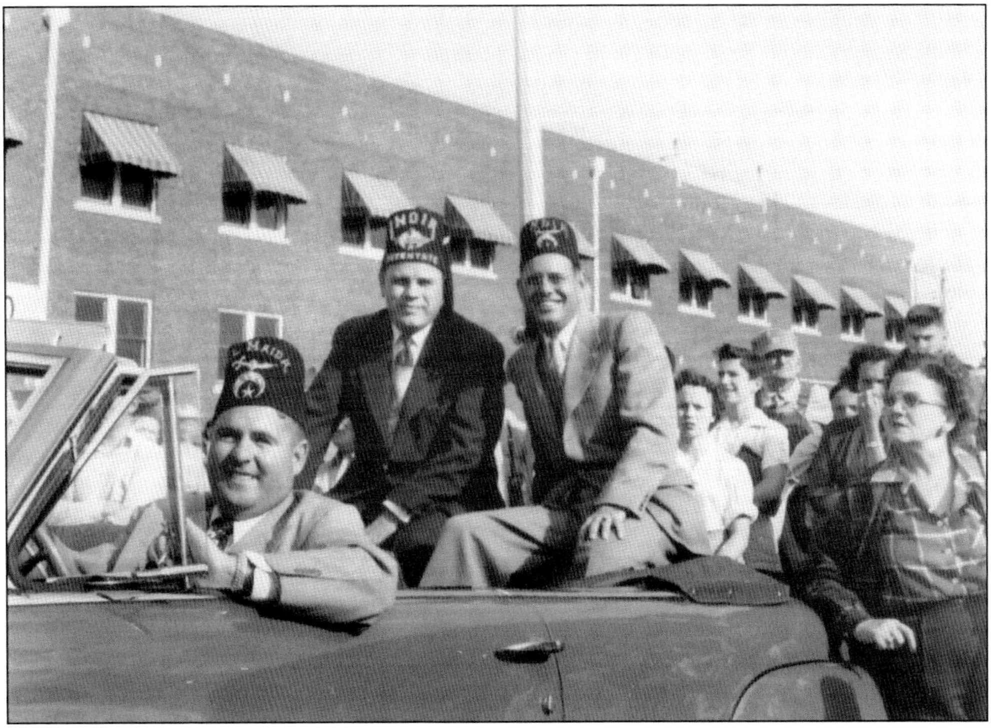

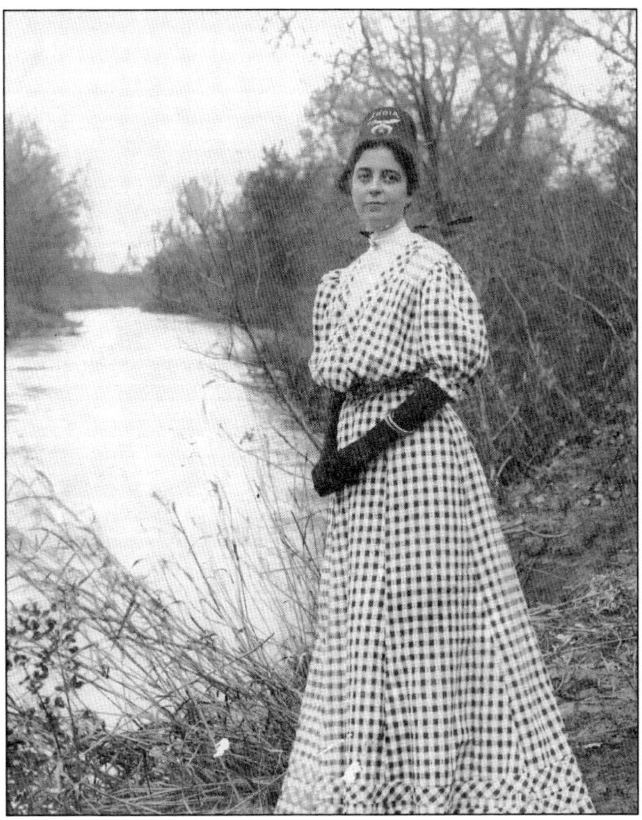

In 1898, the *Chickasha Express* lists several organizations associated with the Freemasons: the Chickasha Lodge No. 79, AF & AM; the Chickasha Chapter No. 17, RAM; the Alpha Lodge of Perfection; and the Ella Morris Chapter of Eastern Star. The men in the picture are probably visitors from Oklahoma City. The fez hats worn by the people in both pictures have "India" written across them. "India" was the name of the Shrine Center that still exists today in Oklahoma City. The man in the dark suit in the parade has the title "Potentate" on his hat, indicating that he was the head of the chapter. The picture of the woman was taken in 1904 by the Washita River, a popular place for groups to picnic.

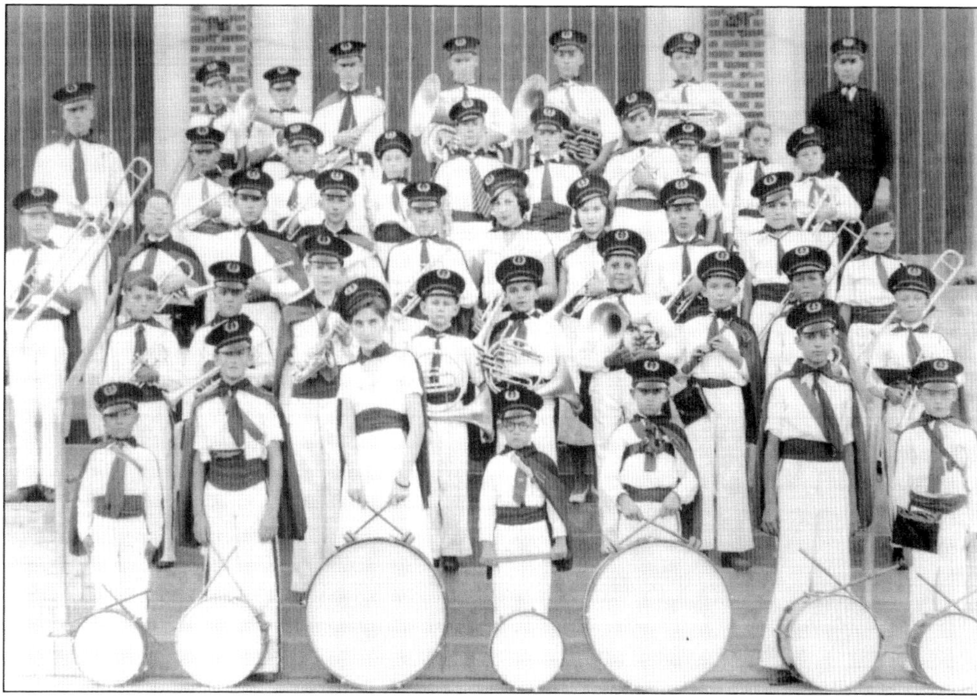

This picture shows a group of local children who were organized into a children's band called the American Legion Auxiliary Kiltie Band. The band members performed in a town Christmas parade in their dark full marching uniforms (as shown later in this chapter).

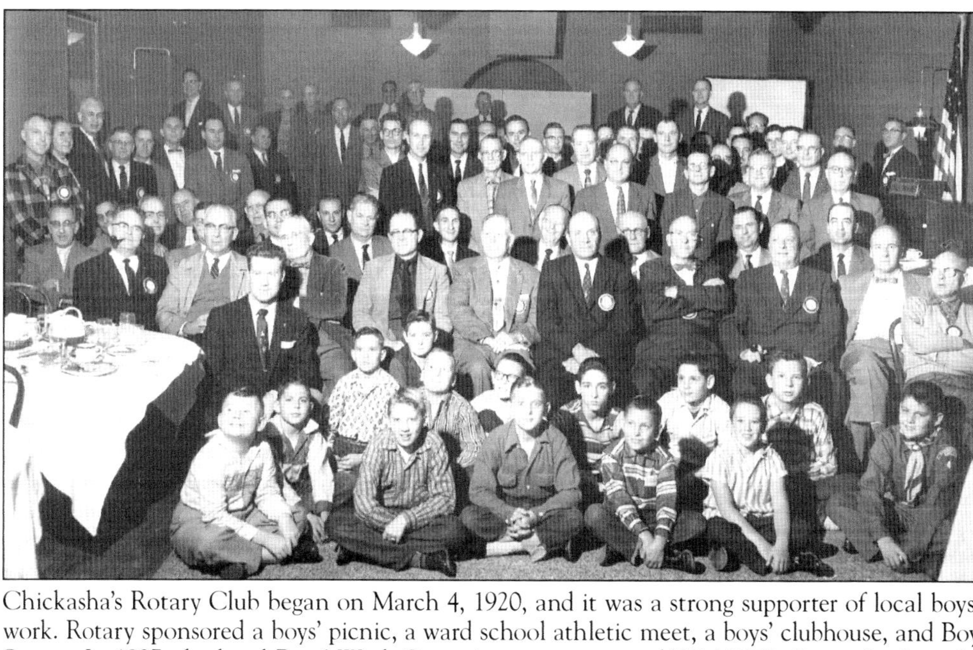

Chickasha's Rotary Club began on March 4, 1920, and it was a strong supporter of local boys' work. Rotary sponsored a boys' picnic, a ward school athletic meet, a boys' clubhouse, and Boy Scouts. In 1927, the local Boys' Work Committee was renamed YRATOR, *Rotary* backwards. Rotary has worked to prevent high school dropouts, and it helped to equip the Jane Brooks School for the Deaf.

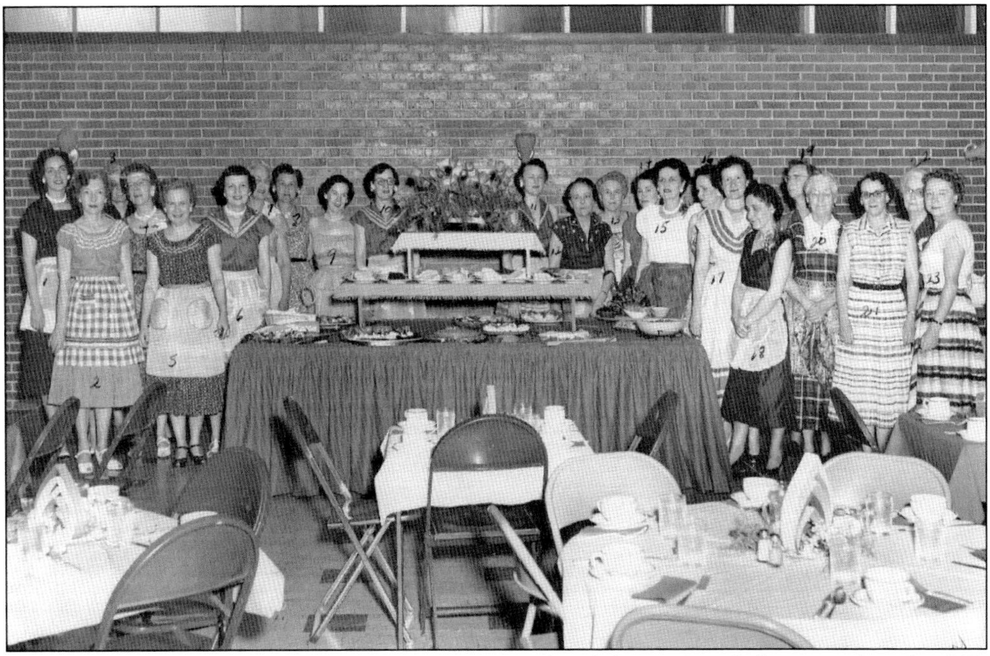

The first of its kind in Chickasha, the Sorosis Study Club was founded in 1896 by Mrs. J.H. Griffin and Mrs. F.E. Riddle. With the motto, "When I Rest, I Rust," its purpose was to share knowledge, ideas, and customs among its members and other social groups in town. This picture shows a Sorosis smorgasbord that took place in April 1954.

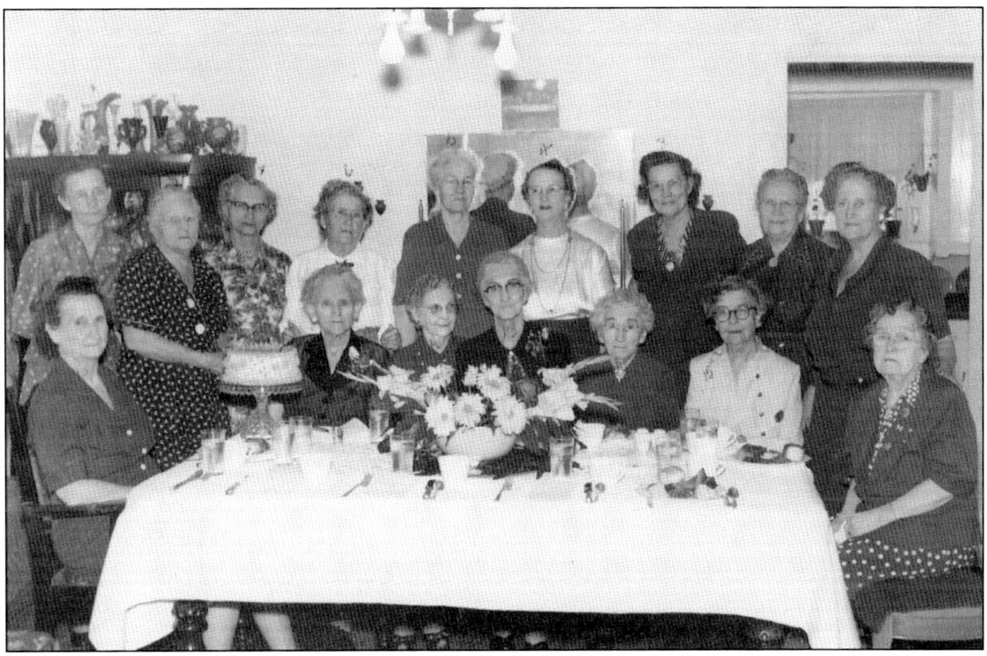

These ladies are gathered together to celebrate a birthday dinner for one of their friends. The celebration took place at the home of a Mrs. Womack sometime around 1950. The women were friends and also members of the Women's Society of Christian Service, which was most likely associated with Epworth Methodist Church.

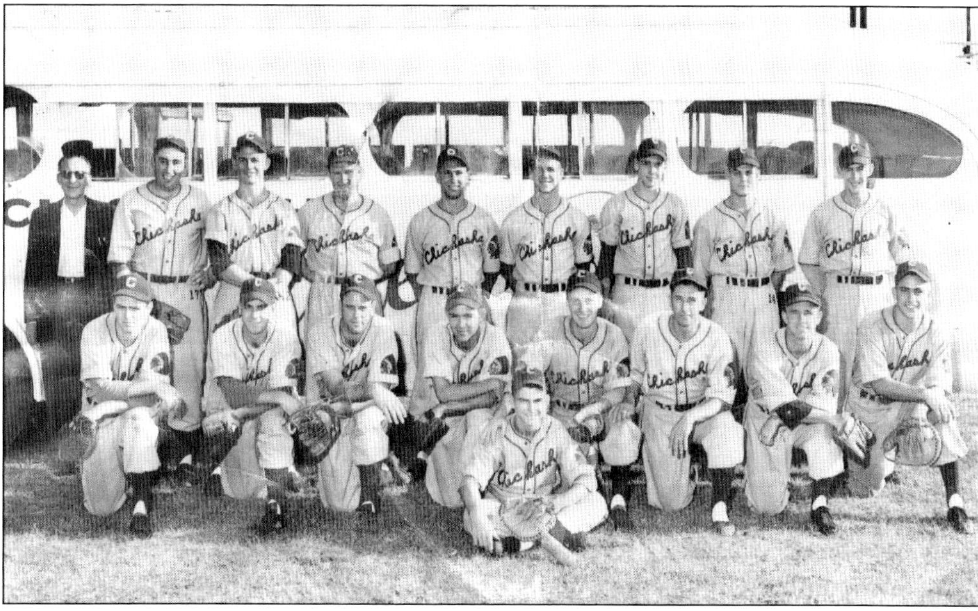

One of Chickasha's first baseball games was held on July 4, 1892, against Minco, and about 500 fans attended. In 1910, Ben Johnson built a new baseball park near Shannon Springs, where streetcars carried large numbers of residents to watch games. Chickasha fully supported its local teams, even sending its semiprofessional team to Little Rock, Arkansas, for training.

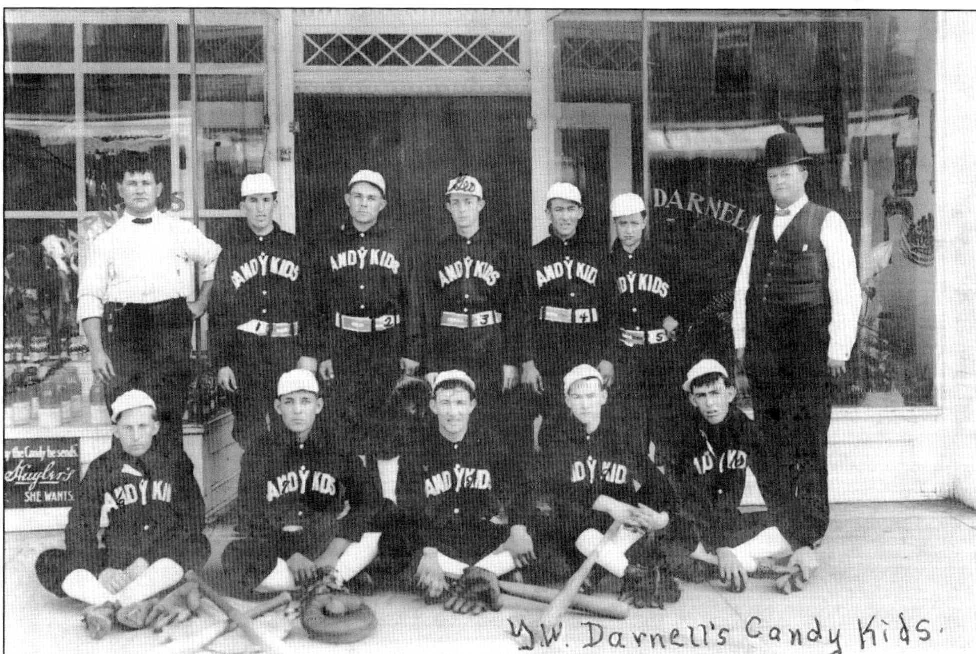

The Candy Kids were a baseball team sponsored by Darnell's Candy Store. Y.W. Darnell opened his shop in 1905 in the 200 block of Chickasha Avenue before it was moved to 305 Chickasha Avenue. He made home deliveries of ice cream by horse and buggy when necessary, and he also served chicken dinners and pie. Shop specialties were black walnut taffy, peanut brittle, and hand-dipped chocolates made by Mrs. Darnell.

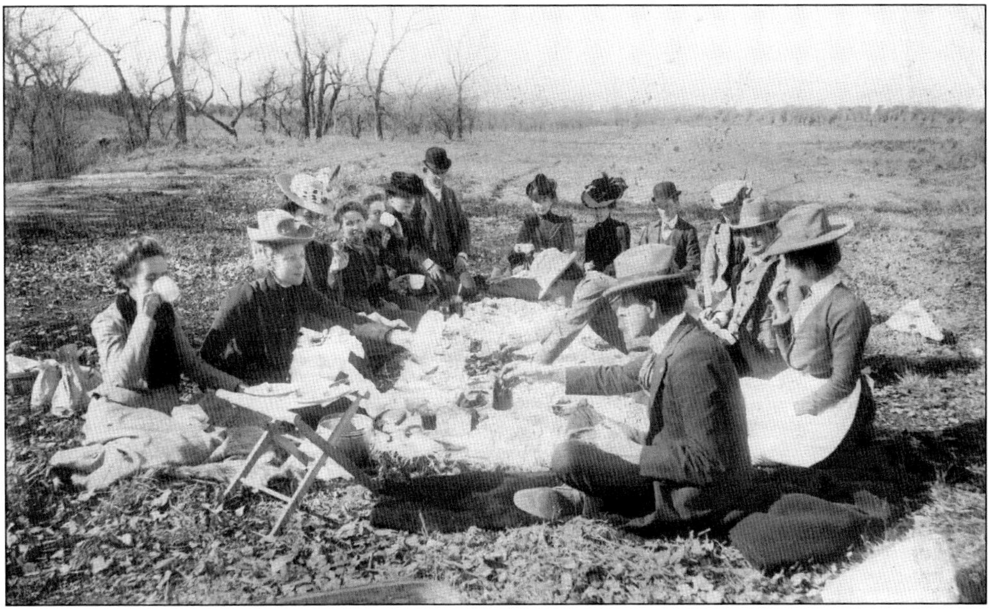

Early Chickasha residents took their picnics in a very different manner than people today. Men and women alike were fully dressed up in their hats, jackets, and nicer pieces of clothing. The picture above shows a large group seated around a picnic blanket stacked with food and tea in a field. The picture below shows a group that went out into the country for some hunting and a picnic near the community of Fred in 1895. The man in the foreground is one of Chickasha's first teachers, Howard Miller. The Grady County Historical Society recreated this scene during its 1983 ice cream social.

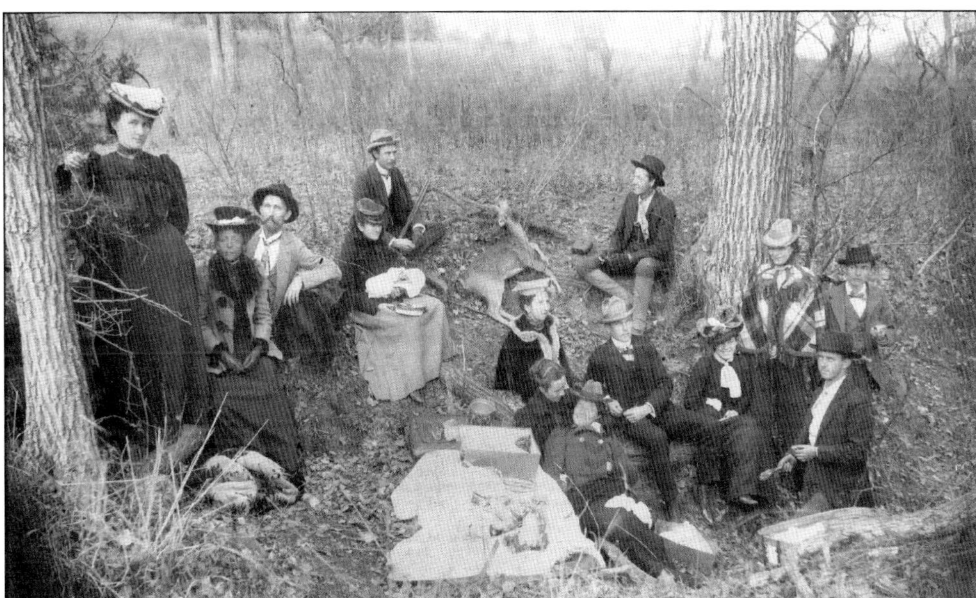

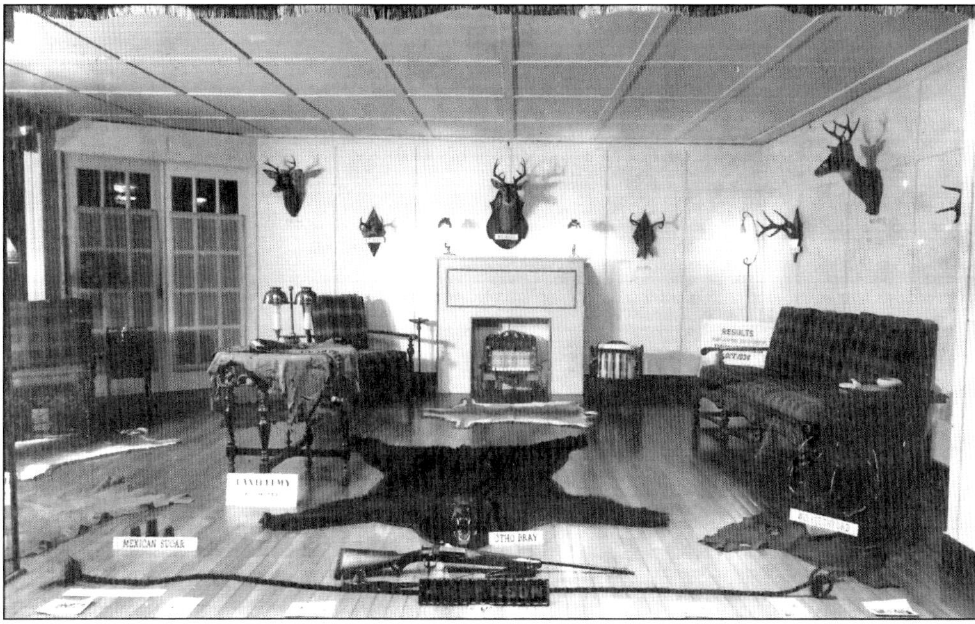

It was a common pastime of Chickasha men to go out into the local wilderness in hunting parties. The previous picture shows a number of people who had gone hunting during a picnic. This photograph shows the impressive amount of game caught by another hunting party during a trip to Mexico. The animals were proudly displayed in the storefront of the Anderson Furniture Store in 1934.

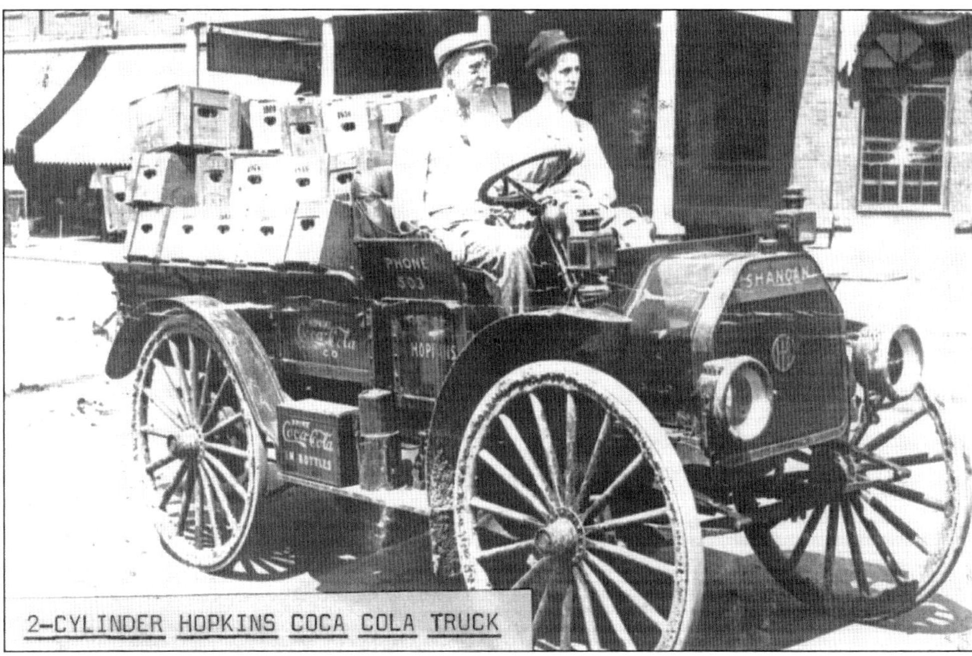

In 1910, W.H. Hopkins opened a bottling company in Chickasha at 120–126 North Third Street. The company was then converted into a warehouse for Coca-Cola in 1930. This picture shows two workers, Charlie Venable and Jack Malone, driving their two-cylinder delivery truck through Chickasha while making their rounds with crates of the soft drink.

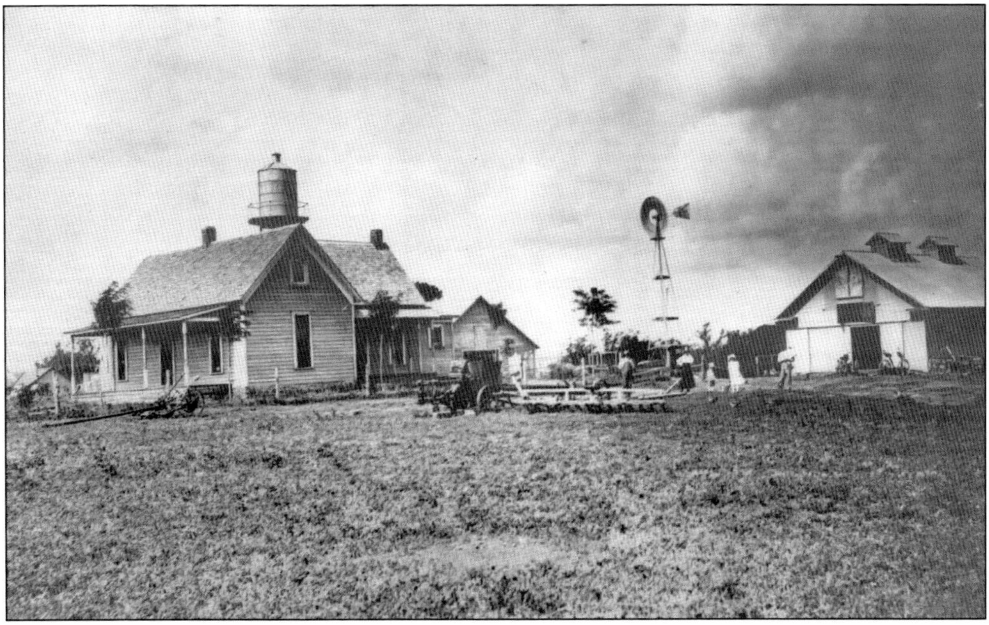

The original homes in Chickasha were dugouts built by settlers. Soon afterwards, residents built more stable homes that were more suited for the farming lifestyle of the area. The town had a number of farms, especially to supply the cottonseed oil mill and the demand for cottonseed meal for animals, cattle ranchers, and dairy farms like the Garland Dairy Milk House.

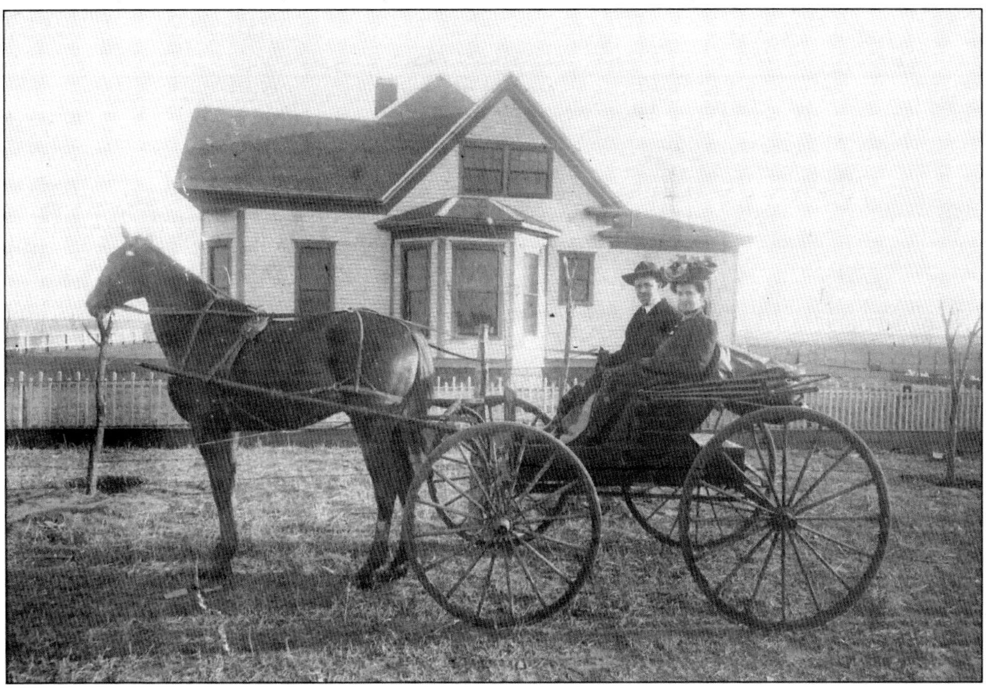

This picture shows Willis R. Kilgore and his wife, Ava Hollingsworth Kilgore. The couple is sitting in their horse-drawn buggy, parked in front of their home. Willis was the son of Willis S., a prominent Grady County official who had served as county treasurer. Willis R. and Ava had a daughter named Hattie and two sons.

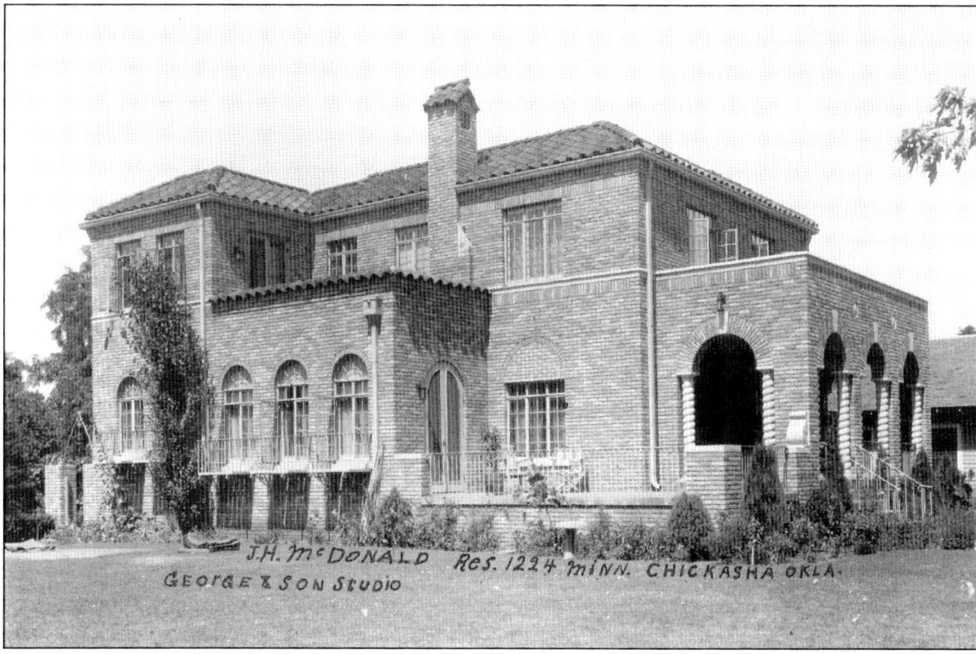

This home was built by a J.H. McDonald of Chickasha. It still stands today at 1224 Minnesota Street. It is an incredibly unusual style of house with twisted columns, faux window balconies, and two actual balconies off of the second floor. Like several homes in town, it was built in a Spanish style with yellow brick, tiled roof, and dark green trim.

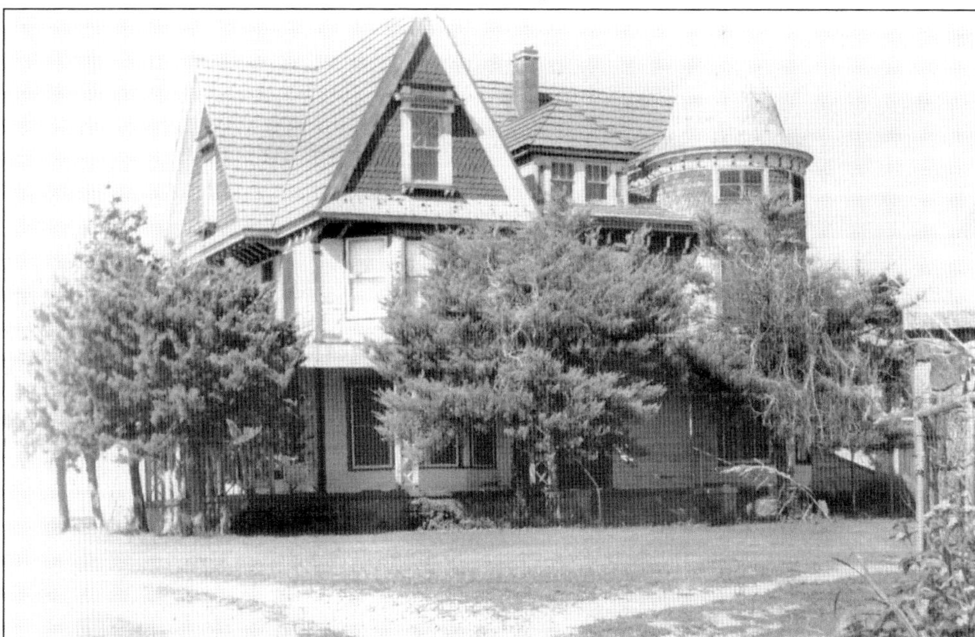

The Dave Hill House was built by David Hill on the 100 acres allotted to his Chickasaw Indian wife, Nellie Atkinson, in 1902. The house had three floors, a large basement, a bedroom for each of their seven children, and a top-floor ballroom. There was also a nine-hole golf course built next to the house.

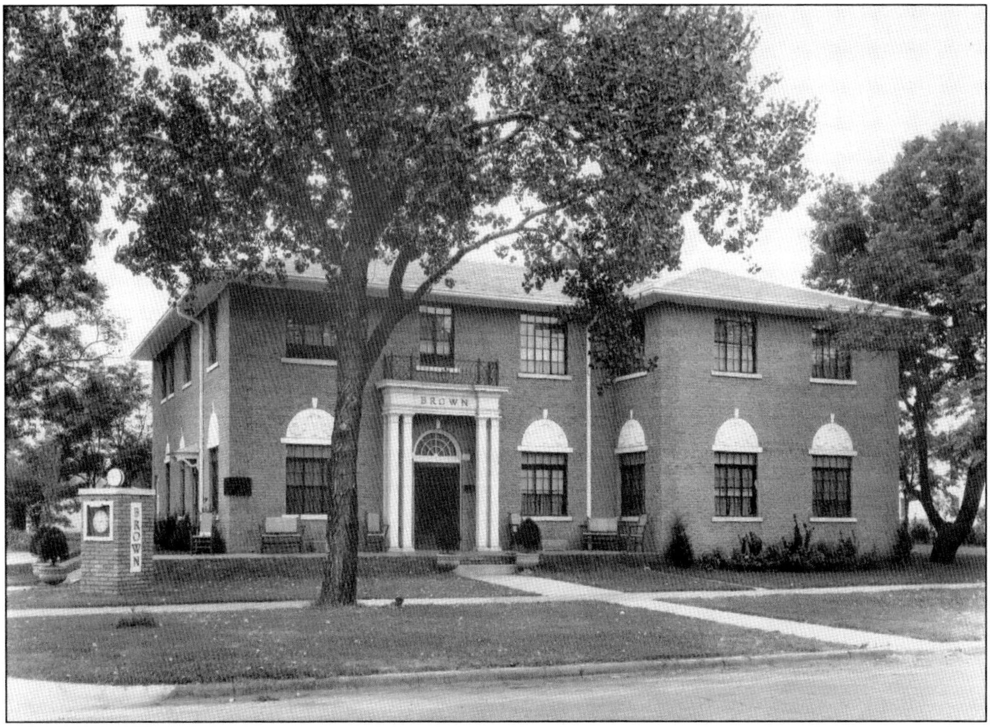

The Browns were a socially influential and connected family in Chickasha. J.W. was the first Brown to move into the area, buying a local ranch in 1890. The Brown Funeral Home was a family business opened by Walter and Golda Brown in 1922. It became the Brown-Binyon Funeral Home and moved into this building in 1929. Today, this structure is the McRay Funeral Home.

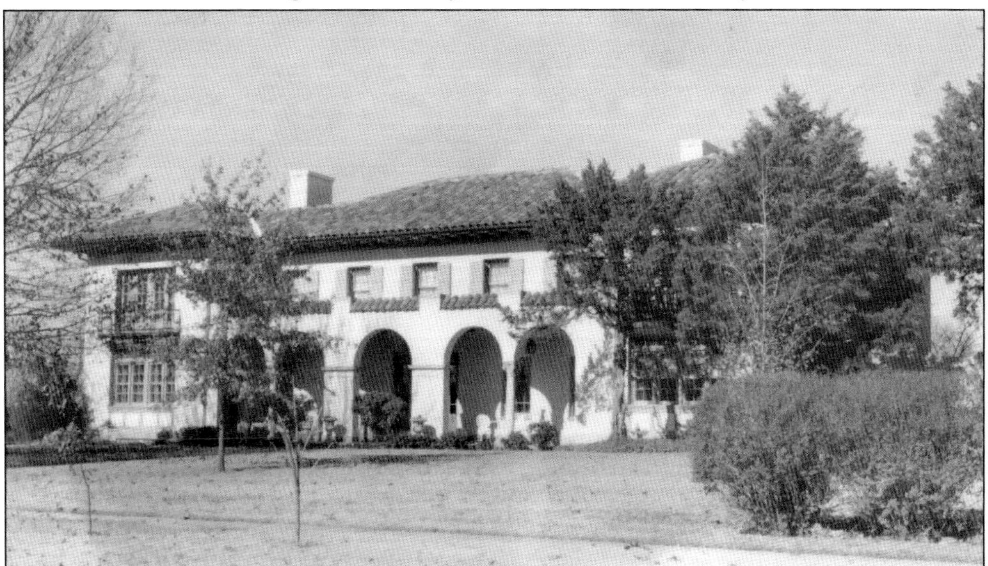

M.E. Humphrey was one of the men in charge of the Chickasha Milling Company, which was established in 1899. The mill produced several specialty brands of flour, such as Full Cream and Queen of Dixie, as well as cornmeal and feed items. Like many homes that belonged to prominent Chickasha residents, Humphrey's home still stands today at 1308 Colorado Street.

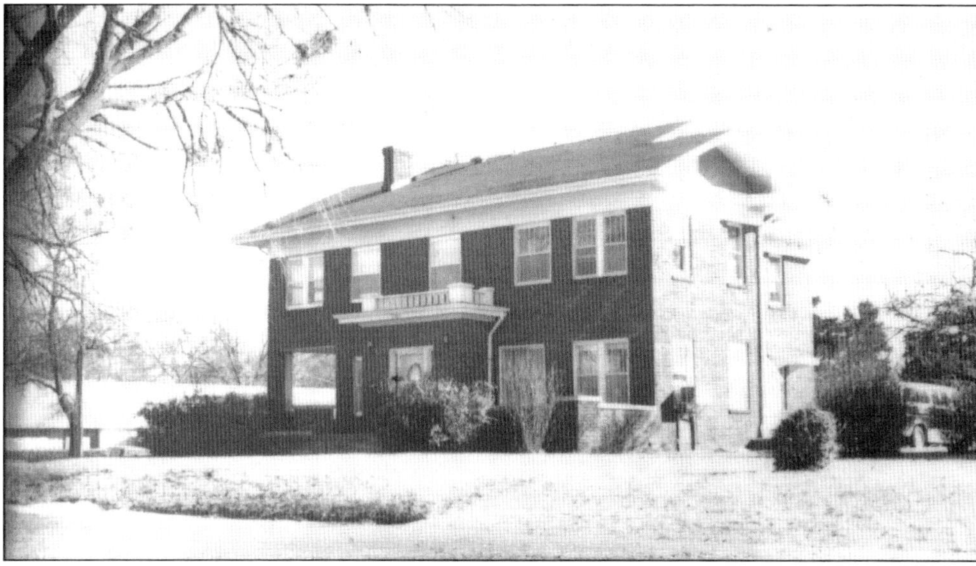

Since 1901, the Owsleys ran the Haltom and Owsley Jewelers jewelry and optician store at 304 Chickasha Avenue, as well as the Owsley Marble Company run by J.R. Owsley. Shown in the photograph above, the Owsley home was built at 1301 Chickasha Avenue, where it still stands today. In the photograph below, the Owsley family poses on the banks of the Washita River with the Sigmons, another prominent Chickasha family. The two are gathered in their finest for the wedding of J.W. Owsley and Julie Sigmon on June 8, 1908. The Sigmon Furniture and Carpet Company was opened at 319–321 Chickasha Avenue before 1905.

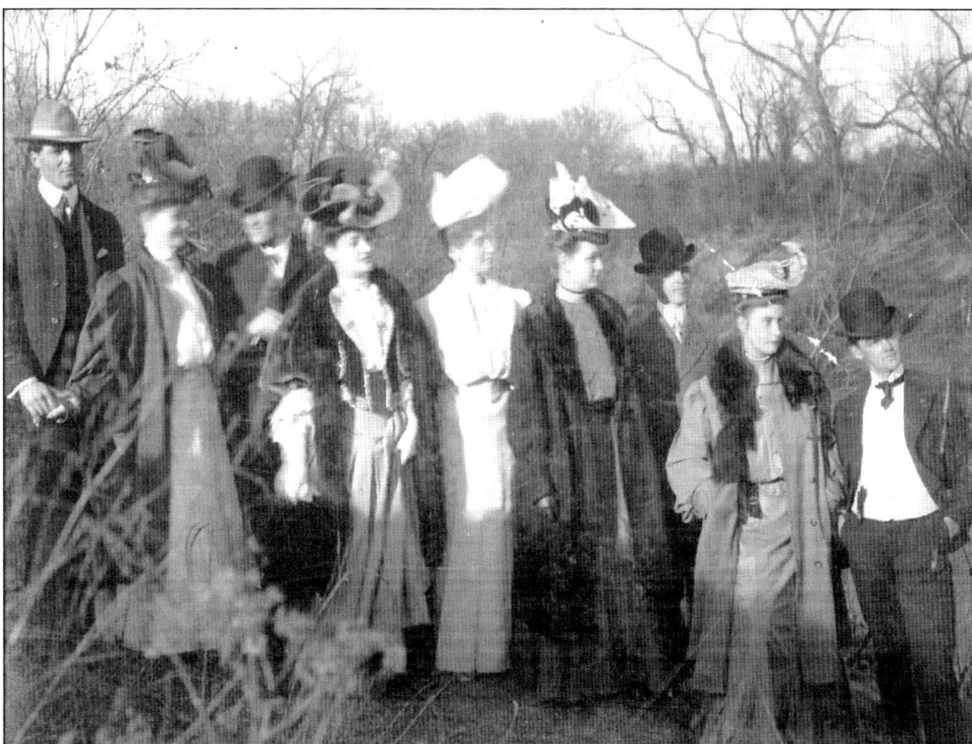

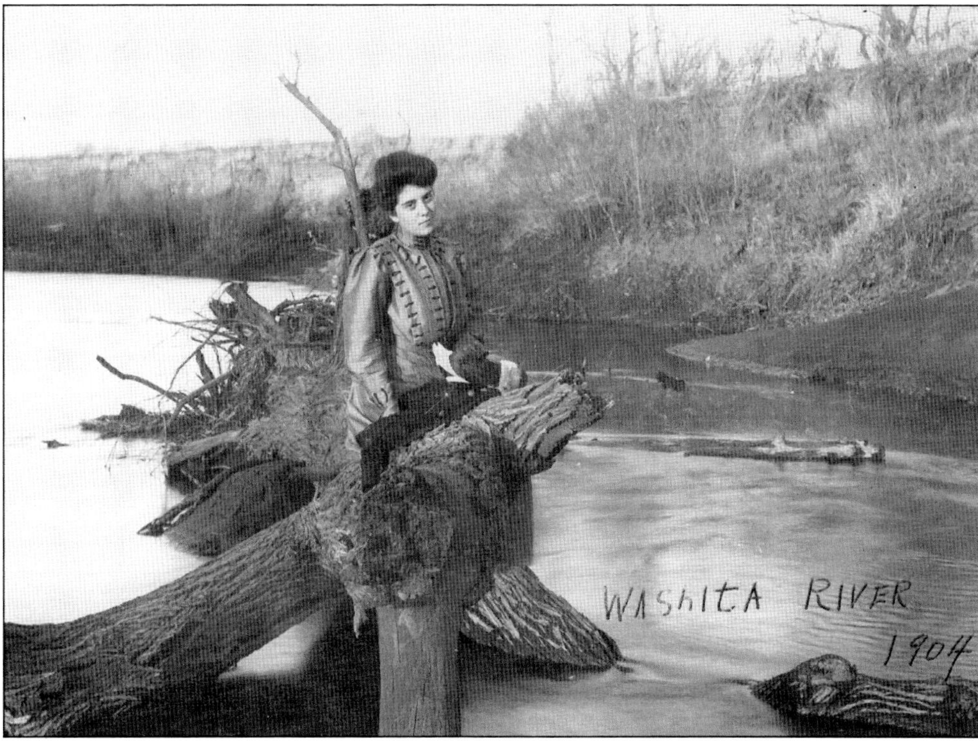

The picture above shows an unidentified woman sitting on a fallen tree in the Washita River in 1904. Although her name is unknown, she was the girlfriend of H.C. Gilkey. The photograph below shows a group of girls posing on a leaning tree in the country around Chickasha. The girls have a tight grip on the tree and each other as they wait for the photographer to hurry and take the picture. The photographer is also unidentified, but it is evident from the shadow cast at the bottom of the picture that it is a woman.

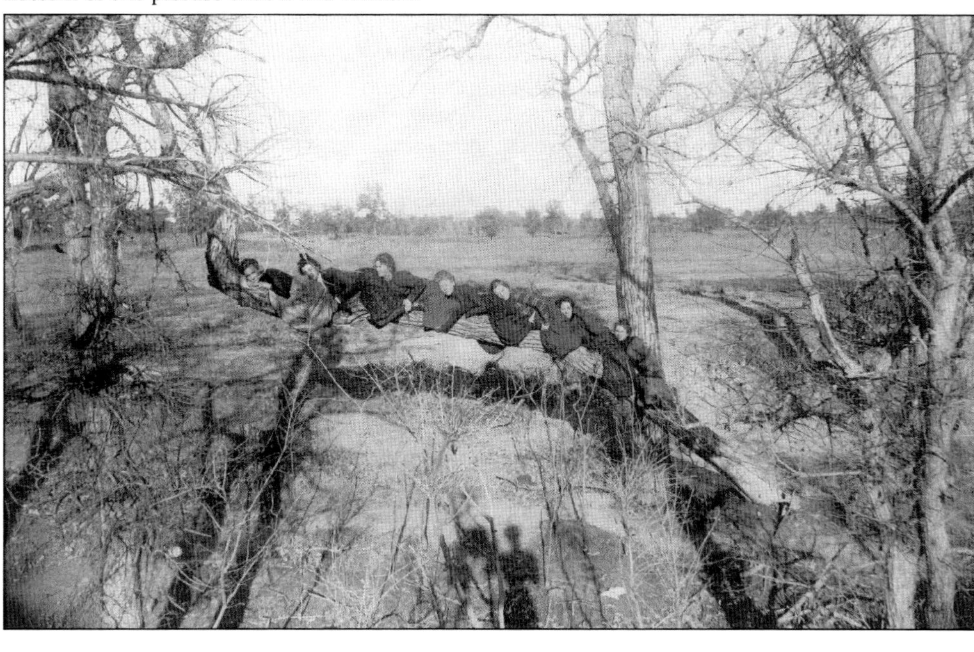

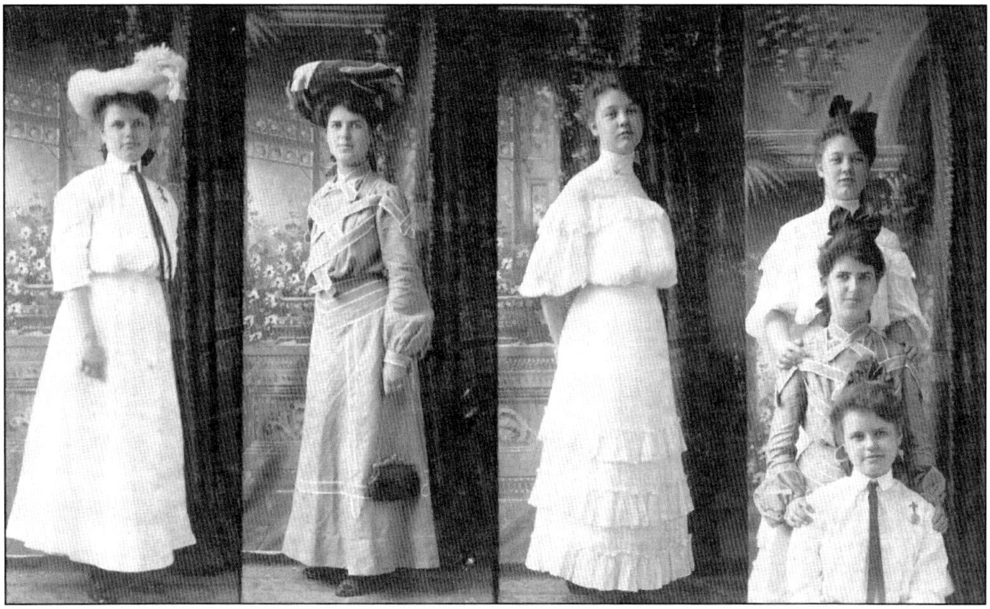

Adorned with layered dresses, oversized hats, and hair bows, this group of girls poses in the fashion of the times. There were several fashionable shops in historic Chickasha, such as the Dixie and the Eagle Mercantile Co. Stressing the importance of being in style, an old advertisement for the Eagle Mercantile Co. states "the safe way is to select only those dresses whose style authenticity is securely established."

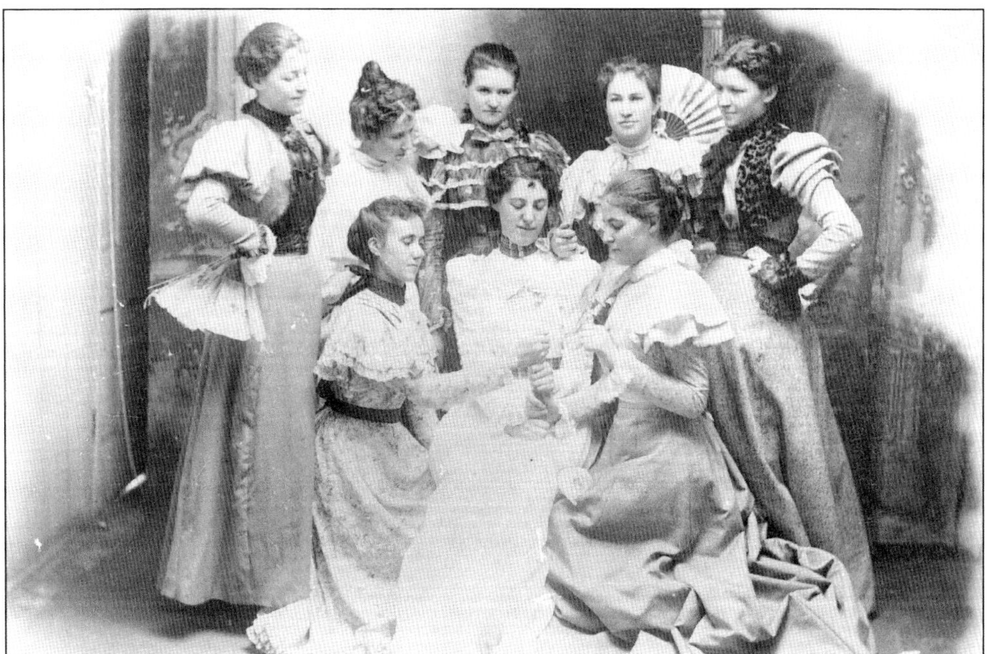

These girls came together and organized themselves into the First Girls' Club of Chickasha in 1894. The club consisted of Ethal Emby, Lille Rose, Josie Kendall, Bertrude Kendall, Nettie Munsell, Mary Williams, Bessie Tye, and, at the center, Blanche Johnston Dews. They were also charter members of the O.F.F. Club.

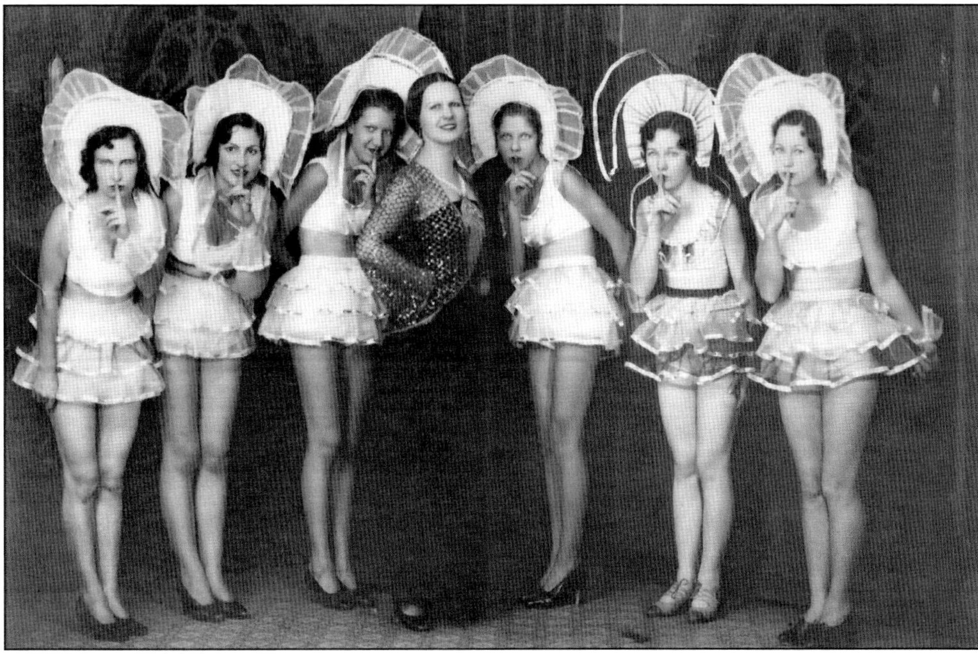

Six of these seven dancers are dressed in their ruffled skirts and oversized bonnets. The seventh dancer stands apart at center in her long, dark dress and sparkling jacket. Whether part of a play put on by the Oklahoma College for Women or an act at one of Chickasha's many theaters, the dancers definitely stood out in their day.

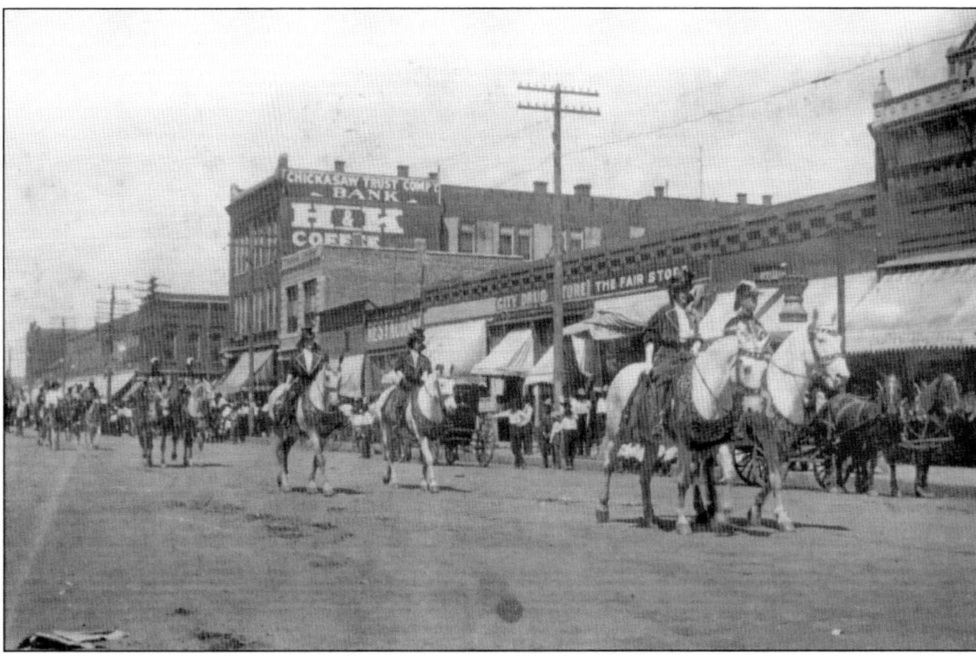

In 1906, the circus arrived at Chickasha, meaning the residents were entertained with a parade. There were a number of traveling circus groups that camped out in the area for a time. When in town, the circus would pitch its tents on a vacant lot or field and give a one-night performance of trick shooting or roping.

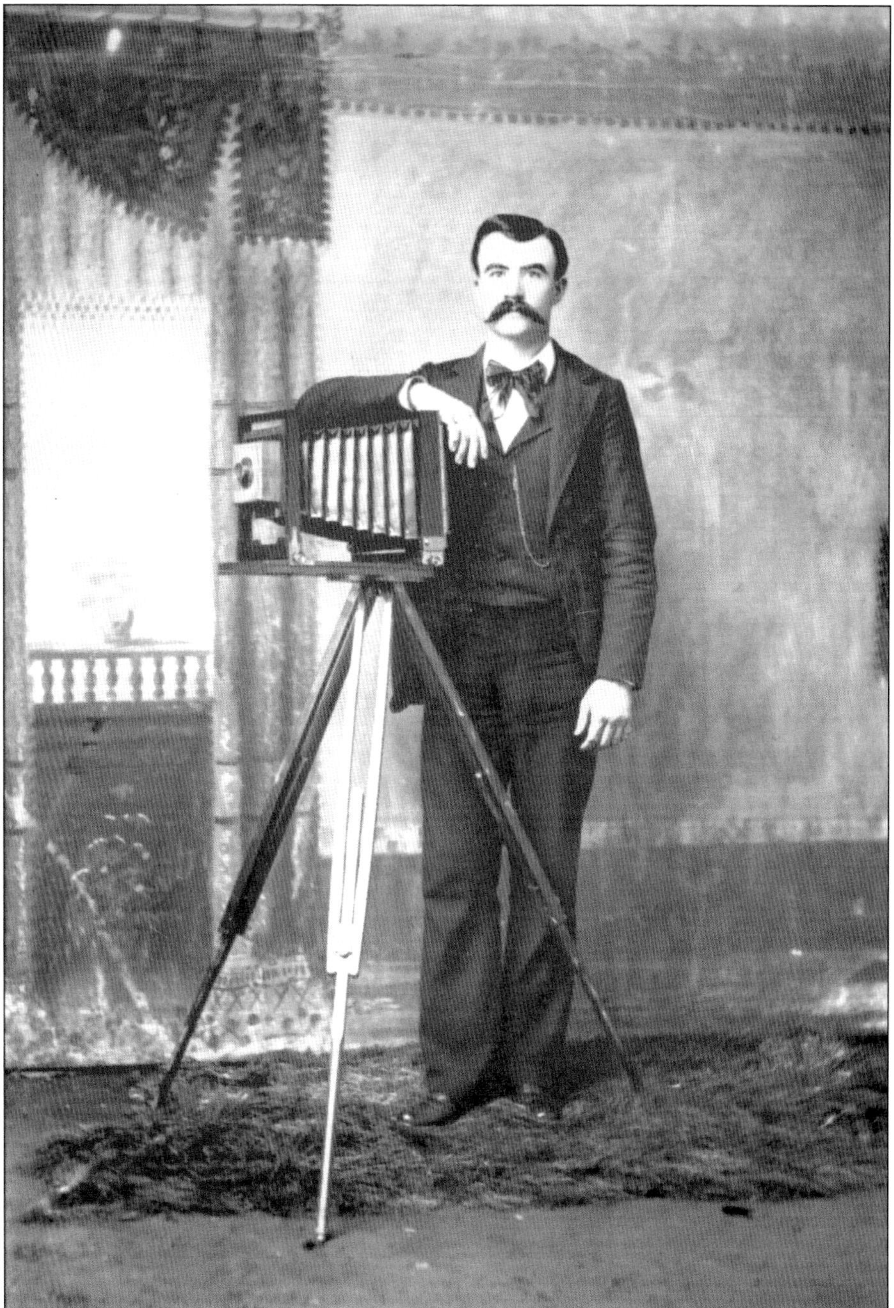

In this picture, W.E. "Ed" Irwin stands in his Chickasha studio, posing with his camera. He was a local photographer who worked in the 1890s and early 1900s during the time Chickasha was still part of the Indian Territory. Irwin took a large number of photographs of local Native American groups such as the Chiricahua Apache, Comanche, and Kiowa tribes, who lived around the Anadarko and Fort Sill areas. The majority of the Native American pictures Irwin took were staged portraits. Irwin would have the participants dress in their traditional clothing and then pose with traditional or native props in order to more accurately document the tribes.

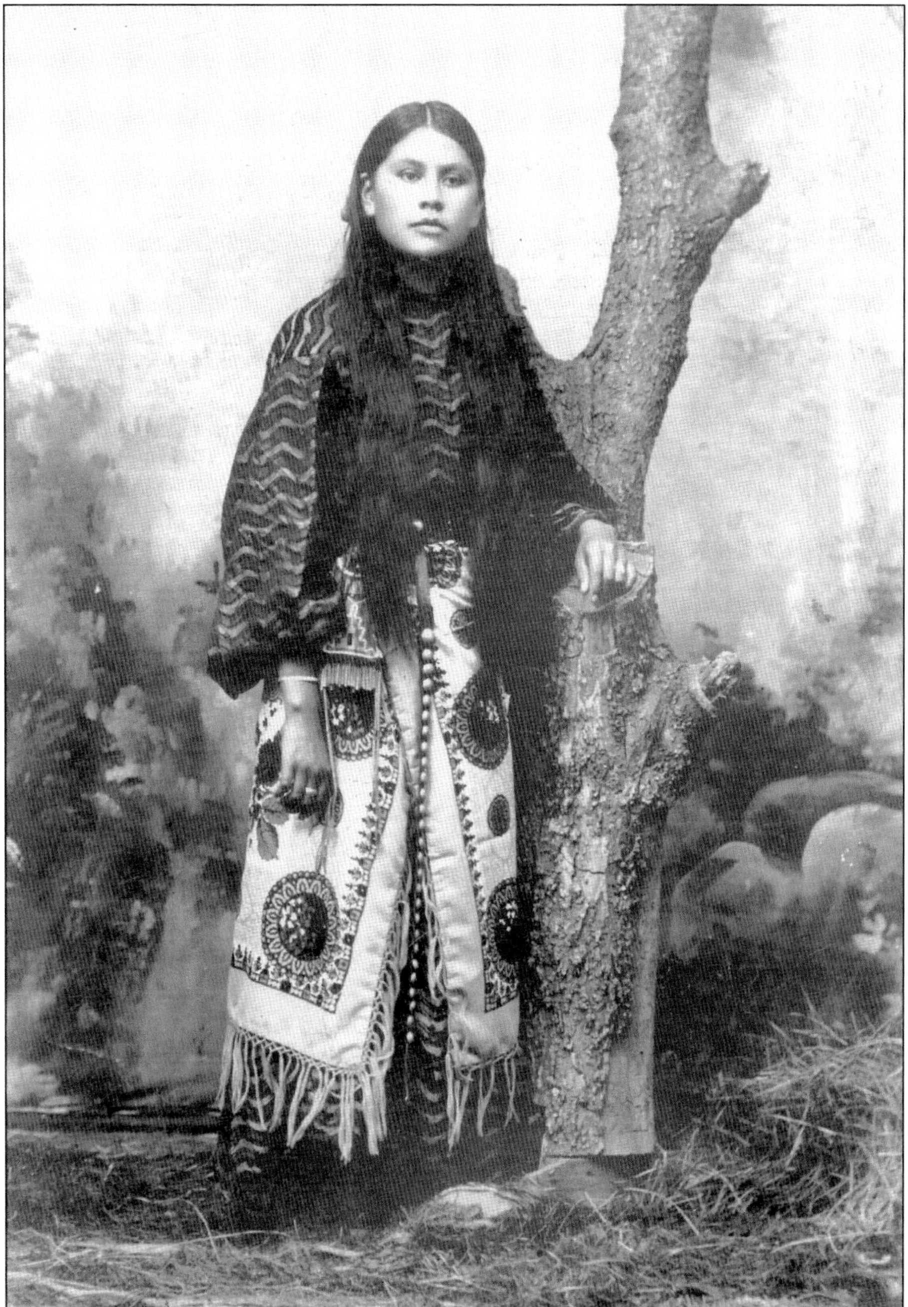

This is one of Ed Irwin's portrait photographs of the local Native American tribes. The Indian girl in Irwin's photograph is named Needle Parker, and she was the daughter of the famous Comanche chief Quanah Parker. Quanah was the leader of the Quahadi Indian band as well as a major figure in the Native American Church. Needle was Quanah's daughter by one of his many wives. Irwin also took a picture of Quanah at this time. Like many of Irwin's pictures, Needle is dressed in her traditional Native American clothing, and she is posed with a tree limb and grass as natural props.

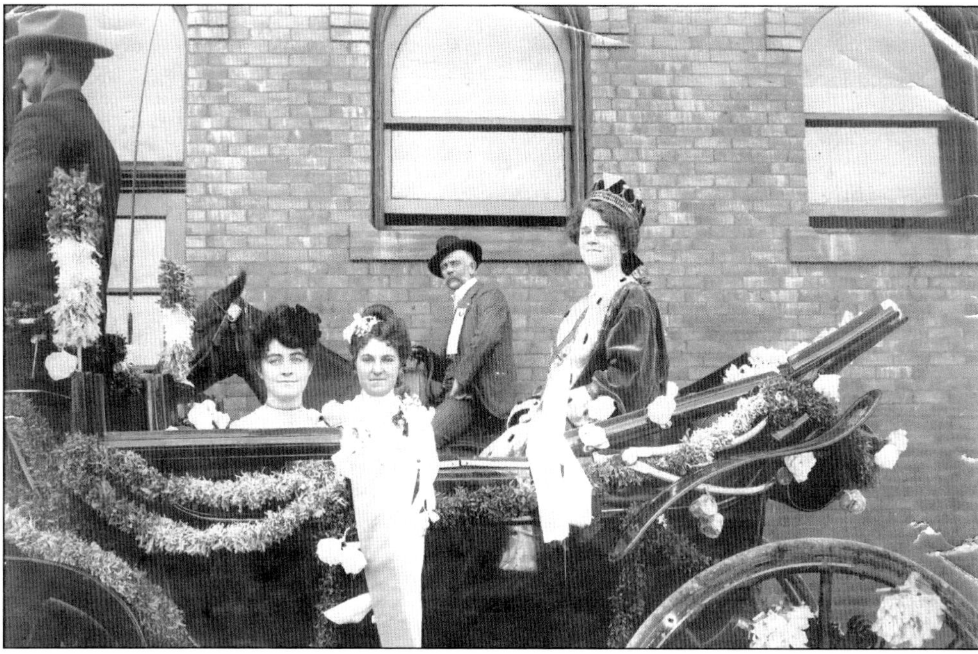

Chickasha held its first carnival and street fair on October 7, 1902. The first picture shows queen Genevieve Scoffern, who was crowned at noon that day before riding through the streets in her decorated carriage with her two attendants, Erin Murray and Mary Barton. Scoffern's father, Chickasha mayor R.F. Scoffern, rode beside her carriage on horseback. The streets were filled with spectators ready to see their new Chickasha queen and to enjoy the band and parade that followed the crowning. During the crowning, carnival official Buford Bond bestowed "all power . . . unlimited by the laws of man . . . circumscribed only by the laws of God."

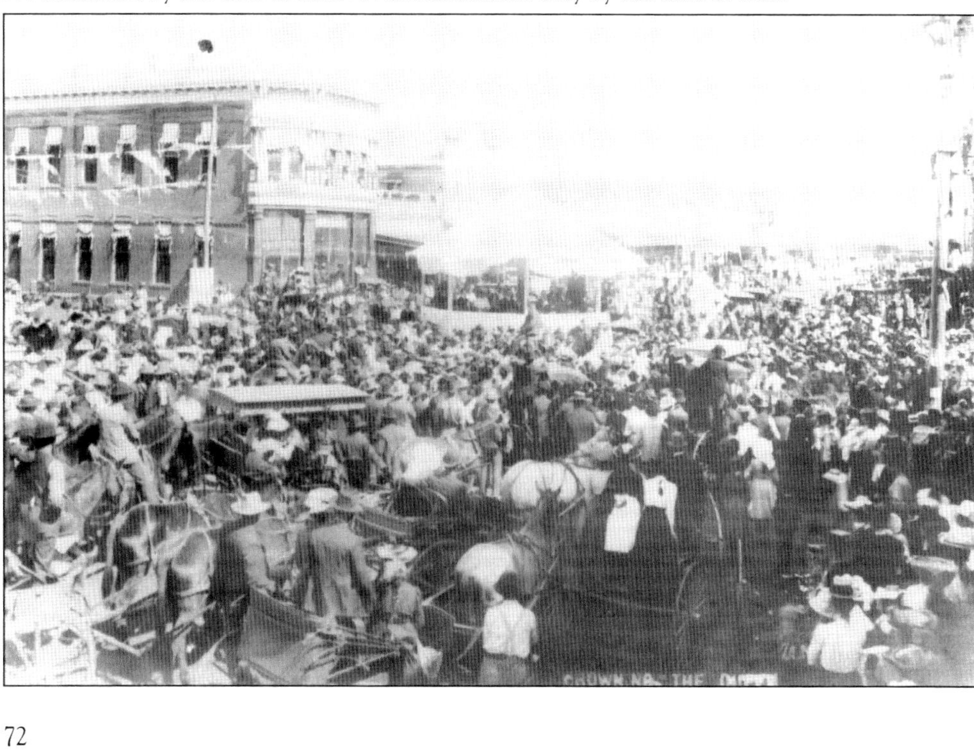

After the crowning of queen Genevieve Scoffern, spectators stayed to watch the carnival and street fair parade. The parade was set to move down Chickasha Avenue, going west to Twelfth Street, coming back, and then ending at Third Street. There were several floats and participating vehicles and horses contributed by residents and local businesses, all of which were judged for the best decorations within their group. Storefronts along the parade route were also judged for having a well-decorated merchant's display. There were even elephants brought in for the queen's parade, as shown in the picture below. After the parade, there was a regular racing program at the fairgrounds and a band of 100 Native Americans holding a powwow and war dance.

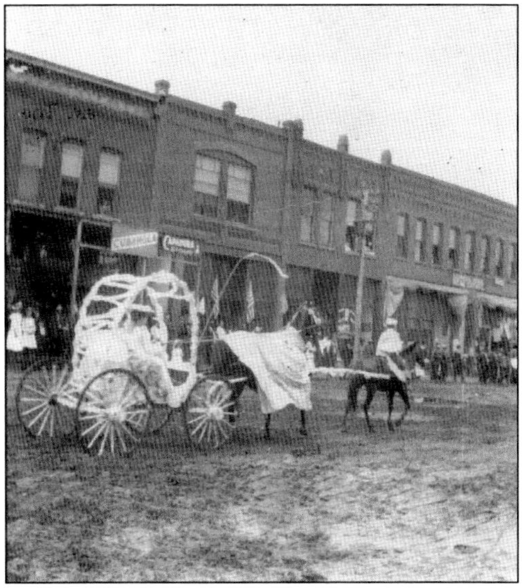

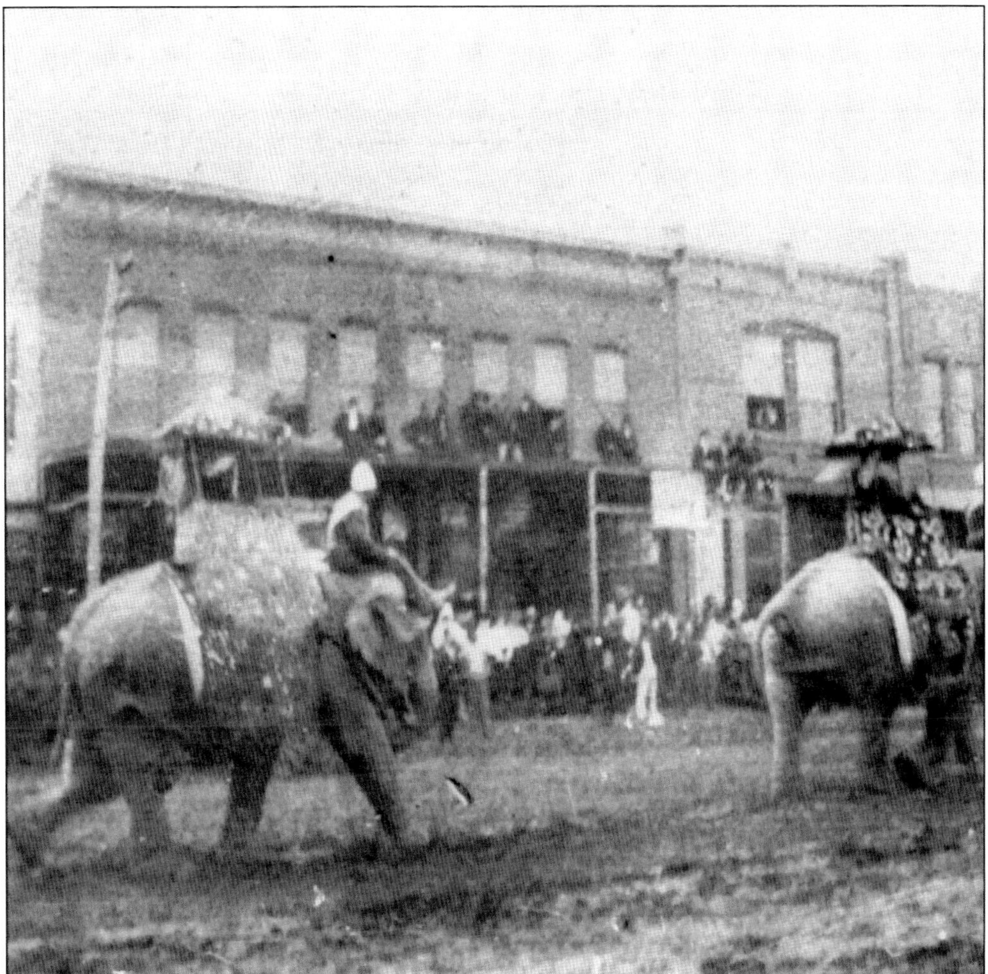

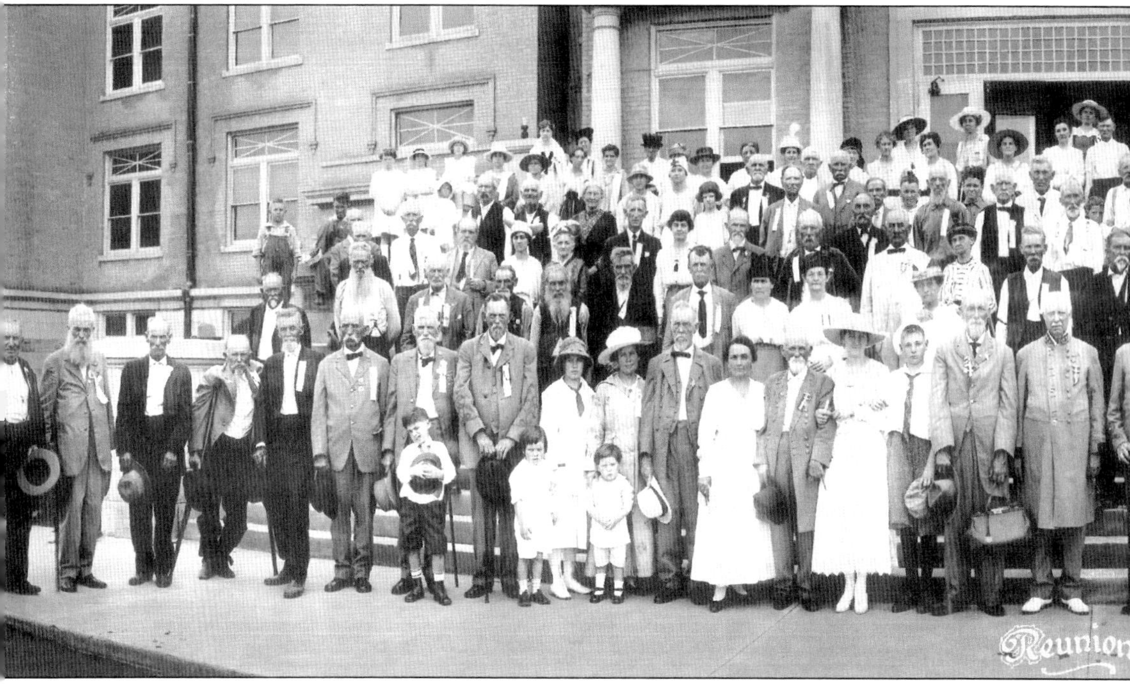

The Oklahoma College for Women (now USAO) was the scene for several reunions of Civil War veterans and their families. The reunions took place at the school between at least 1914 and 1917. State commander of the United Confederate Veterans, Gen. D.M. Hailey, was present at the reunions as were ranking officers like Gen. T.D. Turner, Gen. E.B. Coleman, and Col.

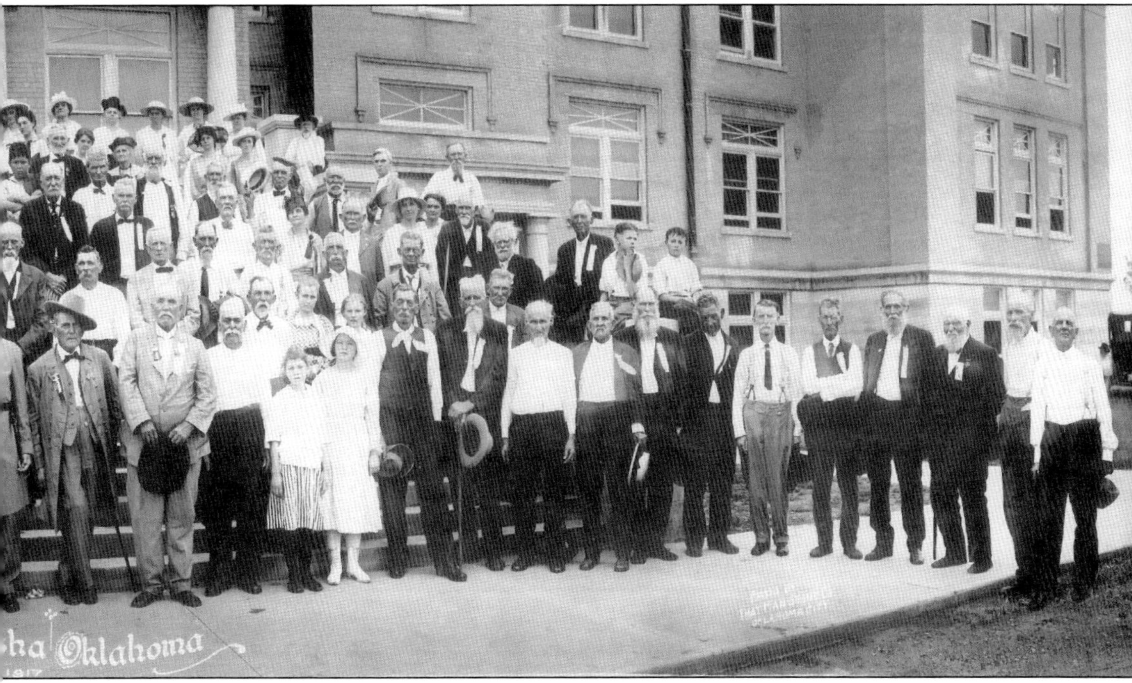

R.A. Sneed. The college provided young men who acted as orderlies during the reunion. These orderlies met the veterans at the Rock Island train station and then accompanied them to the campus rooms they stayed in for their visit.

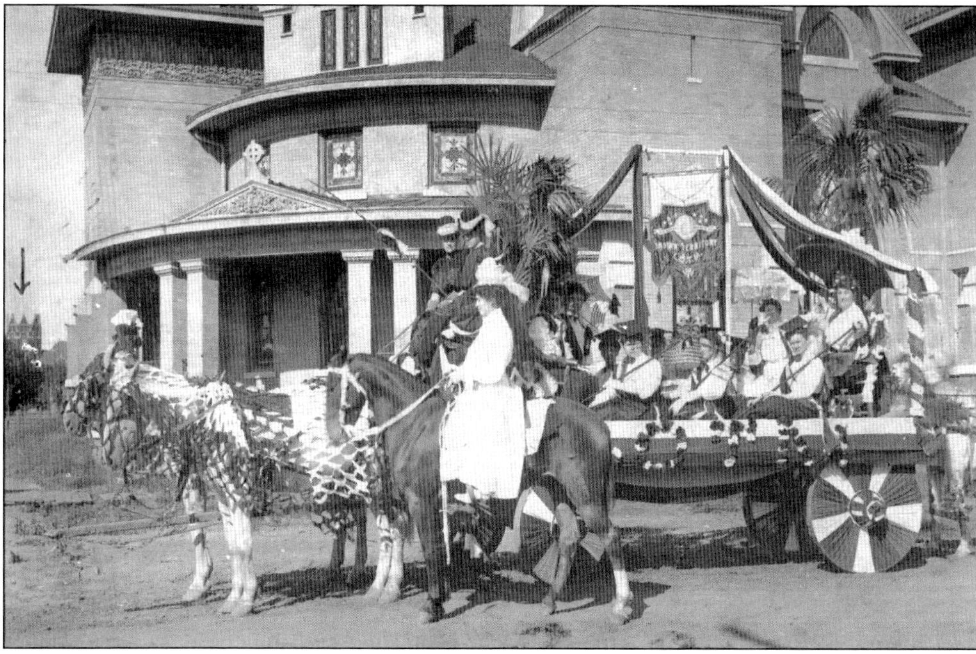

In 1907, Chickasha held a celebration in honor of Oklahoma's brand-new statehood. As was popular in town, there was a parade as part of the festivities. This picture shows the territory float passing in front of Epworth Methodist Episcopal Church at Fourth Street and Iowa Avenue. The initials *LOTM* on the banner and spelled out in flowers on the side of the float most likely stand for the Ladies of the Maccabees.

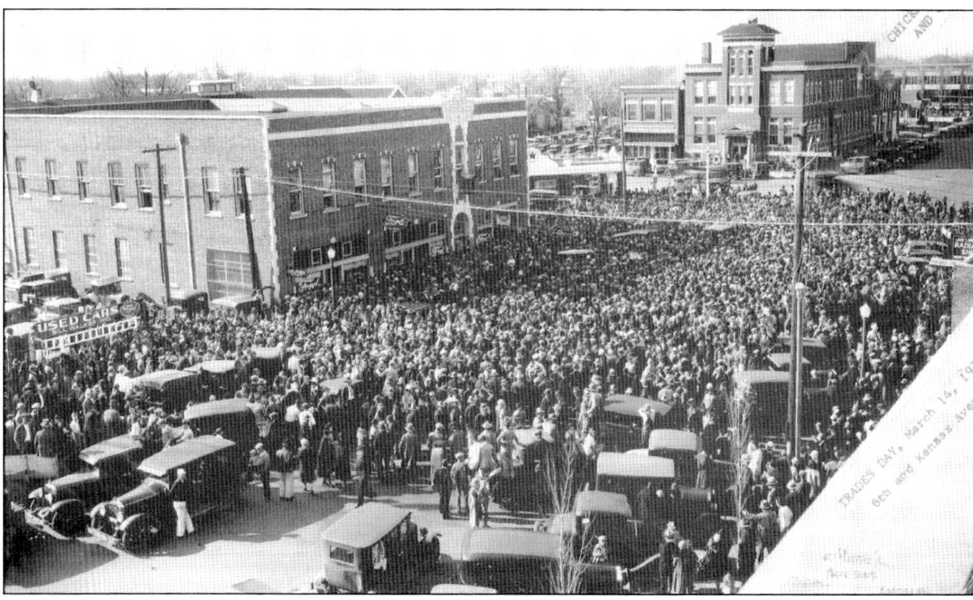

Grady County had a tradition of holding Trades Days in Chickasha multiple times a year. These were special days organized by town merchants. Trades Days were usually on a Saturday, and the idea behind them was to encourage local farmers to come into town to shop. Trades Days, along with parades, carnivals, and theaters, were only a portion of the many ways that Chickasha residents found entertainment.

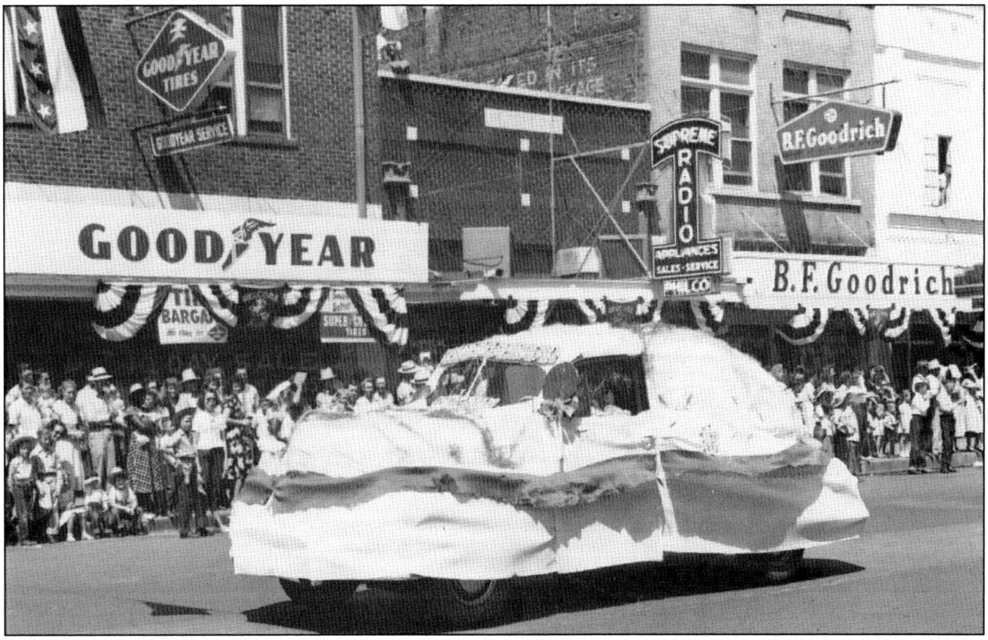

Parades were a favorite way to celebrate anything in Chickasha, and they were filled to the brim with floats in all shapes and sizes. The picture above shows a car that is covered in white paper or fabric, ruffles, tinsel, bows, and giant lollipops. The sign on the windshield of the car reads, "Cate's Candy Company," written in shaped candy canes. The picture below shows a car covered in signs promoting Buicks. The two unidentified men drive along, pulling a smaller car with "Buick" and other words painted on it. A young boy sits in the little pulled car, "driving" and enjoying being in the parade.

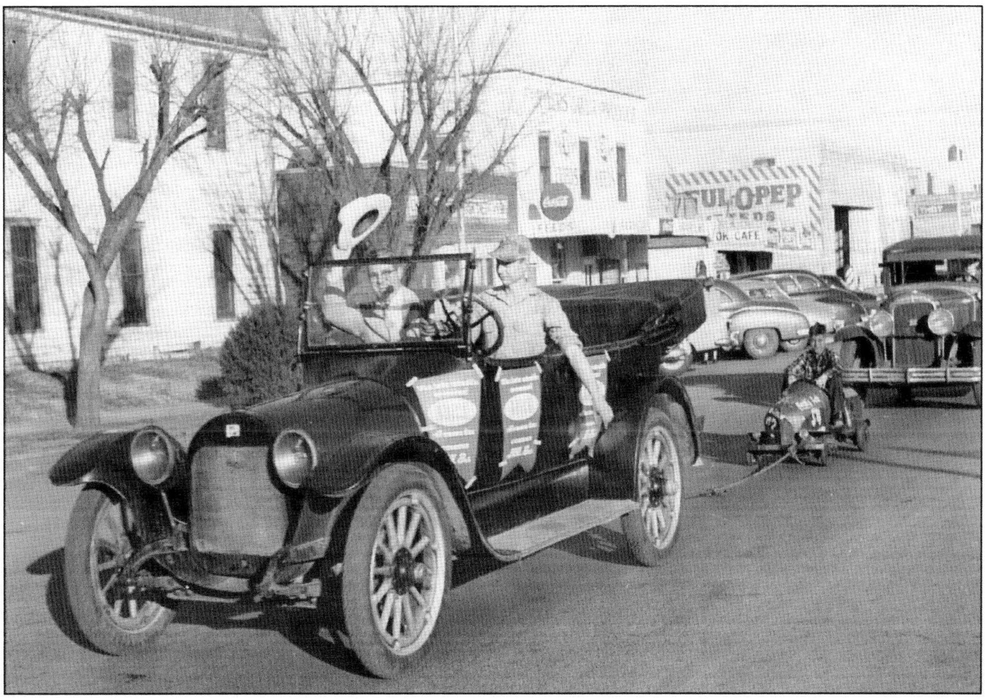

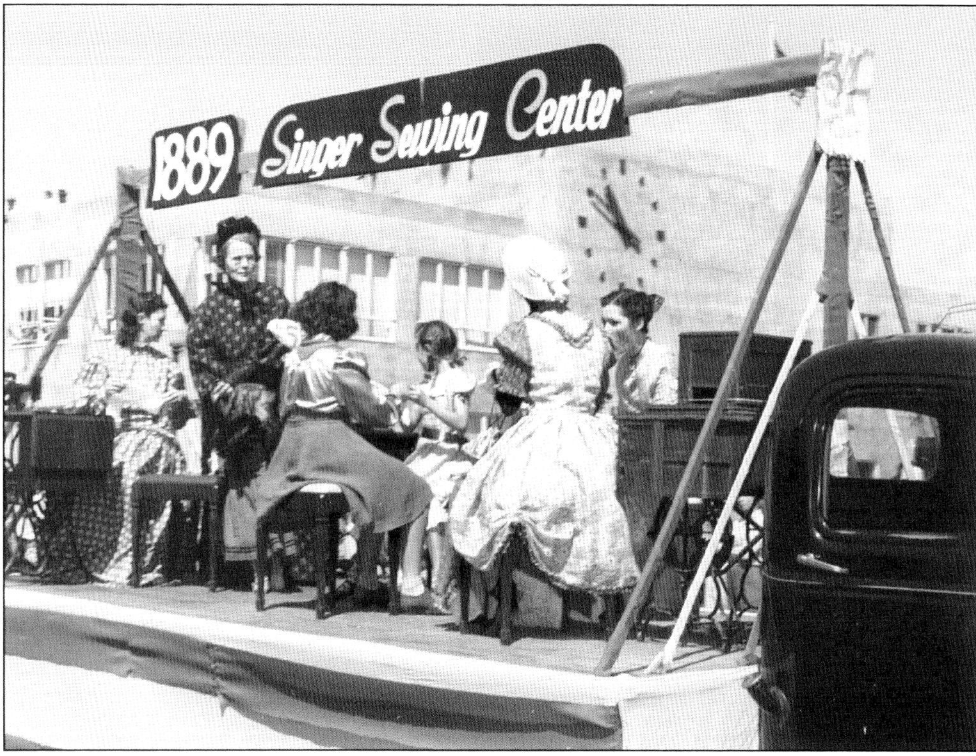

In two other Chickasha parades, there was another variety of floats. The picture above shows a float for the Singer Sewing Center that is part of an unknown parade. The Singer Sewing Center was opened in 1889, and so the women on the float are dressed in clothing that is appropriate for that period. The picture below, taken on November 11, 1931, shows one of the floats for the town's Armistice Day parade. This float was provided by the Southwestern Light and Power Company, which decided to represent a number of military servicemen and women on its float, such as a nurse and a Navy sailor, as well as advertise the company with an electrical worker posing with a telephone pole and power generators.

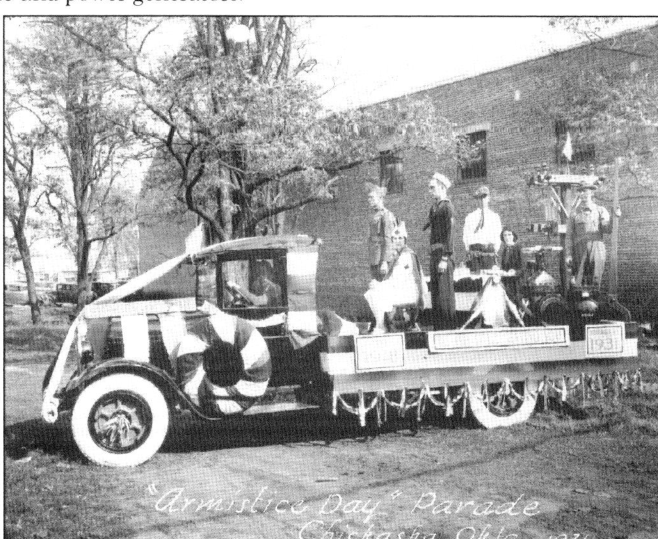

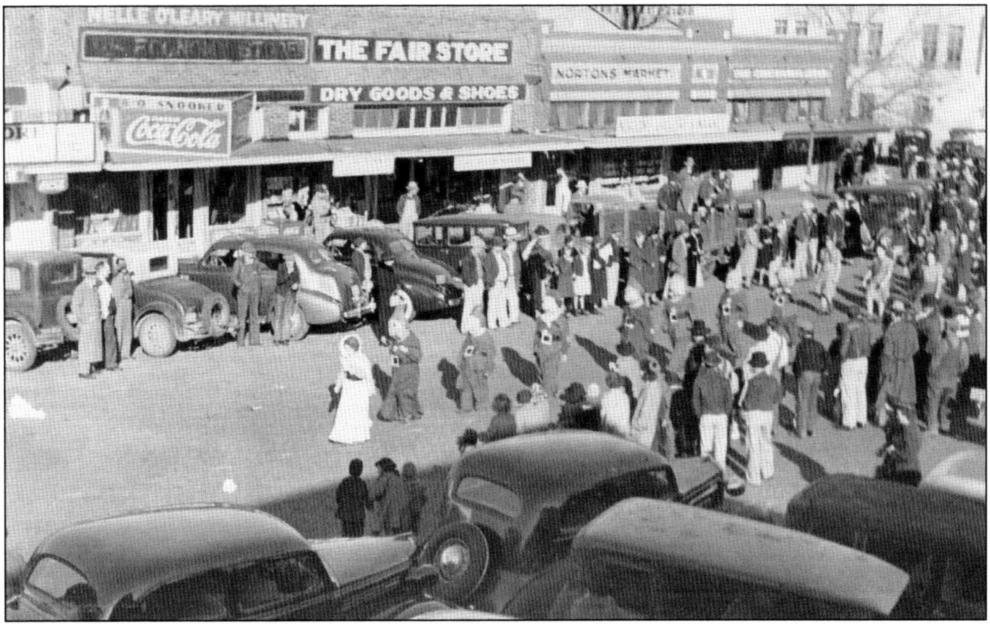

Trades Days were sometimes accompanied by an elaborate parade. The picture above shows a Trades Day held on Christmas Day in 1931. The parade moved down Choctaw Avenue between rows of grocery stores and markets. Despite the cold, a large number of spectators have come out to watch as Snow White and her seven dwarfs march along the street. The picture below shows a Christmas parade. Little girls, daughters of several local families, are dressed up in white and placed on miniature floats or bikes that are all Christmas-themed. The girls are accompanied by members of the Chickasha Boy Scouts.

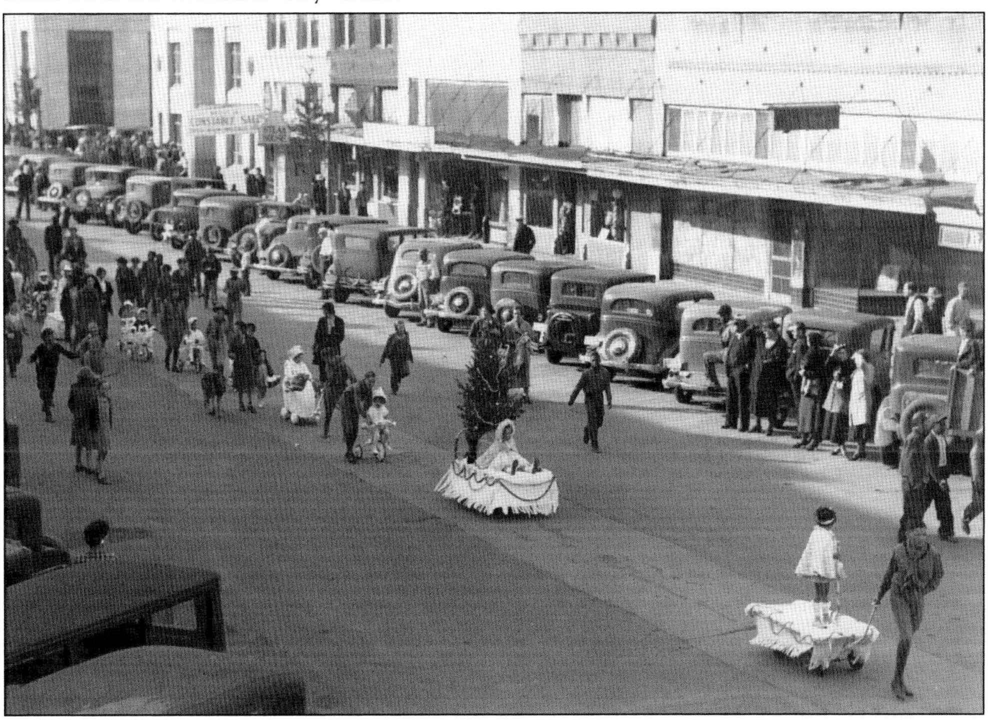

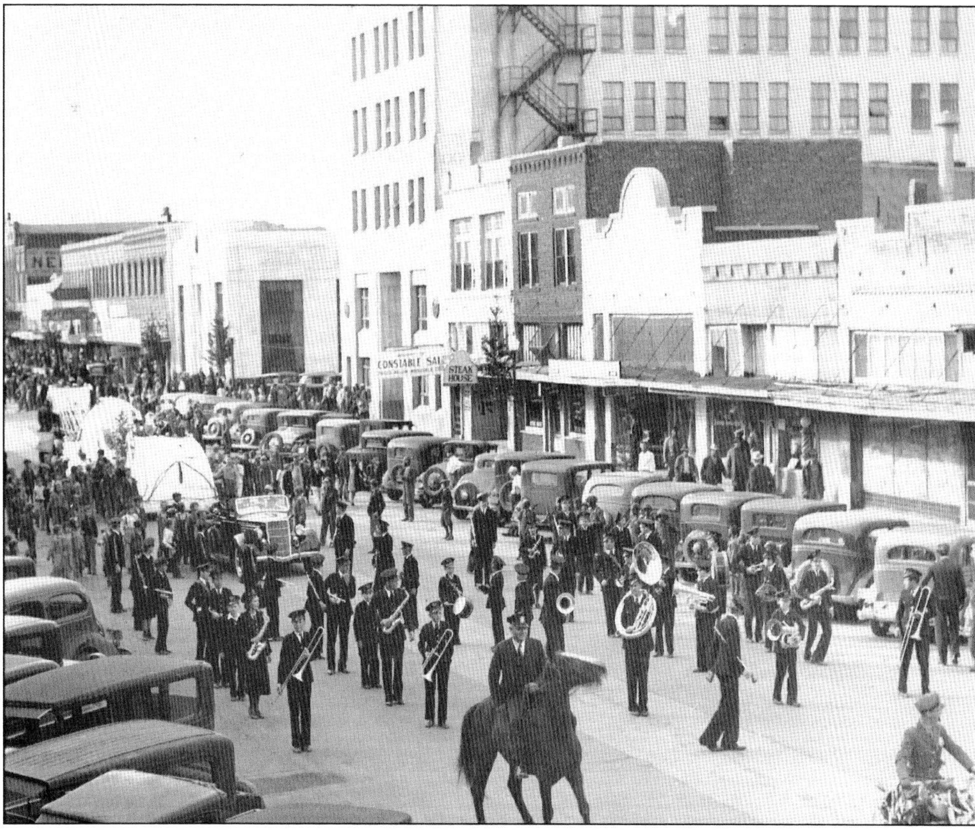

Chickasha parades almost always had a marching band mixed in somewhere between the floats and decorated vehicles. The picture above shows a local children's band in full marching uniforms. The parade the children are playing for is another Christmas parade, celebrated around the 1930s. The picture below was taken as the Chickasha school band played for a parade that moved down Chickasha Avenue. Spectators look on in late spring or early fall as the majorettes literally run through their routine and lead the rest of the band. This second parade took place in 1948.

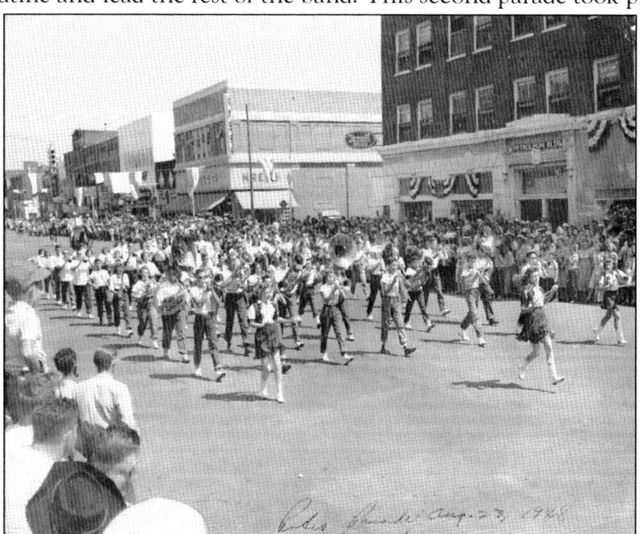

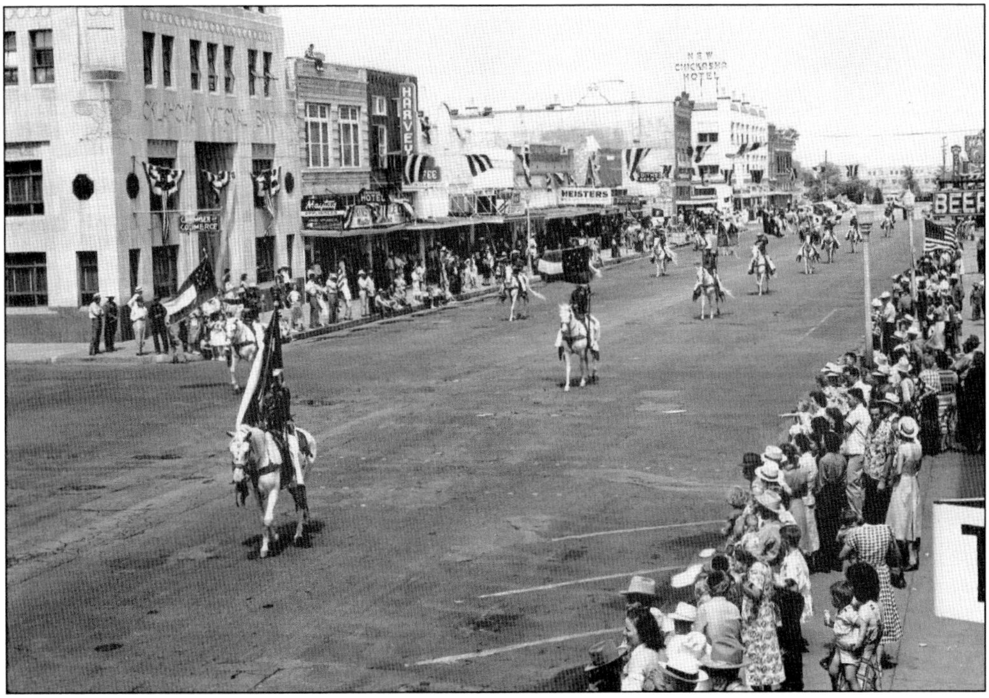

Rodeo parades were a popular event held by Chickasha. These were put on by Chickasha's Rodeo Association and accompanied the town's annual rodeo. The association was started tentatively in 1939 by a chamber of commerce that was wary of rodeos after a con artist had stolen money invested in the town's first rodeo. For the following rodeos, 10¢ from every ticket sold went to the county fair.

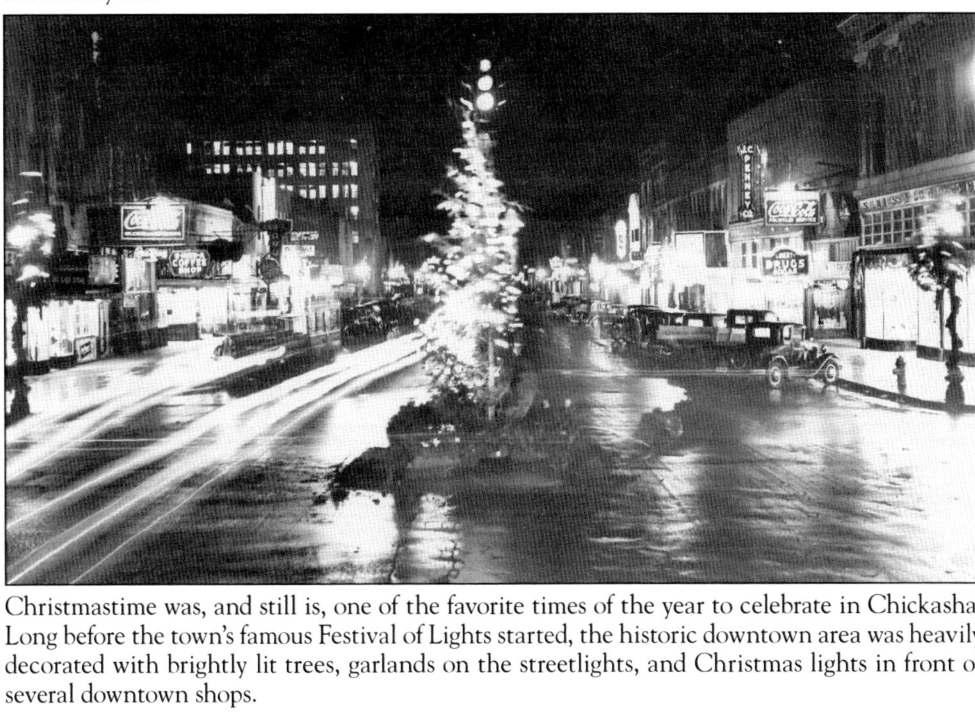

Christmastime was, and still is, one of the favorite times of the year to celebrate in Chickasha. Long before the town's famous Festival of Lights started, the historic downtown area was heavily decorated with brightly lit trees, garlands on the streetlights, and Christmas lights in front of several downtown shops.

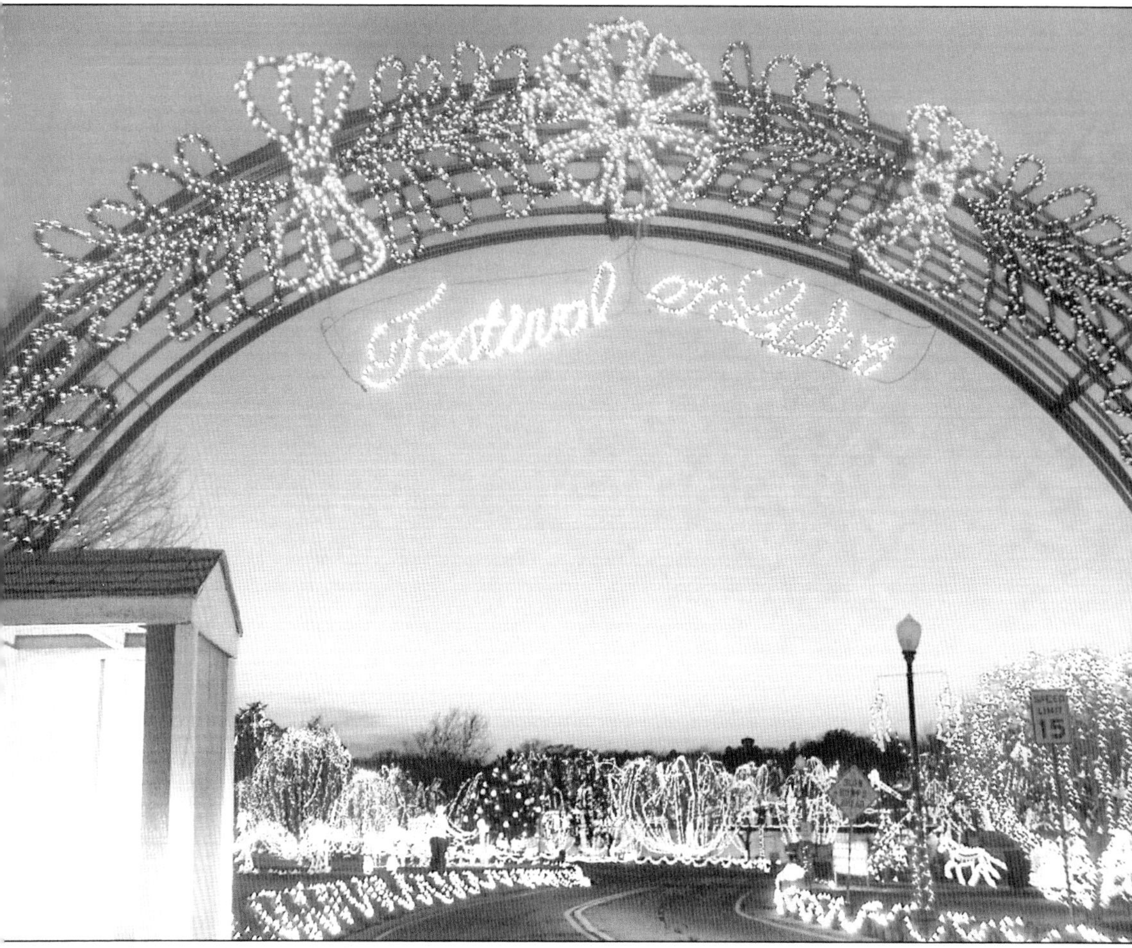

The annual Festival of Lights is Chickasha's claim to fame today. The town had always been heavily decorated for Christmas, as shown in the previous picture in which downtown is covered in lights and garlands and small Christmas trees. The town's holiday decorations can also be seen in the pictures of Christmas parades. In 1993, a group of citizens who wanted to bring even more Christmas spirit and community pride to the town organized the first Festival of Lights. Now, every year, the Shannon Springs Park is completely coated in lights for the festival. (Courtesy of Festival of Light, Inc.)

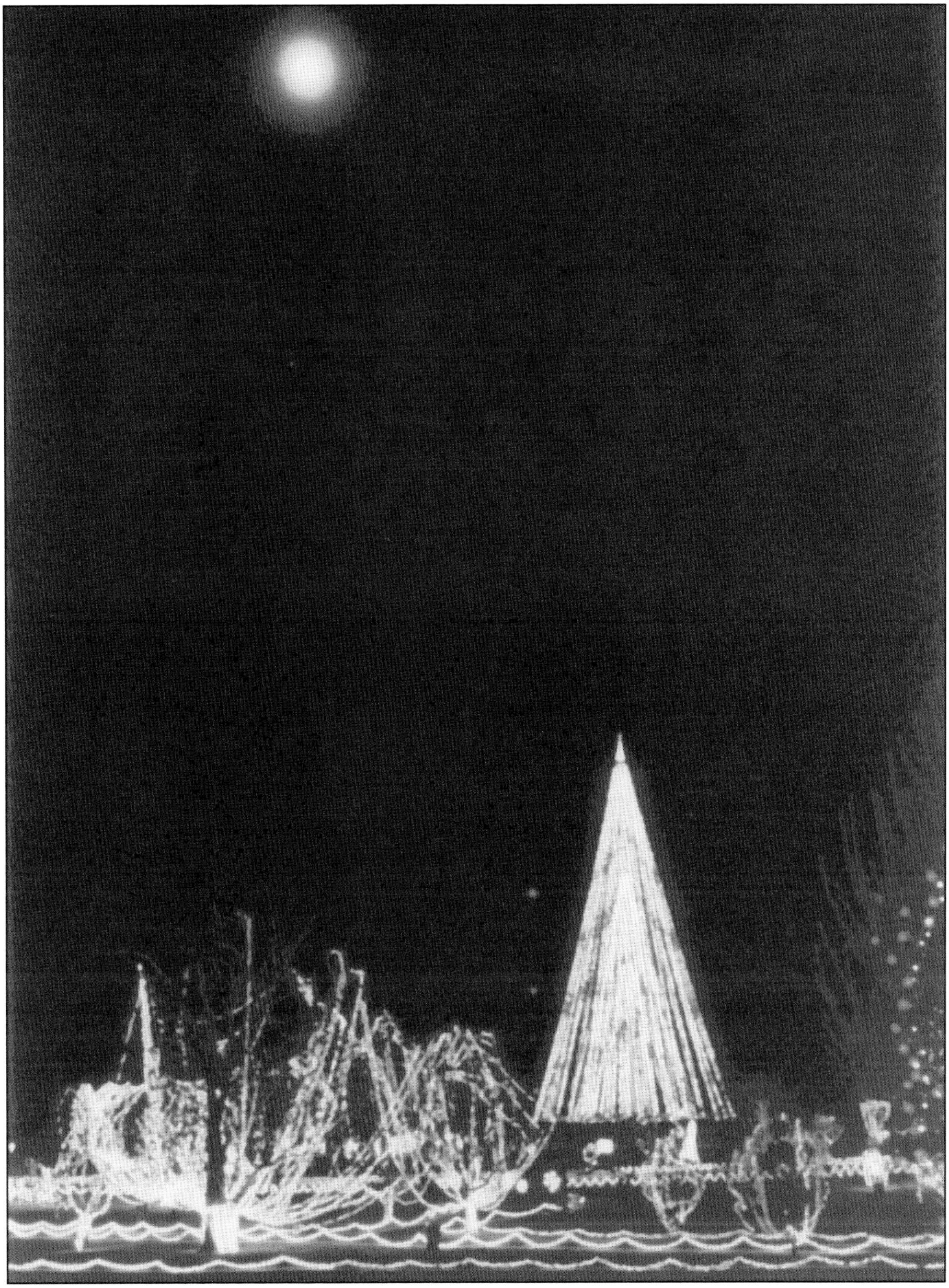

The Big Tree is one of the main features at the light-filled Shannon Springs Park during the annual Festival of Lights. The tree is 16 stories tall and it is lit in different colors every year, with over 25,000 Christmas lights. The tree itself uses as much energy as the rest of the park's displays combined. It is considered good luck by some visitors to stand under the tree's 80-foot diameter base and spin in a circle. Other featured decorations include a wooden bridge that crosses the small lake that is covered in an archway of white lights. There are over four miles of lit walkways in the park. (Courtesy of Festival of Light, Inc.)

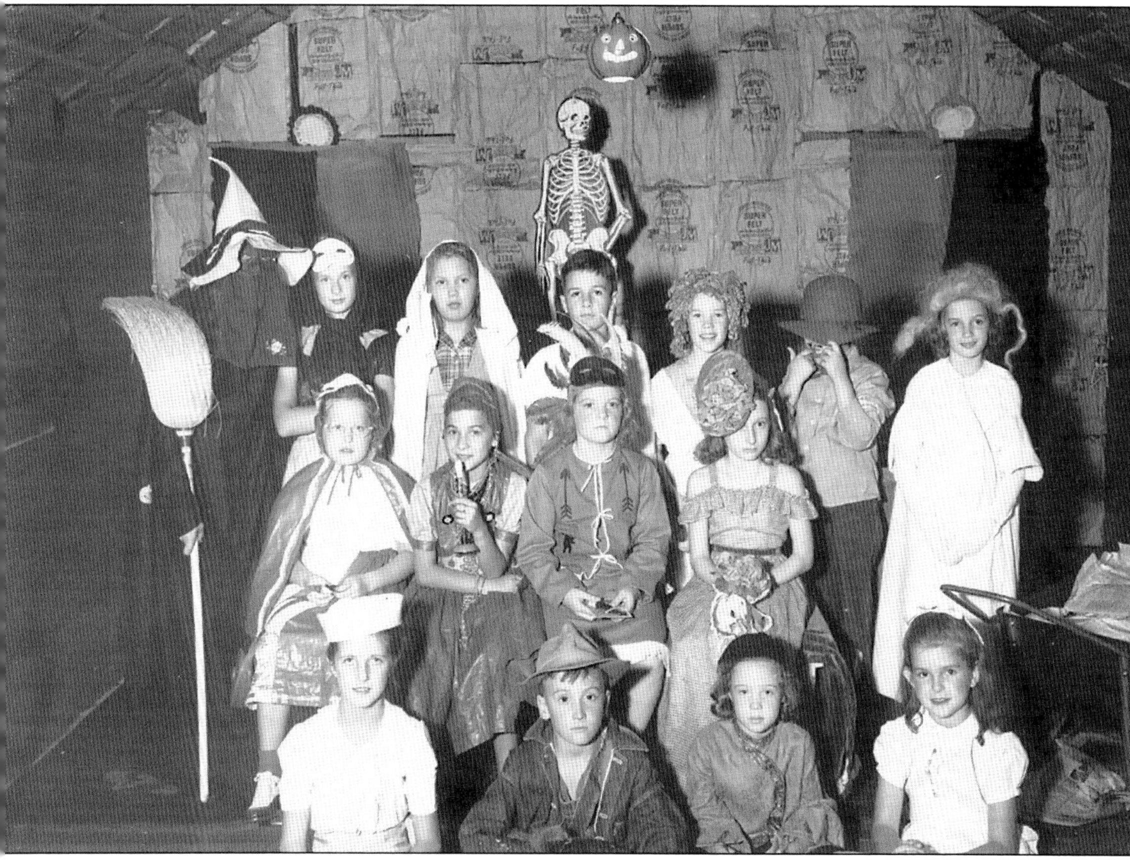

This photograph shows those attending a Halloween party for the Mozart Jr. Music Club of the MacDowell Music Club in 1948. The picture was taken at the home of Janet and Helen Ross. The MacDowell Music Club began in 1911 for the purposes of studying famous musicians and development of music for young people.

Four

Religious Life

Religion has always been an important aspect of life in Chickasha; it was not long after the first tents dotted the landscape that religious organizations formed. The town is spiritually, politically, and culturally connected to the Bible Belt. Oklahoma has a unique religious history because it was designated as Indian Territory. At the dawn of the 19th century, American Indian religions dominated what would later be called Oklahoma. In 1821, the American Board of Commissioners for Foreign Missions (ABCFM) established the Dwight Mission in Arkansas for the purpose of converting American Indians to Presbyterian and Congregationalist churches. Later, in the 1840s, Southern evangelical religions were brought to Oklahoma along the Trail of Tears by the Five Civilized Tribes, including the Chickasaw, who settled on the future site of Chickasha. After the Civil War, Southerners looking for a new start, including freed slaves, arrived in Oklahoma, strengthening the presence of Southern Baptists and Methodists in Oklahoma.

With the land rushes, the new population did little to increase religious diversity in Oklahoma. The religious alignment to the South, with fundamental and revival Christianity, is evident both culturally and politically. Through the 20th century, Oklahoma supported racial segregation and social conservatives. With the Cold War, conservative churches remained strong as they connected their teachings with the evils of communism and the counter culture.

With the founding of Chickasha, all the Christians met together in different stores for a common sermon, but it did not take long for religious cooperation to end. The Presbyterians built the first church and opened its doors to all, and they would soon be followed by other denominations. In 1898, the following churches were listed in Chickasha: Presbyterian, Christian Church, Roman Catholic, Baptist, and Methodist. Over the years, buildings would come and go, with many being renovated and expanded. Today, with what seems to be a church on every corner, Chickasha has retained its strong religious character.

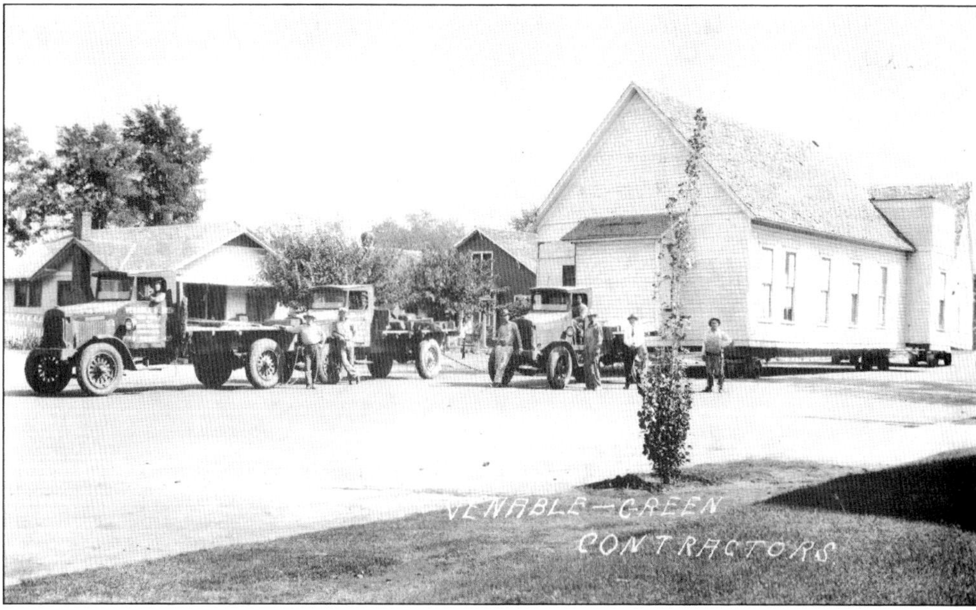

The First Presbyterian Church, which was one of the original four established in the town's inaugural year, constructed the first church building in Chickasha. It was officially organized on June 28, 1892. In the beginning, the church opened its door to other congregations to meet in the building, giving the First Presbyterian Church the name "a mother of churches." The Presbyterians also established the first school in town, which met in their building. In 1922, the church was moved to make room for a new structure.

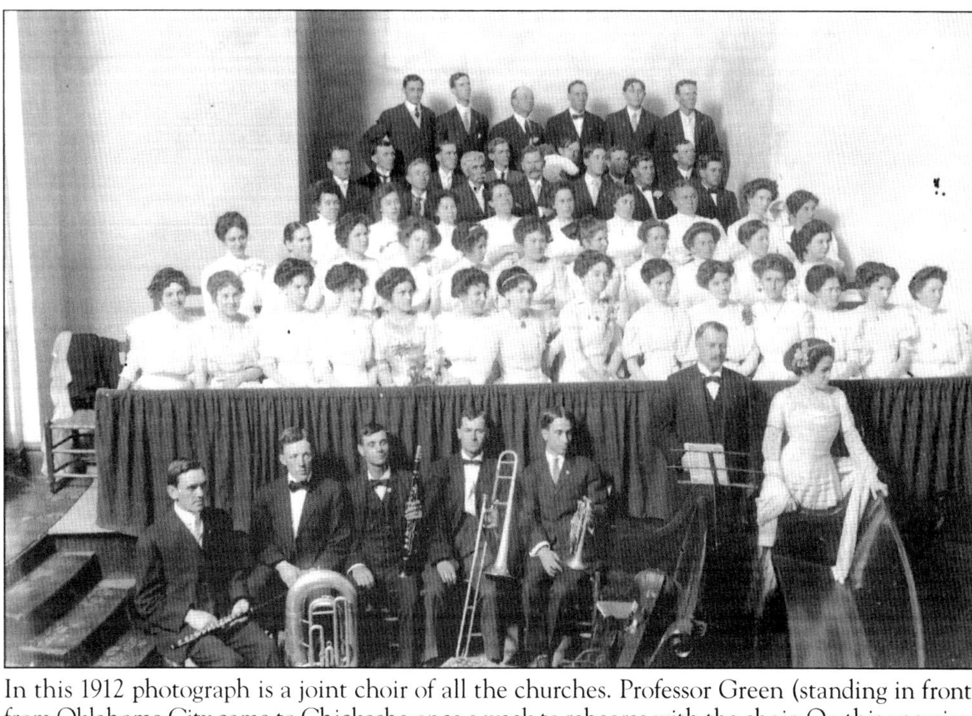

In this 1912 photograph is a joint choir of all the churches. Professor Green (standing in front) from Oklahoma City came to Chickasha once a week to rehearse with the choir. On this occasion, he brought a special guest soloist from Oklahoma City to sing.

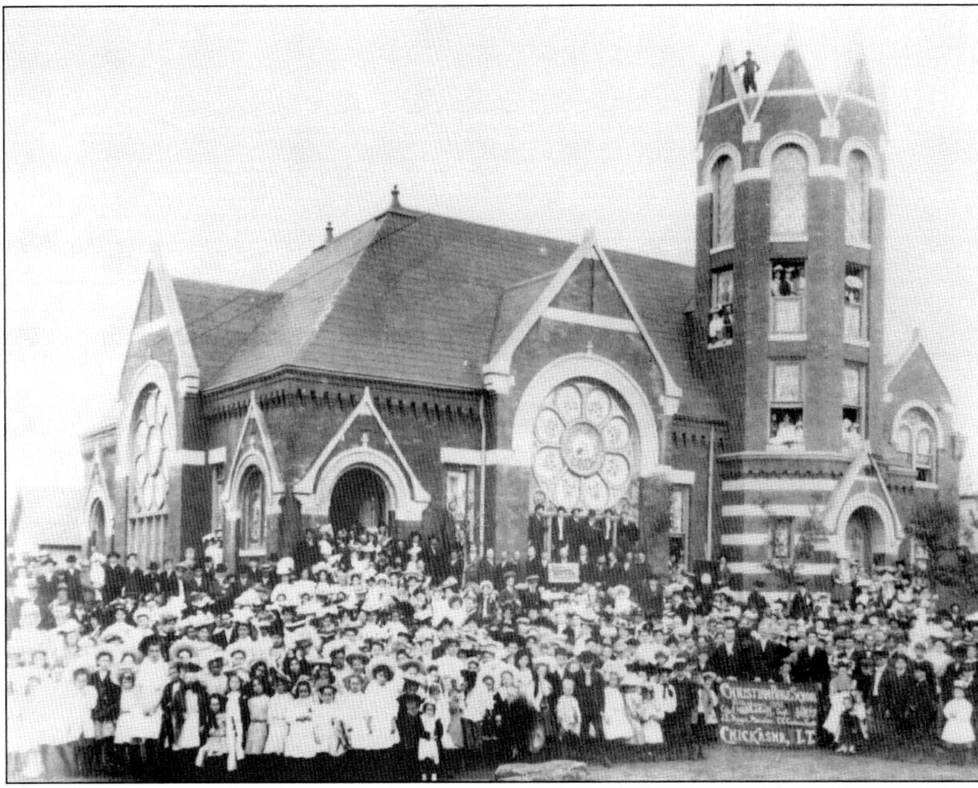

The First Christian Church was another of the four original churches in Chickasha. In 1892, it was organized under the leadership of Lillian Bohart Welsh and S.C. Kennedy. Members erected their first church in 1894, then replaced it with this new brick Gothic-style building in 1904. This 1907 picture shows the Sunday school posing in front of its new home.

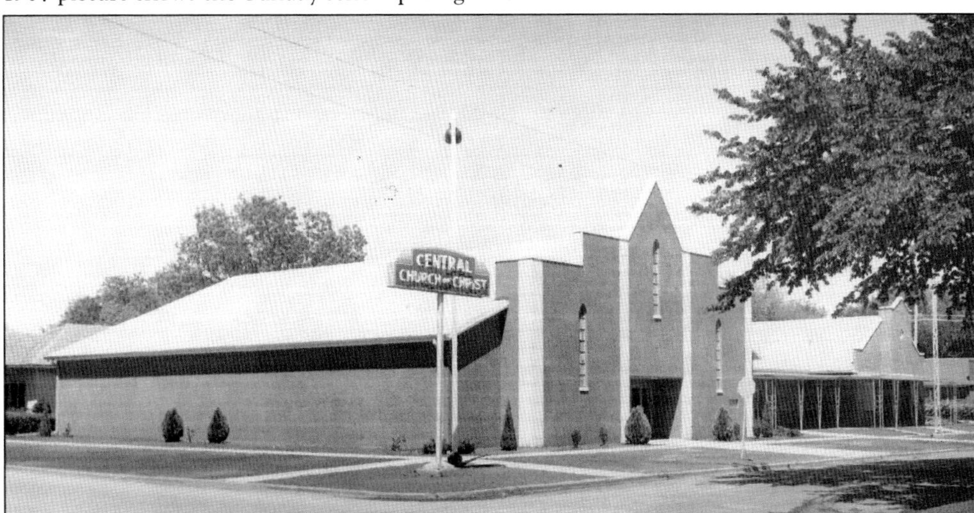

In 1915, the first meeting of the Church of Christ was held in the backyard of a Mrs. Freeman. In 1916, the church began holding services above the Dixie Store. The congregants purchased the building from the First Christian Church in 1926, but they eventually constructed this new building on the lot in 1959. The structure is now the home of Stanley Office Supply.

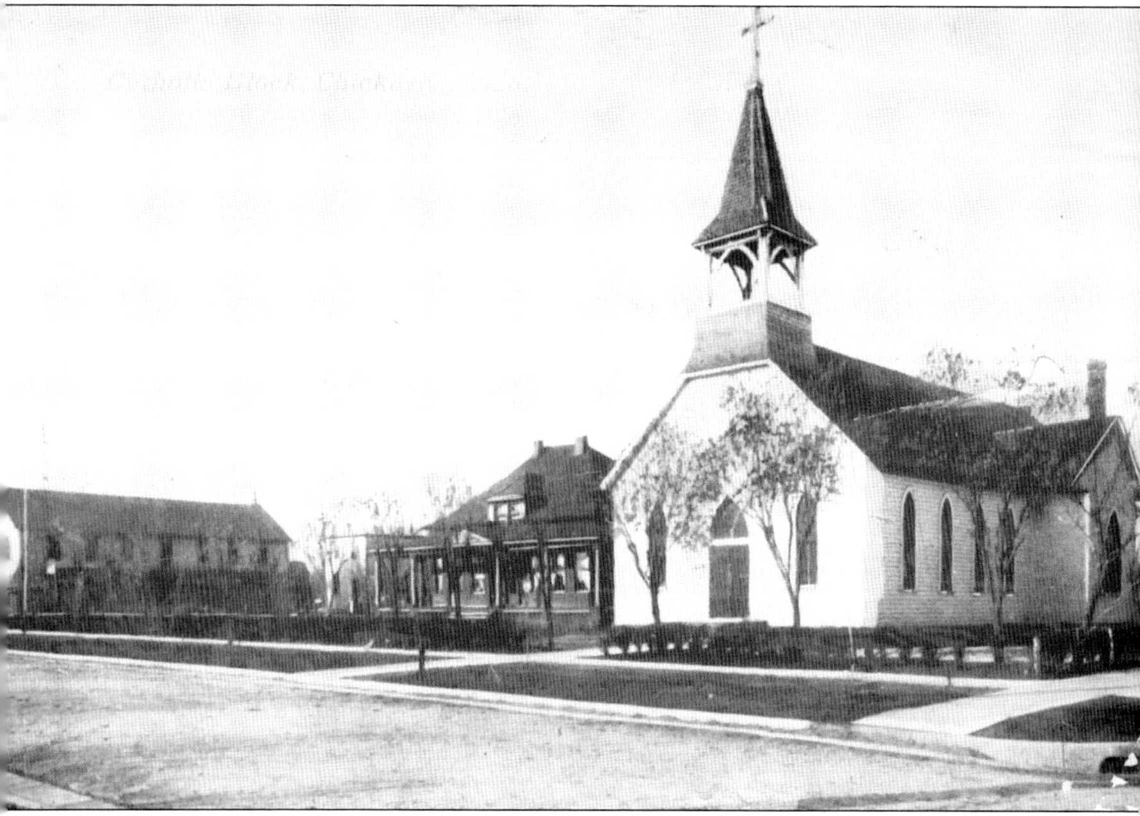

The Holy Name Catholic Church officially began in 1895 under the direction of Pastor Joseph Van Hulse. Without a building, parishioners met in the Fitzpatrick Building on Main Street, and when they outgrew that establishment they moved to the Masonic Lodge. Finally, in 1898, under Fr. Isidore Ricklin, the new spiritual leader in Chickasha, the Catholics' first building was constructed. Also that year, the church took the opportunity to purchase an entire square block of land with a two-story school building. In November 1899, four Franciscan nuns arrived in Chickasha and opened the first Catholic school in their newly acquired school building. St. Joseph's Academy's initial enrollment was 100 students, but by 1902, the number of students was over 160. Finally, in 1902, under the new leadership of Fr. Urban de Hasque, the church building was moved onto the new property at the present-day site of the Catholic church.

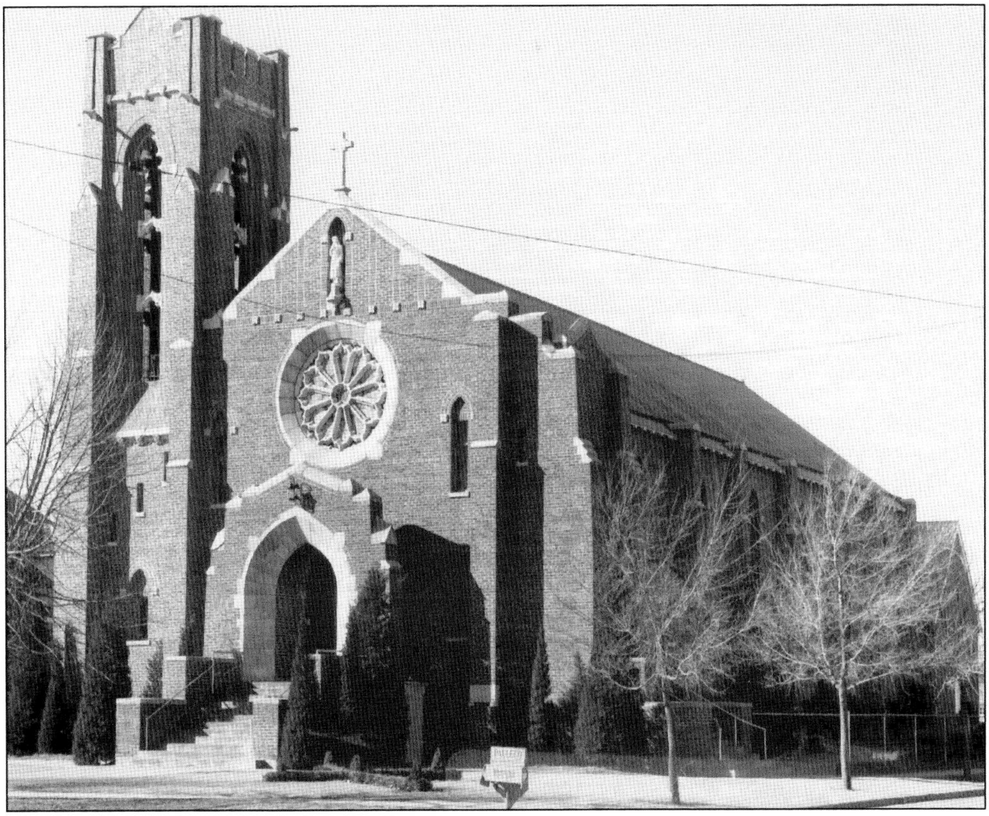

In 1925, Fr. Van Wees took over leadership of the Catholic church in Chickasha and began construction on the new church building, seen above, designed by Harold Gilmeno. It was dedicated on May 5, 1926, by Bishop Francis Kelly. The picture below is a view of the inside of the new church. Though the Catholic church has prospered in Chickasha, it struggled in the early years in Oklahoma. After the lands rushes, the population grew so fast and with so much chaos, the more organized denominations like Catholics and Episcopalians struggled while the less structured denominations tended to fare better. At one point, when Prohibition was in effect in Oklahoma, sacramental wine was even outlawed.

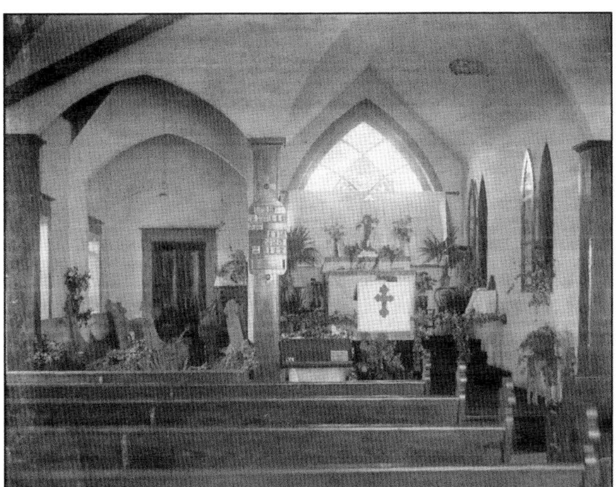

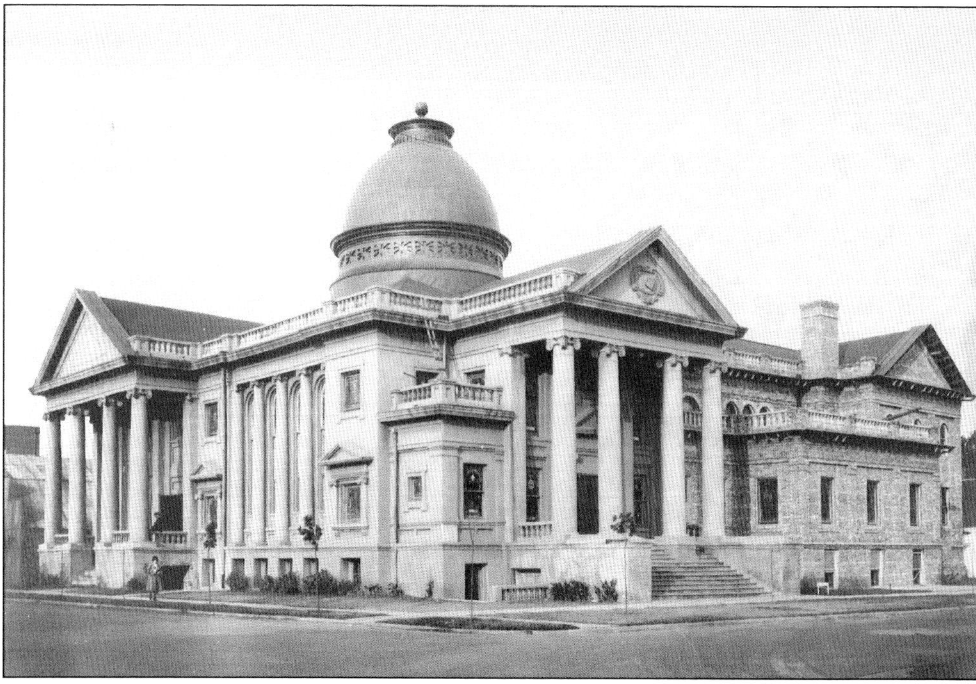

The First Baptist Church began in 1892 under the leadership of R.J. Dyes, and its first minister was T.E. Covington. In the beginning, the Baptists met together with other denominations. However, a local story goes that during a meeting in 1892, an unknown preacher claimed that all Baptists were doomed for perdition, causing the Baptists to break away that very day and form the first Baptists charter. The first Baptist church was built in 1893, but it was quickly outgrown and replaced. The church (above) was built in 1908–1909 with a domed roof. Years later, the dome had to be removed (below).

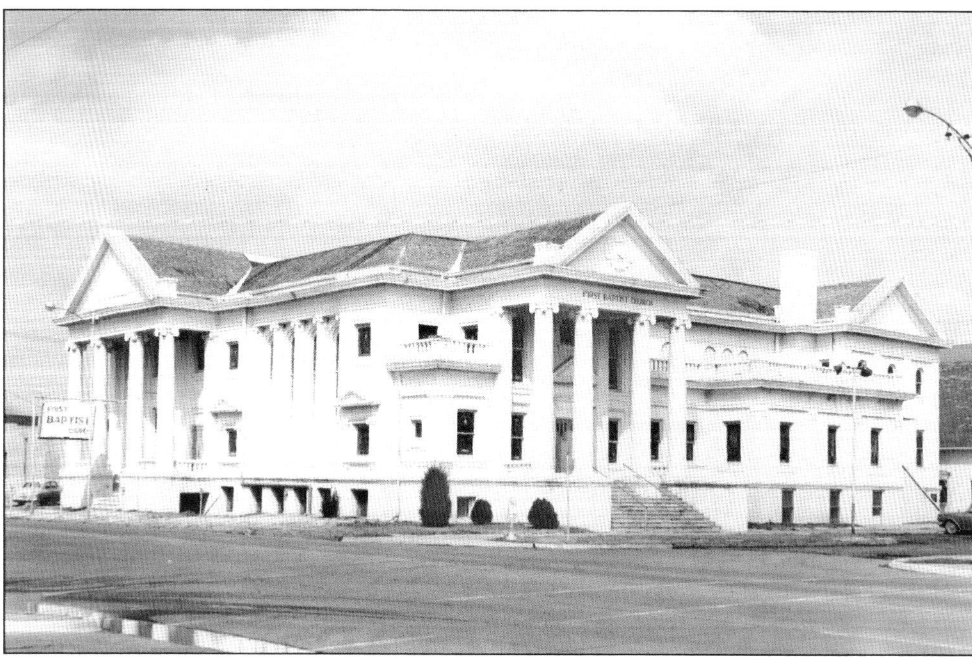

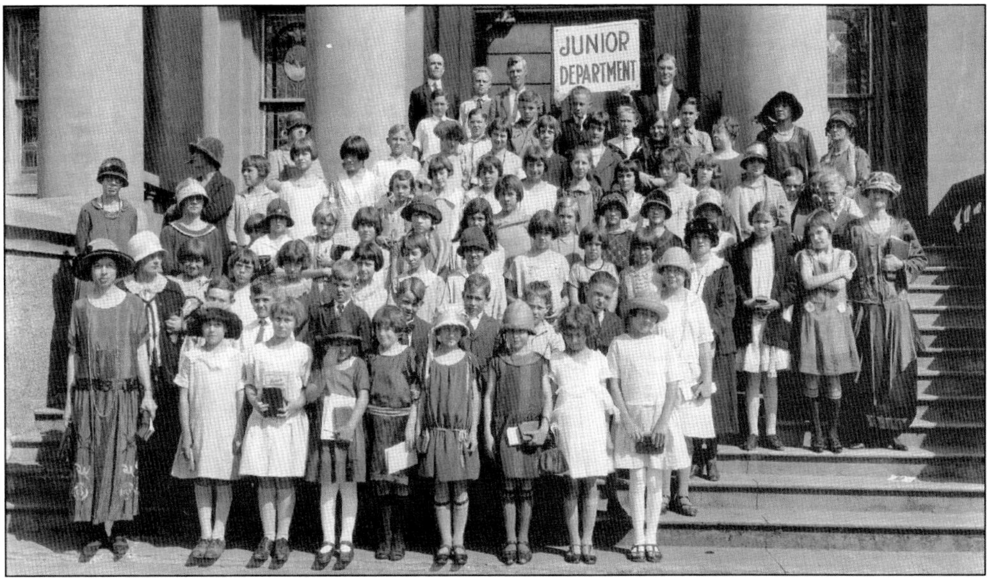

The junior department of the First Baptist Church of Chickasha poses in front of the church building in 1924. The Baptists were one of the original four churches created in the town's first year. The next year, 1893, a second Baptist Church was organized by 20 black families who gathered to worship. At first, they called themselves New Hope, but by 1895, they too called themselves First Baptist Church. There are still two churches called First Baptist in town.

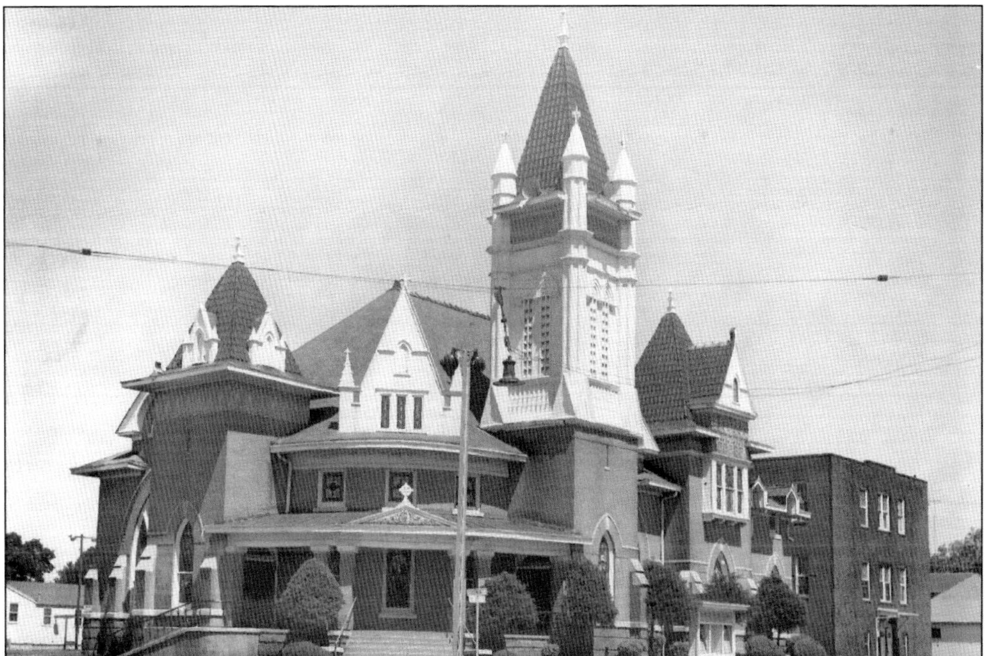
The Methodists can trace their involvement in the area to before the town's founding when J.J. Methvin began missionary work in 1891. The formal organization of what would become the Epworth United Methodist Church occurred in 1894 under the direction of A.B.L. Hunkapillar. This building was constructed around 1904.

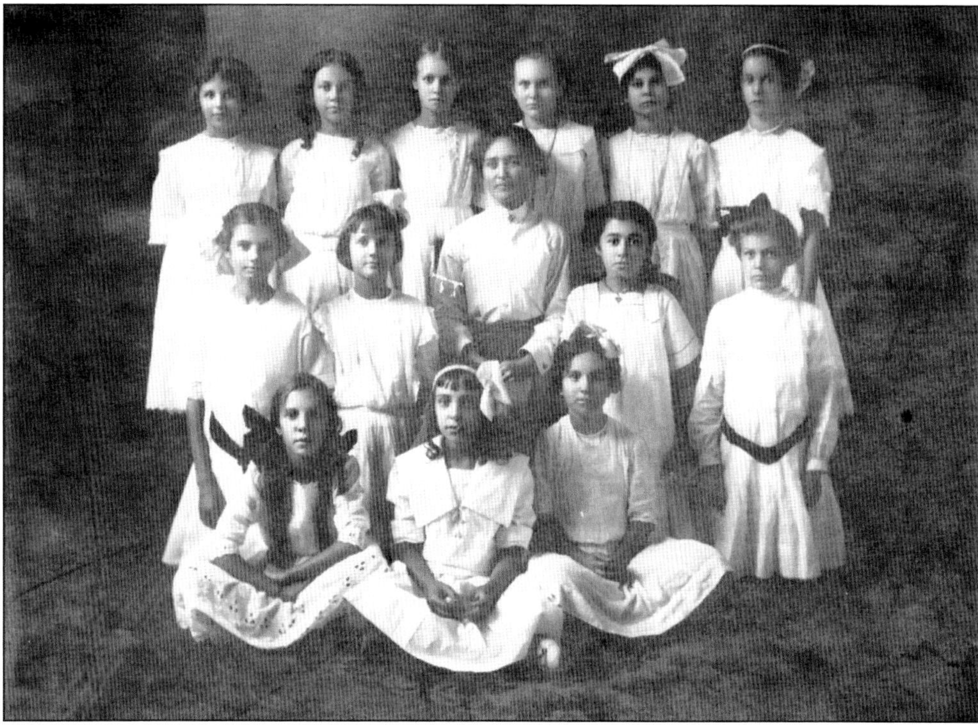

When the Epworth United Methodist Church first organized in 1894, it had only about 12 members, but under the leadership of A.B.L. Hunkapillar, membership over the next four years increased to around 100. In 1902, the church recorded a membership of over 500. The *Chickasha Evening Telegram* reported that the church created two Epworth leagues to take care of the needs of its youth, with both a senior and a junior league. Above are some of the members of the young women's Sunday school class in 1914. In 1904, a new building was constructed, with a new pipe organ, shown below.

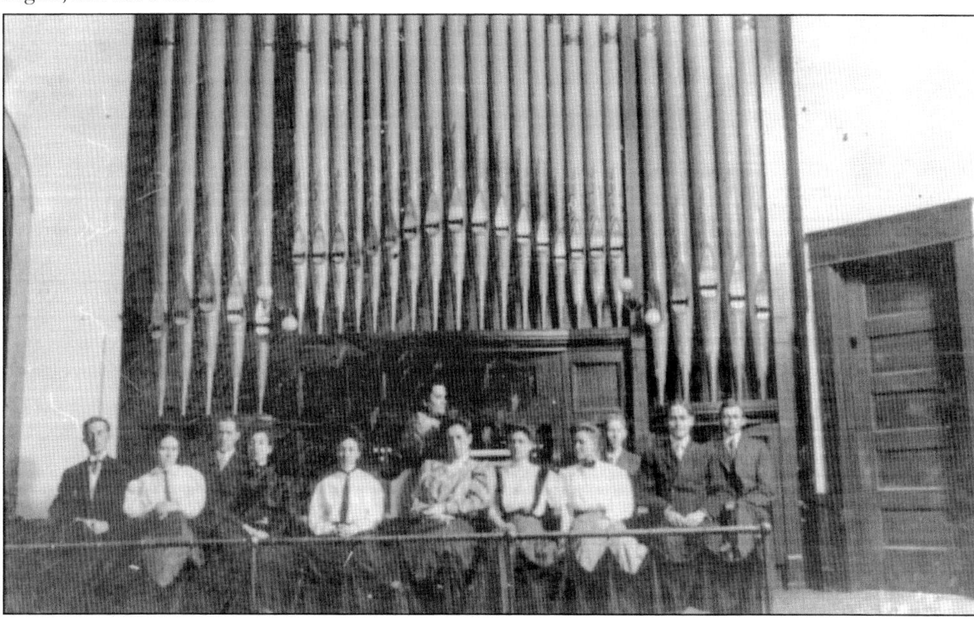

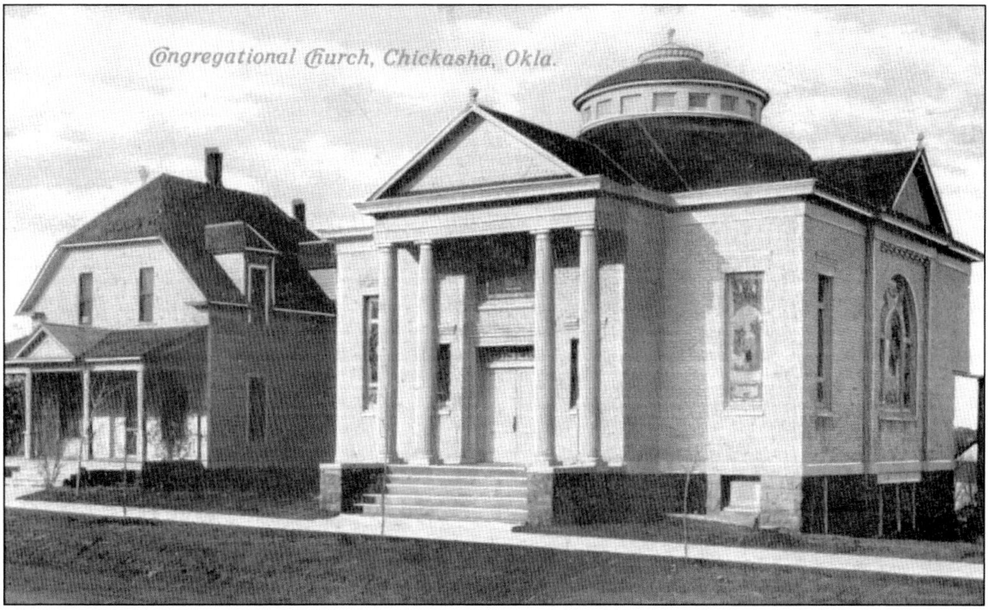

The first record of the Congregational church shows up in 1910. It was on 902 South Ninth Street and listed John C. Trent as pastor.

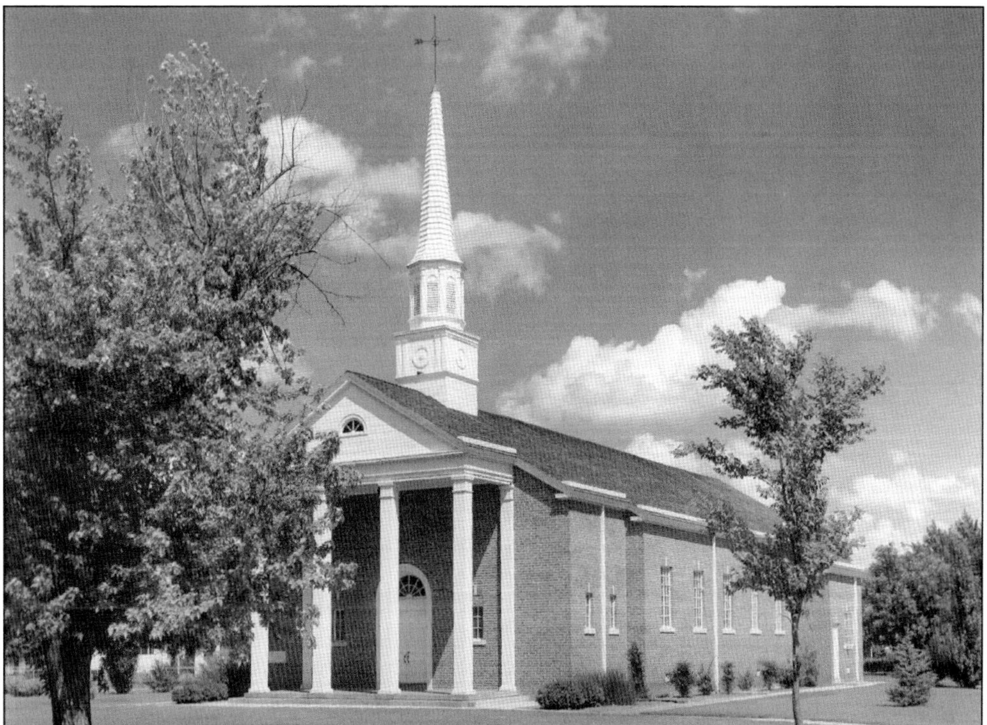

The First Church of Christ, Scientist has roots to the very beginning of Chickasha. On one of the first trains into town was Jane Robinson, a student of Christian Science. Eight years later, she was joined by A. Jones, who after being healed moved to Chickasha. The church was organized officially in 1906, with five members at the home of a Mrs. McClure.

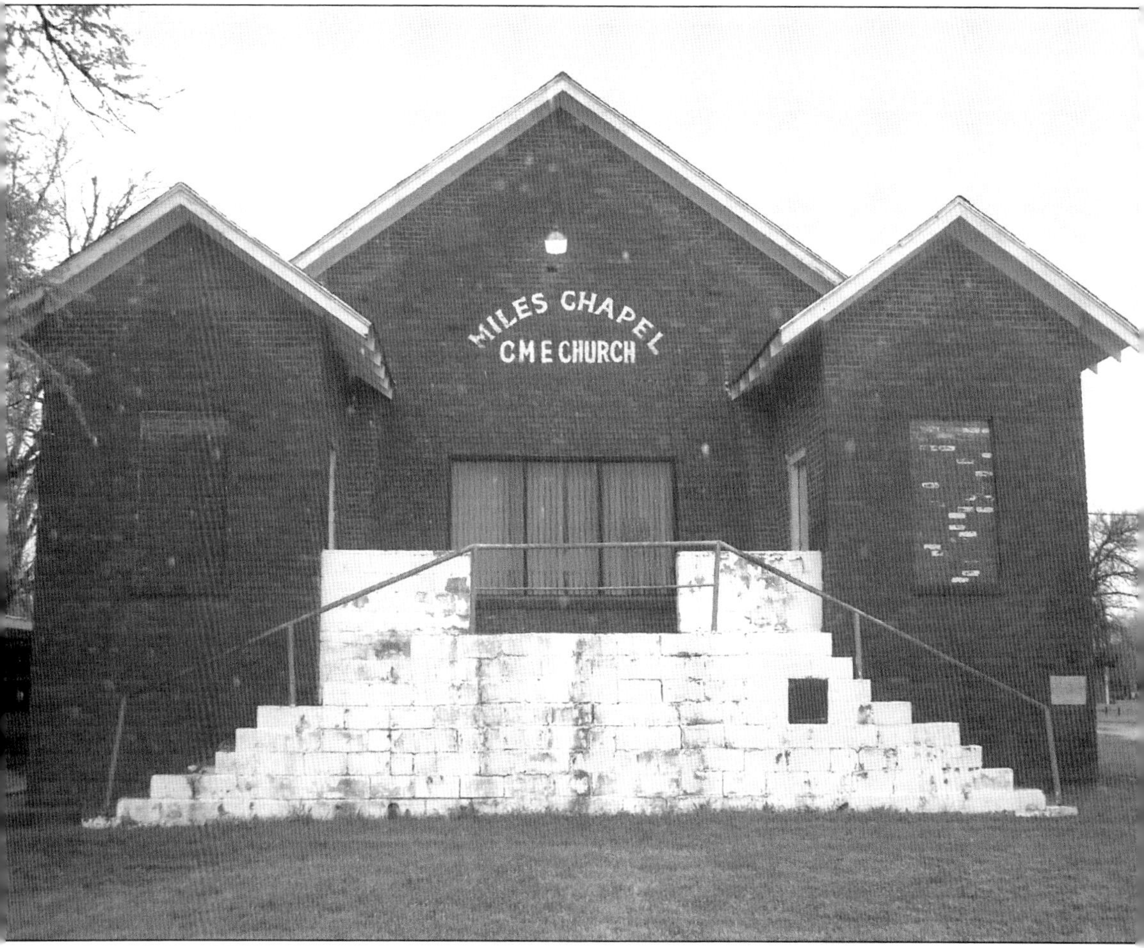

There has been a thriving African American community in Chickasha since the beginning, mostly concentrated on the east side of town. One of the first congregations began meeting 1909 and organized the New Hope Baptist Church in 1910. The church has moved several times but is now located on South Shepherd Street. The Colored Methodist Episcopal Church, pictured here, was organized even sooner than New Hope, its congregants began meeting in 1906. In 1957, the congregation changed its name to the Christian Methodist Episcopal Church.

Five

EDUCATION

Chickasha's educational system began with private schools. The town was on tribal lands, so no taxes could be raised to build public schools. The first private school in Chickasha was the First Presbyterian Church school in 1892, with Howard Miller as teacher. Other early schools were held in the homes and stores of local citizens. The townspeople themselves built another private school in 1893.

In 1898, the Chickasaw Indians surrendered their land rights with the Atoka Agreement, allowing Chickasha to raise taxes and begin a public school system. The first public school opened in the fall of 1900 with 400 pupils under the leadership of supertintendent Dr. James Cook. Chickasha grew rapidly, and by 1902, the student body increased to 900.

There was also a school for black children in the area. These 85 students were taught by Oscar Spencer in a small Baptist church at the corner of First Street and Dakota Avenue in 1900. In 1909, the school expanded into the ground floor of the Odd Fellows Hall in order to hold the 650 enrolled students.

In 1901, Chickasha voted a bond issue of $60,000 for four redbrick, two-story buildings, each with four classrooms per floor. These were the Washington, Jefferson, Lee, and Lincoln Schools, simply called the North, South, West, and Lincoln Schools, respectively. The Lincoln School was built as the town's public school for the black community.

In 1912, Chickasha reorganized its original school system to create Oklahoma's first junior high school. The schools expanded in the 1910s and 1920s, and fires in the 1930s moved classes to local churches and the Oklahoma College for Women during rebuilding. Beginning in the late 1950s, Chickasha schools began to gradually desegregate, mostly allowing black football players into the high school; but in 1960 complete desegregation shifted school designations as Lincoln school transformed from a K–12 school to an elementary school within the Chickasha school system. A new high school opened on October 16, 1968, on the old World War II Borden General Hospital grounds.

Chickasha also had the Jane Brooks School for the Deaf. It was moved from Purcell to Chickasha in August 1953 and was supported by all aspects of the local community. The school was founded by Margaret Brooks in 1929, and it was named for her daughter, who had been crippled by meningitis.

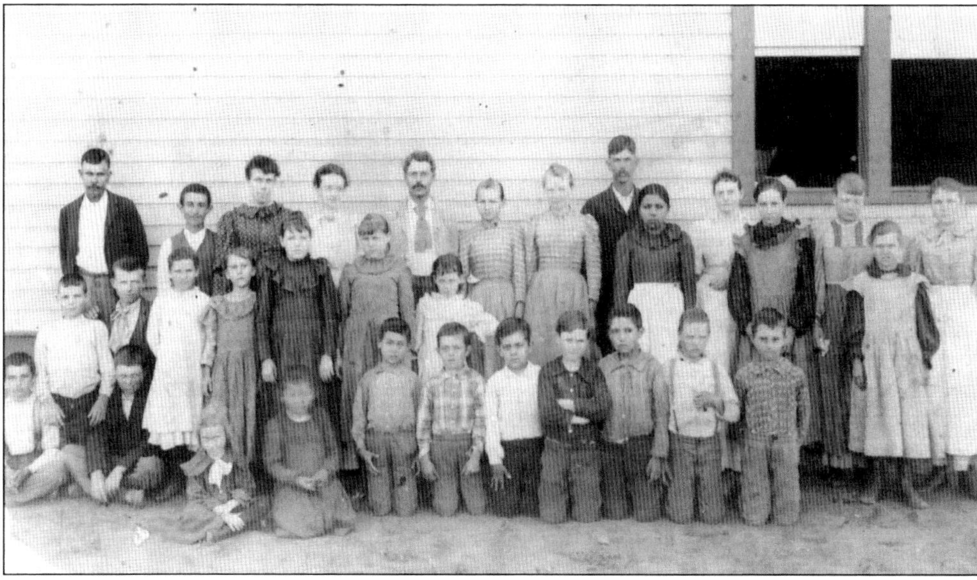

The first schools in Chickasha were private schools known as tuition schools, because students were expected to pay on average $1.50 a month to attend. This system was different then other states, where taxes were used to pay for primary education. The first tuition school in Chickasha was organized in 1892; in 1893, town residents came together to raise $3,000 to build an actual school building. The first teacher was Lillie Miller (shown below). The school did not last the year, as parents who were not accustomed to paying fees did not pay, and the school was closed.

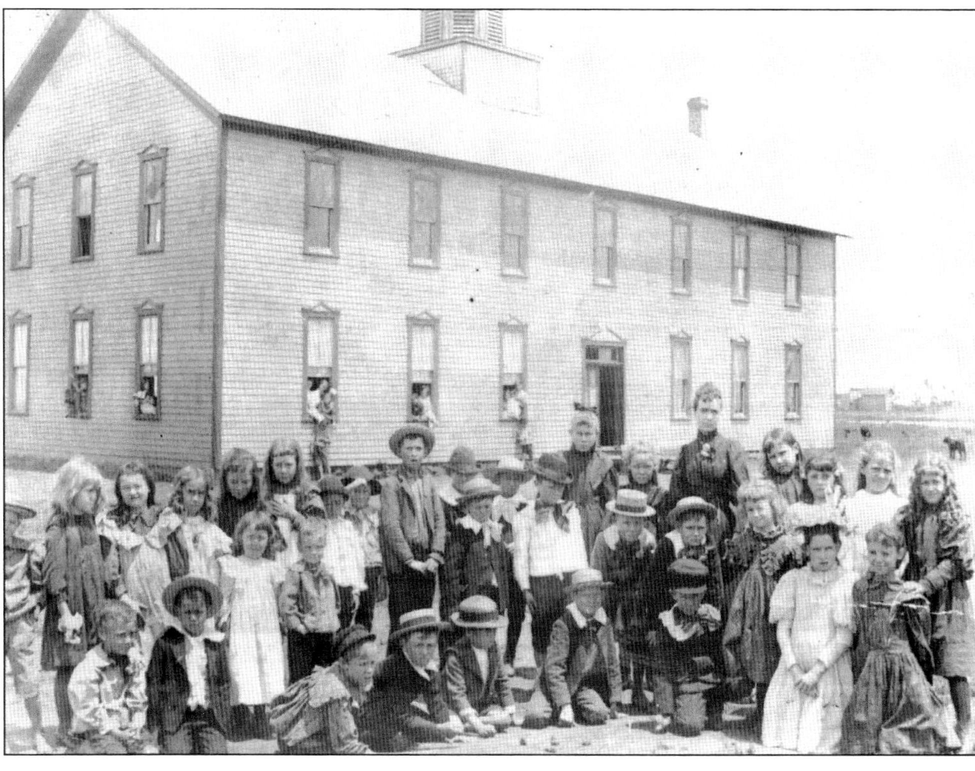

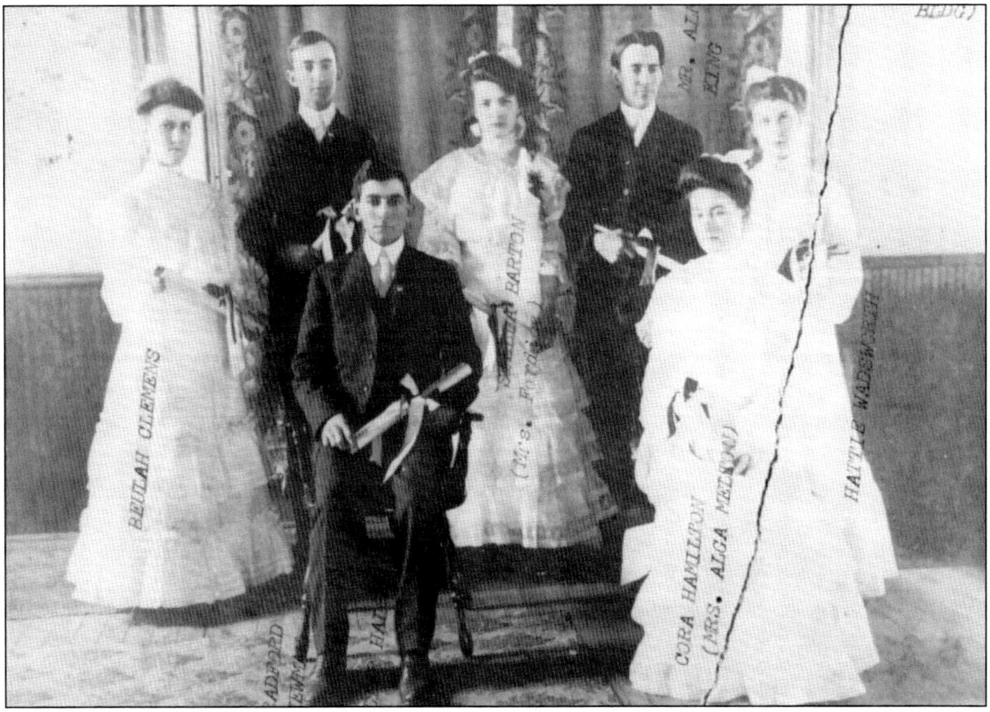

The first graduating class from Chickasha High School was in 1904. Standing, from left to right, are Belulah Clemons, Bradford Newman, Stella Fardice, Alma King, and Hattie Wadsworth. Seated are Walter Hulsey and Cara Hamilton. It is interesting that there were more girls than boys in Chickasha's first high school class.

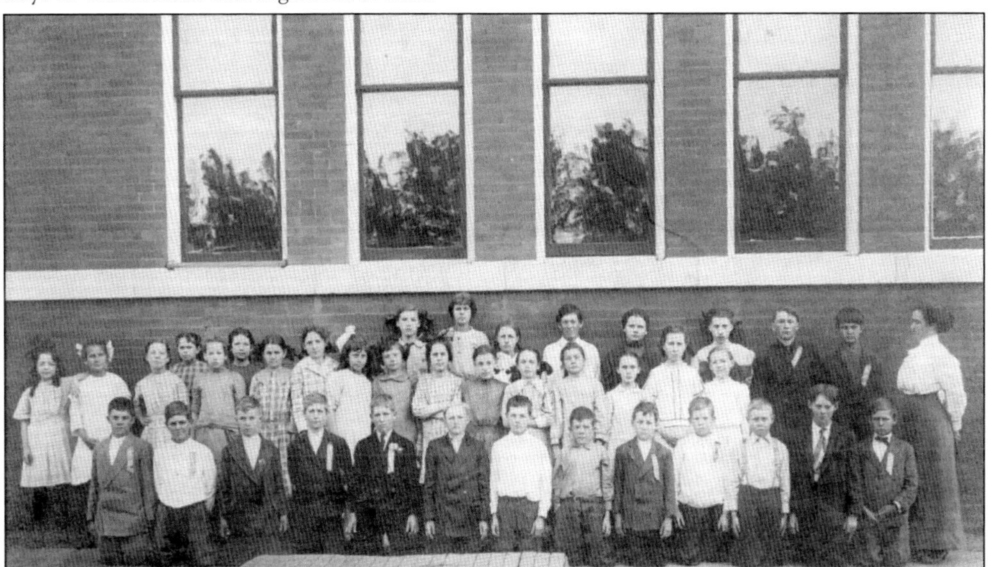

A group of Chickasha children pose in their best school outfits for their class picture sometime in the early 1900s. The building they are standing in front of is one of the four constructed with a $60,000 bond issued to Chickasha between 1901 and 1902. The schools built were the Washington (North), Jefferson (South), Lee (West) and, for the black community, Lincoln Schools.

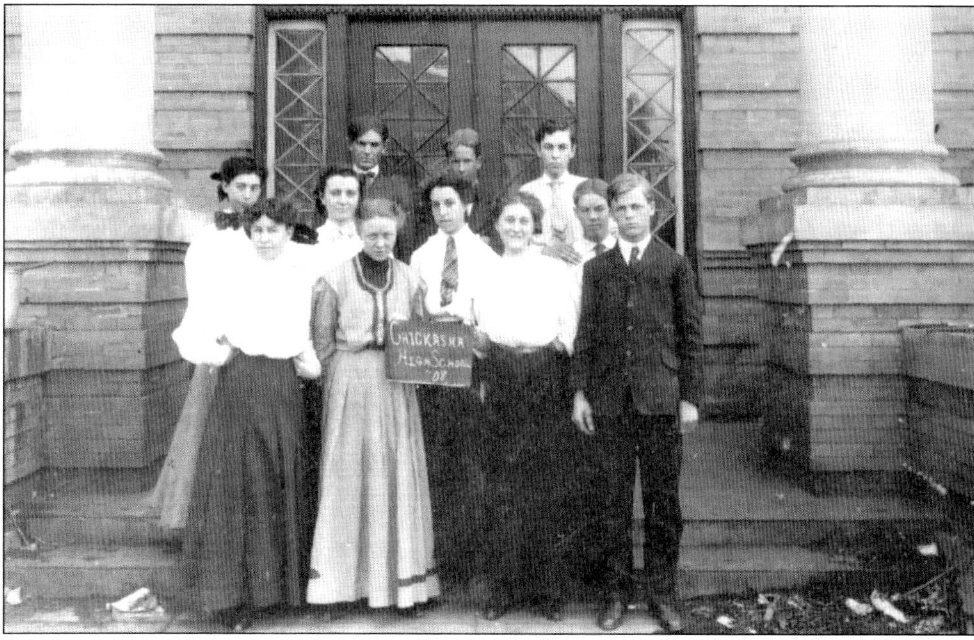

These pictures show the Chickasha High School graduating classes of 1908 (above) and 1909 (below). The group attended high school at the West School until the new high school building was finished in 1909, which explains why the class pictures were taken in front of the Carnegie library. Constructed for the price of $90,000, the new high school stood on Ninth Street, between Washington and Florida Avenues. The cost of the new building was a far cry from the $3,000 paid by Chickasha residents for their first community school only 16 years before and indicated the massive growth of the town's education needs. Several of the girls in the picture above went on to enroll in the Oklahoma Industrial Institute and College for Girls.

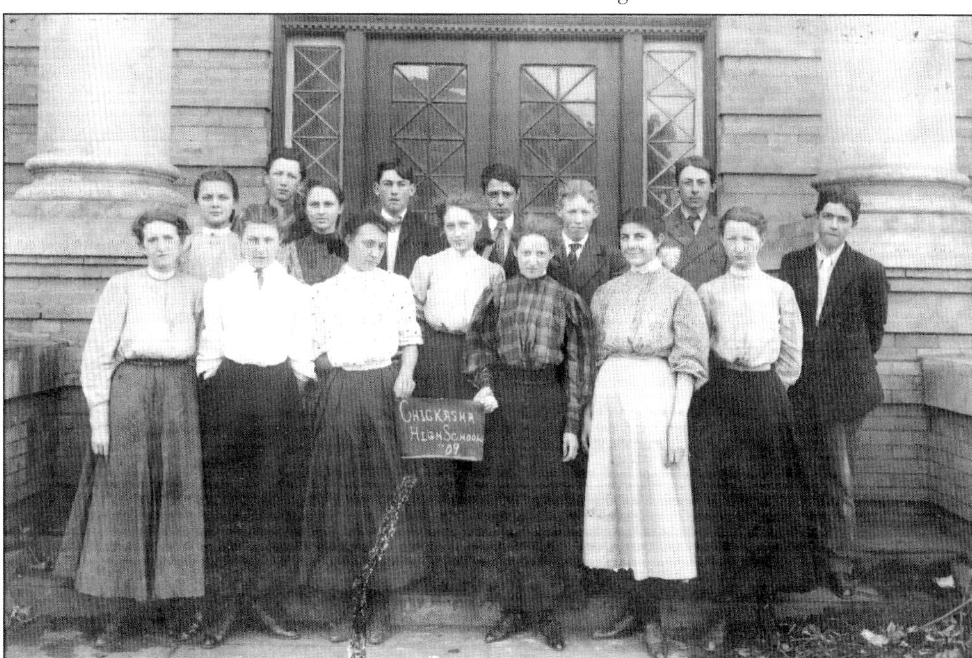

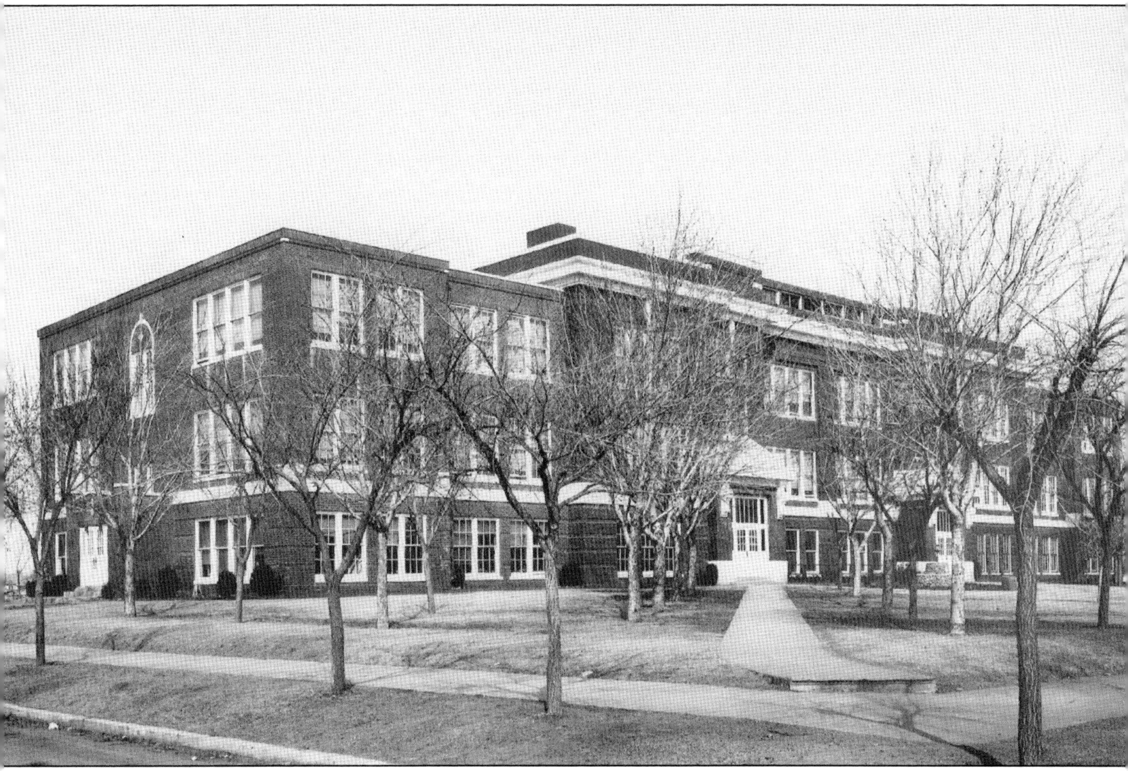

This picture shows the new Chickasha High School that was built in 1909 on Ninth Street between Washington and Florida Avenues. The West School (Lee High School) was the first high school constructed in Chickasha, but the student body population quickly outgrew the school. In 1923, the students again became too numerous thanks to the growing population of Chickasha, and major renovations were added to the high school, which doubled the building's size. In 1933, however, a fire destroyed the renovated high school. Classes did not have to be canceled, but were instead held in the Methodist and Baptist churches, as well as at the Oklahoma College for Women.

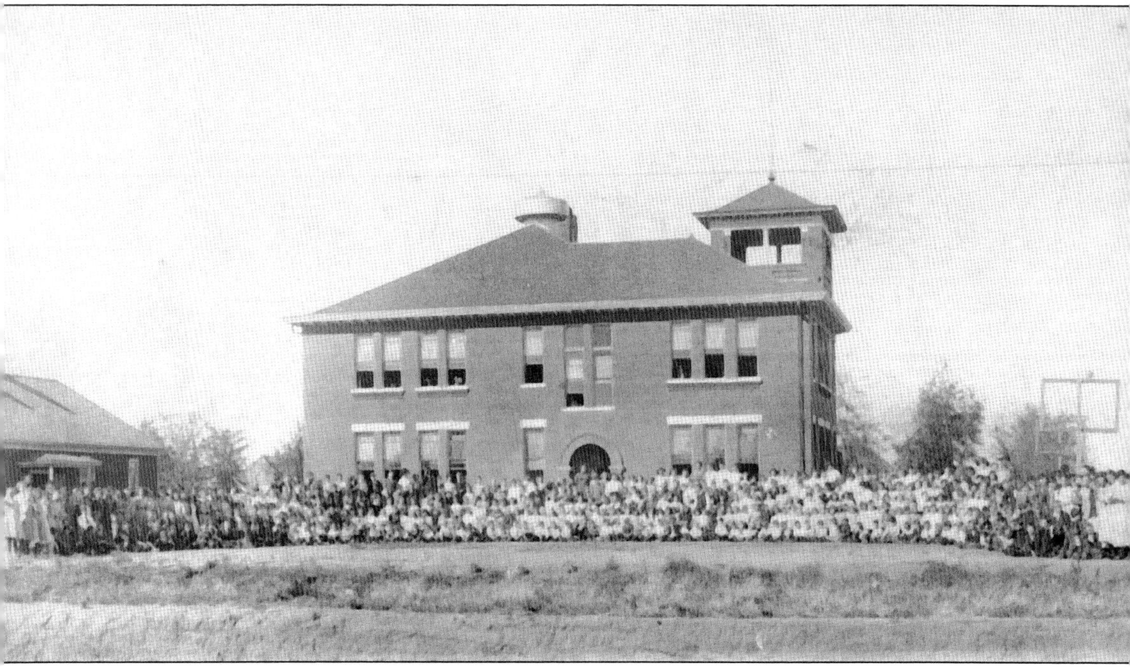

In 1901, a bond was issued for $60,000 for the creation of four public schools for the city. They each had names but over time three of them became known by their locations—North School (Washington), South School (Jefferson), and West School (Lee); the fourth was Lincoln School. This picture is of the West School, but all four were identical, two-story redbrick buildings with four classrooms each and restrooms and offices in the basement. West School was used as the first high school until 1909 when a new high school was built. The Lincoln School not only stands apart as the one that kept its name, but in segregated Oklahoma, Lincoln was used for the education of black students.

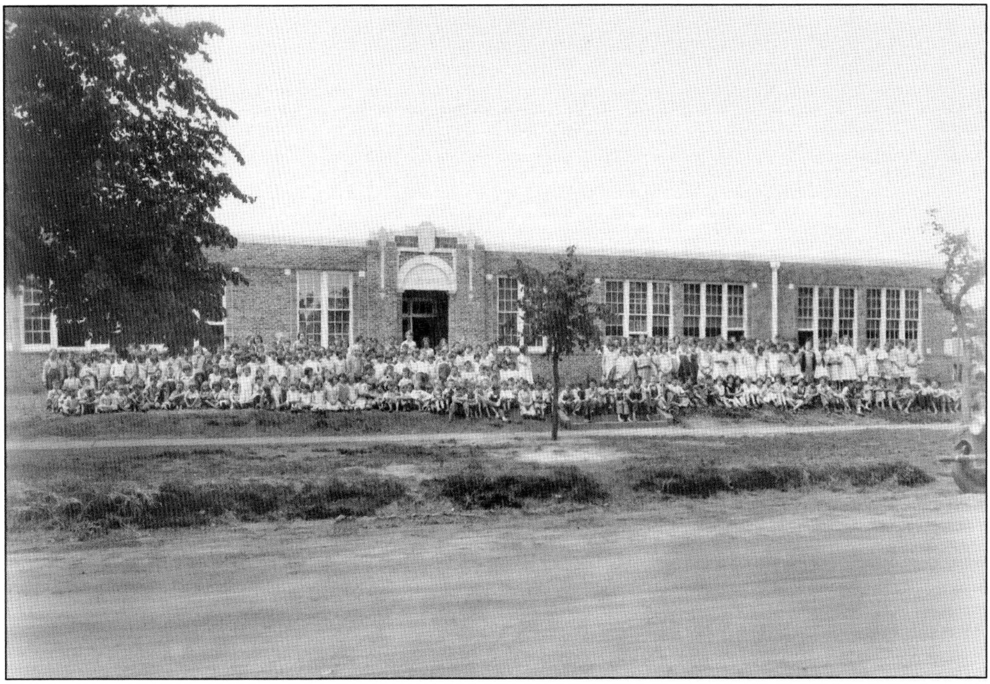

The city built four public schools, and by 1930, they were in disarray and unsafe for the children. Three of the schools—North, West, and South—were demolished, and new one-story buildings were put in their place. The only school to remain was Lincoln, which had major renovations but was not new. This is a picture of North School.

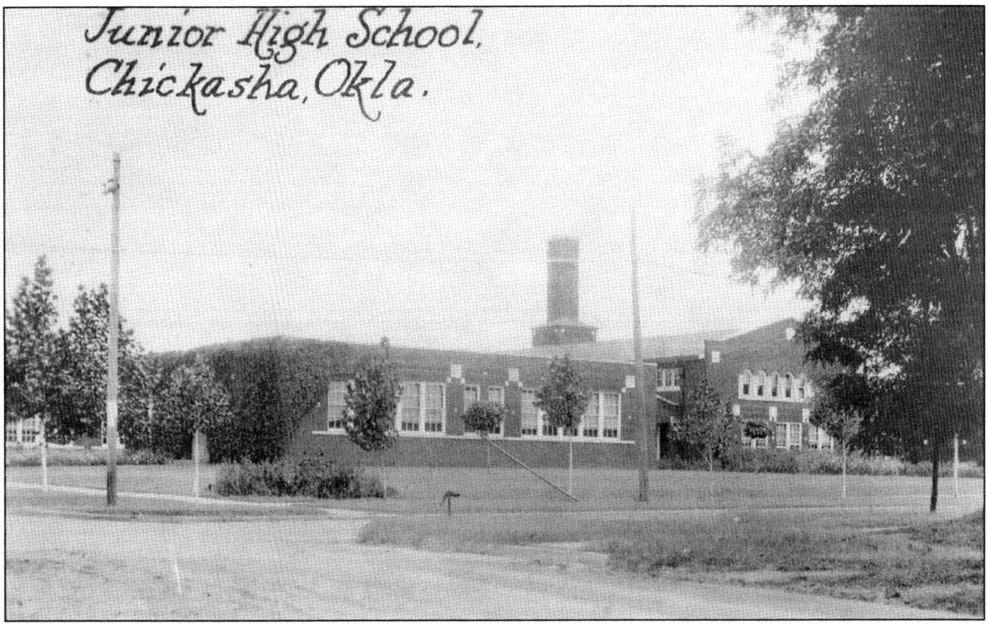

The early schools were designed to have first through eighth grades in elementary school and ninth through 12th in high school. In 1912, this concept changed to incorporate a junior high school. Under the leadership of superintendent William Ramey, a new junior high was built in 1916 for grades seven through nine. Chickasha Junior High was the first of its kind in the state.

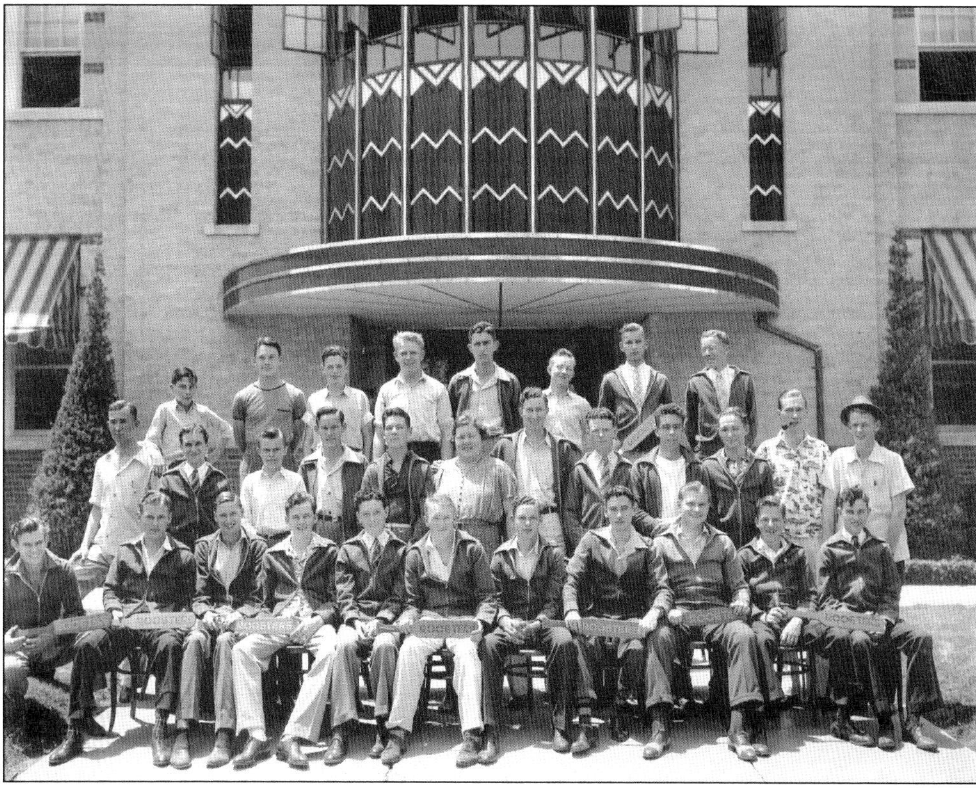

The Roosters were a boys' pep club at Chickasha High School. The club was first organized by Hayden Roberts in 1928, and Nellie Waterman was its first sponsor. Its initial purpose was to further athletics at the school, but it later expanded into involvement in most school activities. Members of the Roosters wore distinct jackets of purple and gold, the Chickasha school colors.

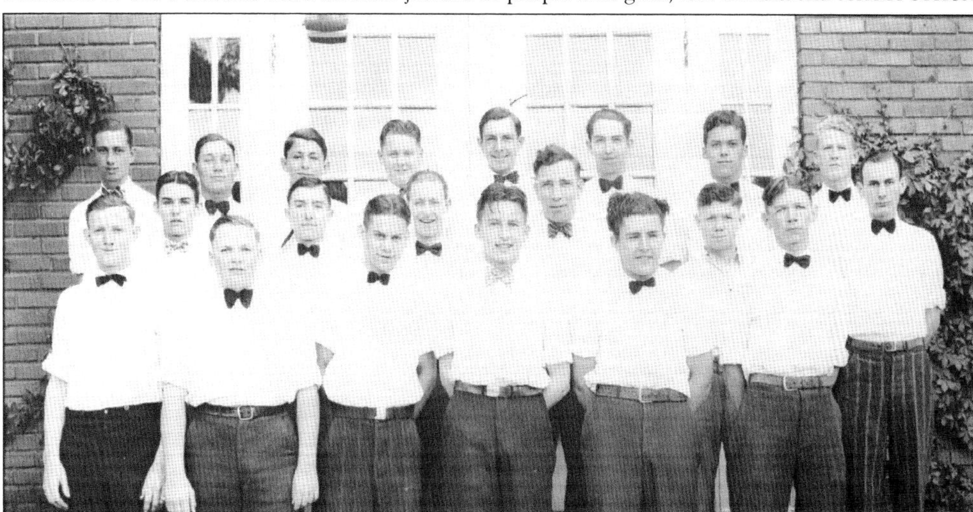

Started in 1928 or 1929, the Honyoks, like the Roosters, were a boys' pep club at Chickasha High School. The two clubs were actually rival pep clubs at the school, playing against each other in both football and basketball. The Honyoks organized a small pep band that played at basketball games throughout the season.

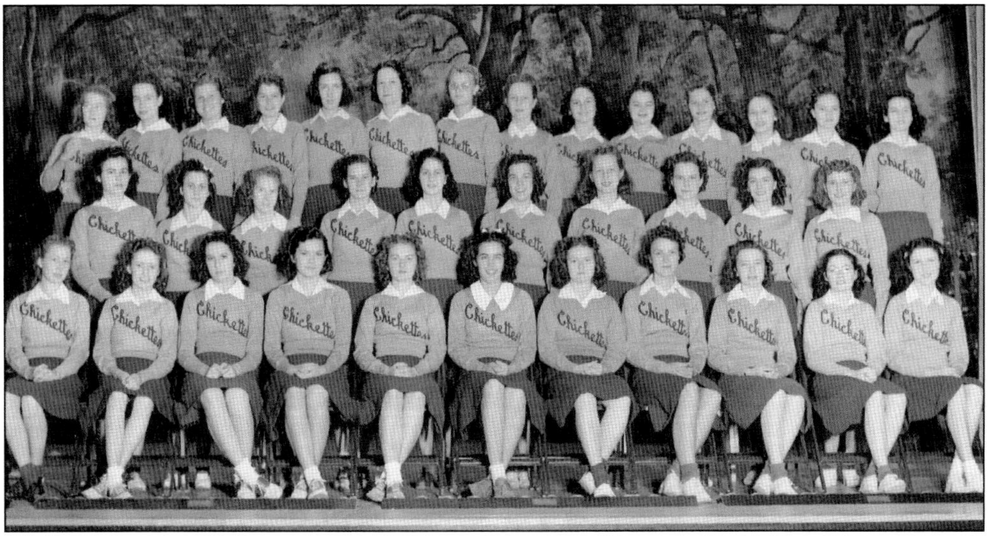

The Chickettes and the Pepettes were Chickasha High School's two girls' pep clubs. The original pep clubs were actually all boys' clubs. The first girls' pep club was the Peppy 12 started in 1921, which cheered and also had dances, parties, and a weenie roast. After the Peppy 12, the Chickettes were the second pep club, started in 1927. The group was involved in cheering for football and basketball games, school queen coronations, and holding breakfasts to kick off annual events and banquets to close out the football season. The Pepettes were an offshoot of the Chickettes. The club's annual activities began with a "getting acquainted tea" followed by football and basketball cheering, spring picnics for all of the sports teams, and closed with another breakfast.

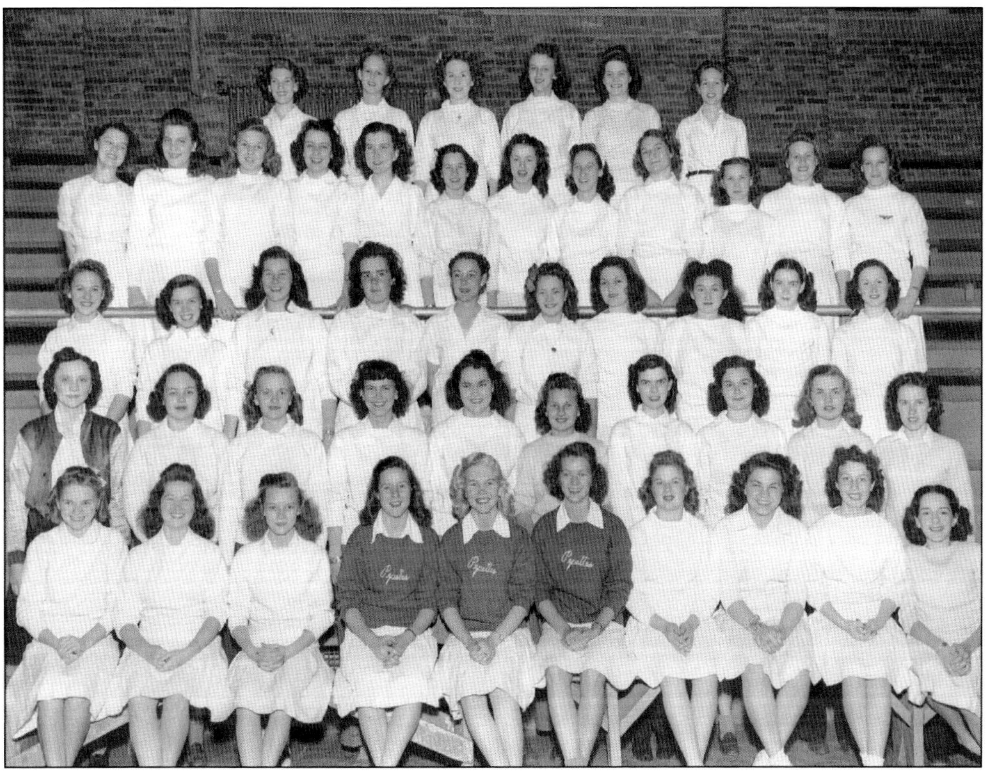

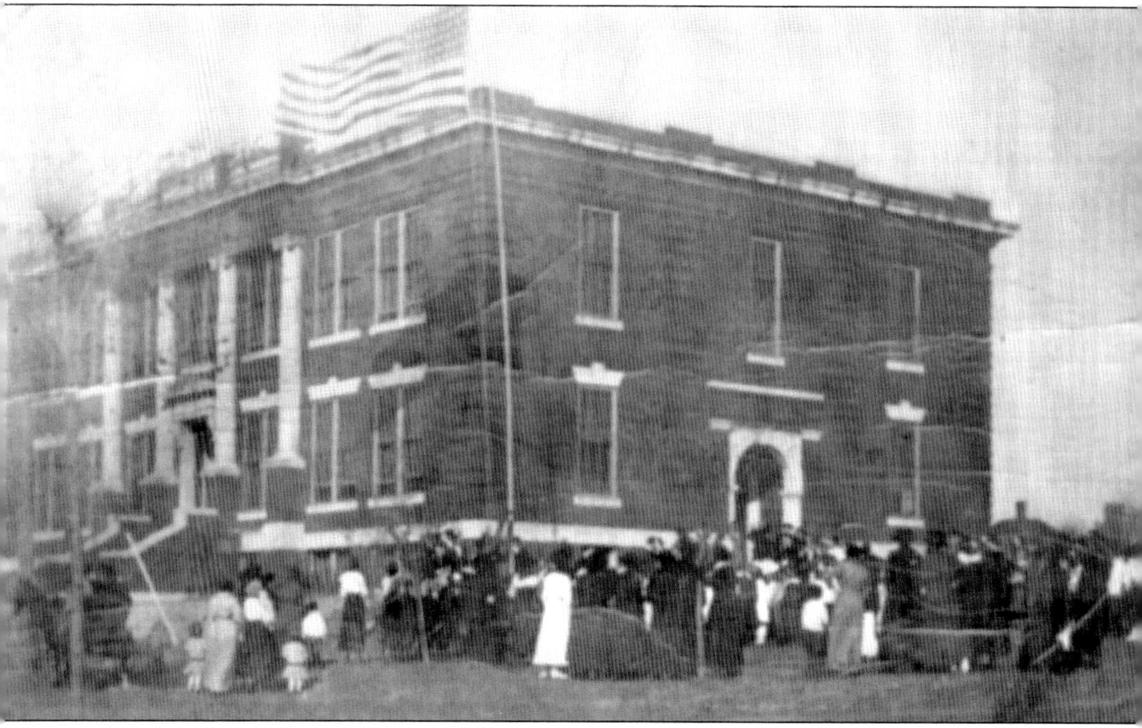

A school for Chickasha's African American students was first organized by J. Oscar Spencer in September 1900. In the beginning, classes met in a Baptist church on the corner of First Street and Dakota Avenue. By 1909, the school was overcrowded, so its 650 students moved into the ground floor of the Odd Fellows Hall. As the school continued to grow, it moved again into a newly constructed building located at 103 Dakota Avenue, where it still stands today. Lincoln sported groups such as the Hi-Y boys' club and Y-Teens girls' club. In 1960, the school was integrated into the rest of the Chickasha Public School system and was used as the elementary school for first through sixth grades. In 1970, it was reassigned again, this time into a fourth grade center for the entire district. Today, Lincoln Elementary houses Chickasha's fifth and sixth graders.

Six

The University of Science and Arts of Oklahoma

The University of Science and Arts of Oklahoma is Oklahoma's only public liberal arts university and has recently been described as a "hidden gem" by the American Council of Trustees and Alumni. What sets USAO apart from other institutions is its interdisciplinary approach to learning. All core, or IDS, classes, are team taught by professors from different disciplines. An American civilizations class may be taught by a history and economics professor one semester, then a history and political science professor the next, while a physical science class may be taught by a physicist and a geologist. This approach to teaching allows students to truly acquire a liberal arts education by tackling a subject from different perspectives. Because of the size of the student body, a little over 1,000, students at USAO receive personal attention from their professors.

When classes first began in 1909, the college had a different set of goals. The state legislature desired an institution to provide "a school for the high literary and industrial education for white girls." Chickasha was chosen to house the Oklahoma Industrial Institute and College for Girls. In 1916, the school underwent its first name change to the Oklahoma College for Women. It still strove to improve the intellect of girls, but also endeavored to prepare them as homemakers and social, civic, industrial, and educational leaders. In 1965, the school underwent another name change as well as its largest transformation. Males began attending, and the name changed to the Oklahoma College of Liberal Arts. The name was changed for the last time in 1974 to the University of Science and Arts of Oklahoma, as the state legislature renamed all its four-year colleges to become universities.

Moving into the new millennium, USAO has continued to make a name for itself. In 2001, the campus was listed as a national historic district—the only campus in Oklahoma with such a distinction. In 2005, the president announced the Mission Enhancement Plan, which has harnessed all institutional energies into refining USAO's mission and vision. Among its many successes: no institution in Oklahoma has higher admission standards.

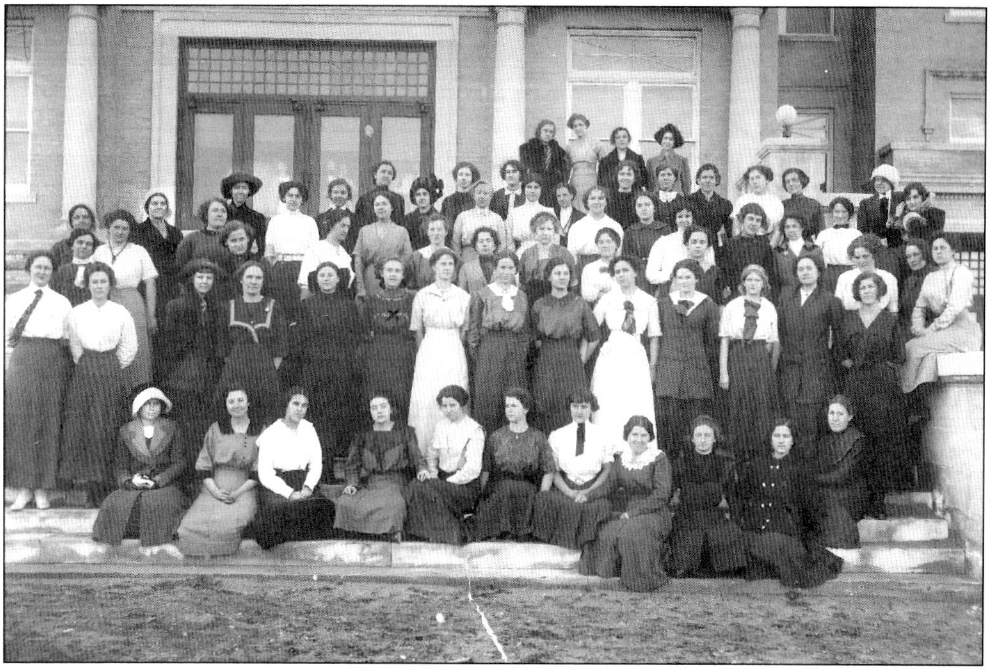

Pictured here is the 1911–1912 student body of the Oklahoma Industrial Institute and College for Girls (OIICG). Beginning in 1909, the student body was made up of women from Oklahoma between the ages of 12 and 35. All incoming students had to "pass satisfactory examinations in reading, arithmetic, geography, English grammar, and United States History" and "possess a good moral character."

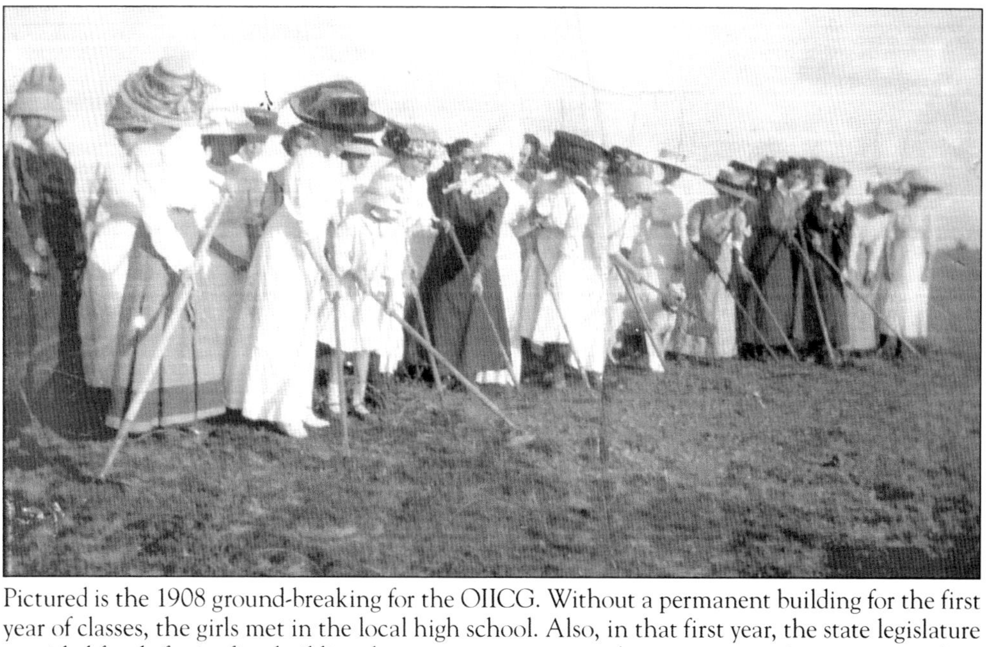

Pictured is the 1908 ground-breaking for the OIICG. Without a permanent building for the first year of classes, the girls met in the local high school. Also, in that first year, the state legislature provided funds for its first building, but not operations or salaries; so women's groups went door to door in Chickasha soliciting funds to operate the college. Once the legislature reconvened, it voted to fund the institution.

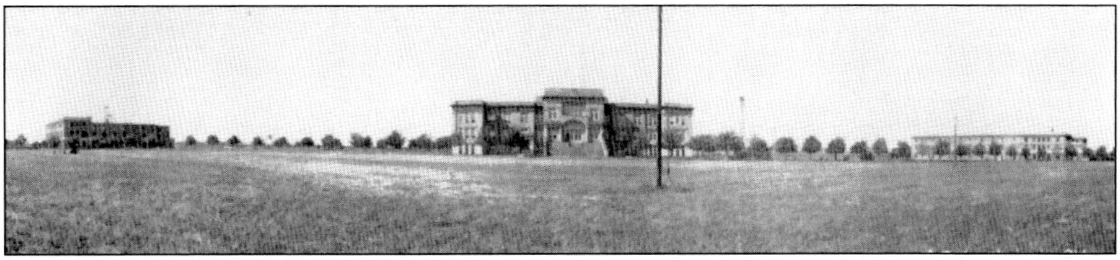

The administration building, now Troutt Hall, was the first structure built on campus. It was designed by the firm of Smith and Parr, famous for its design of the Oklahoma City Civic Center Music Hall. Originally, the first floor was the cafeteria, the second had classrooms and labs, the third had a dormitory for about 40 girls and a library, and the gymnasium was in the basement. The main auditorium was added in 1926, now named in honor of Te Ata, a famous Chickasaw folklorist and 1919 graduate of the Oklahoma College for Women. In 1995, the building was renamed after Roy Troutt, the longest-serving president of the university—from 1975 to 2000.

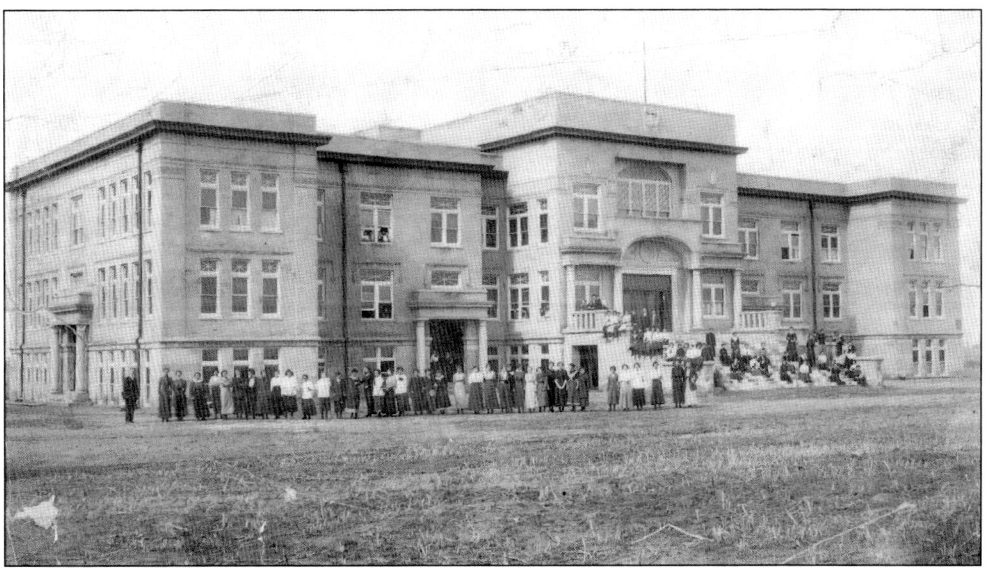

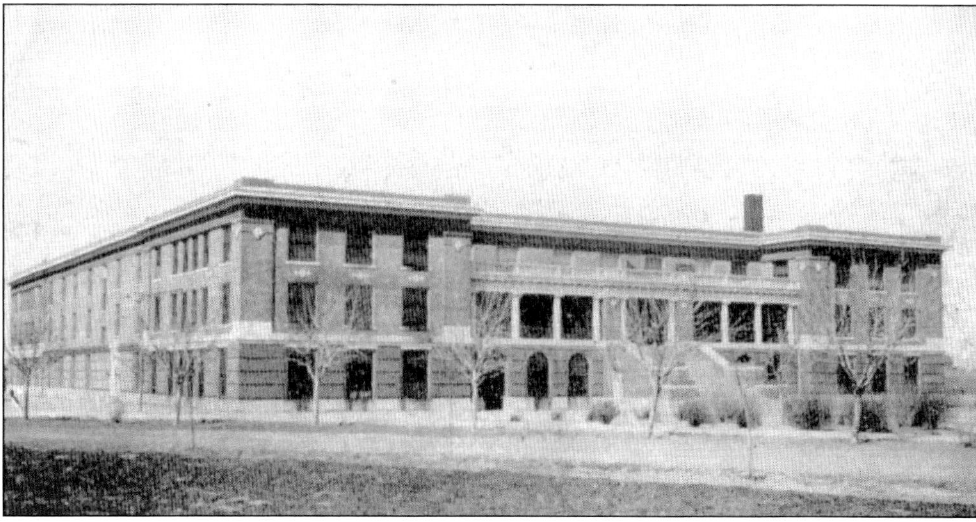

Nellie Sparks Hall was the second building on campus and the first dormitory. It was designed by famed architect Solomon Andrew Layton and dedicated in 1914. The 20 acres of land upon which the college was built were donated by J.B. Sparks, a local rancher who married a Chickasaw woman. The dorm was named in honor of his daughter Nellie, who had left Chickasha to attend a women's college in Missouri. While at school at age 19, Nellie died. Sparks donated the land for a women's college in Oklahoma so no other girls would have to leave their families to receive an education.

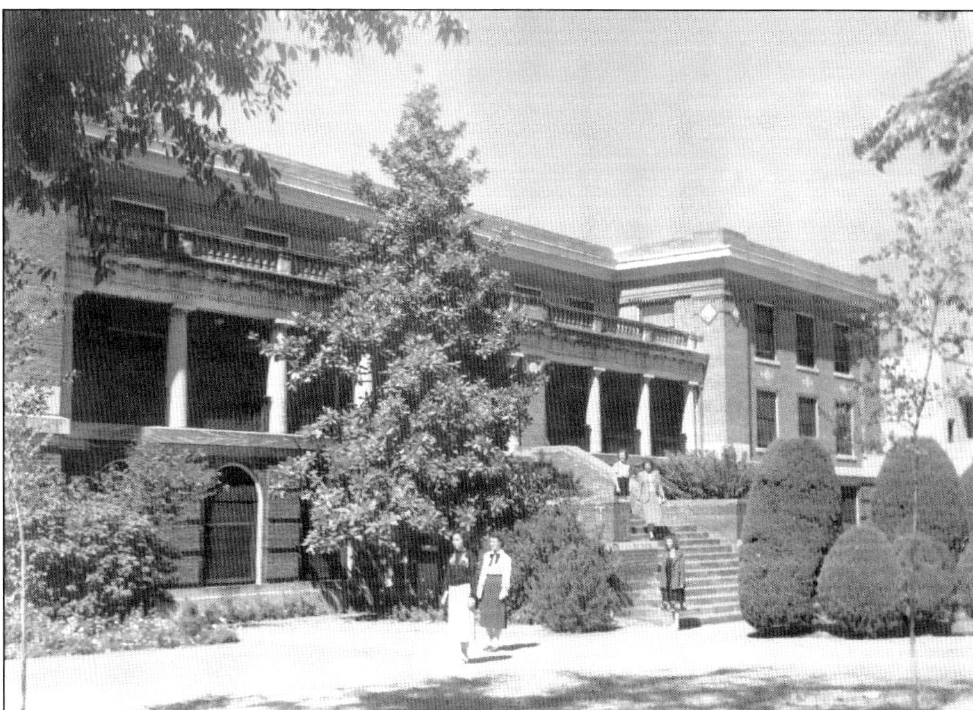

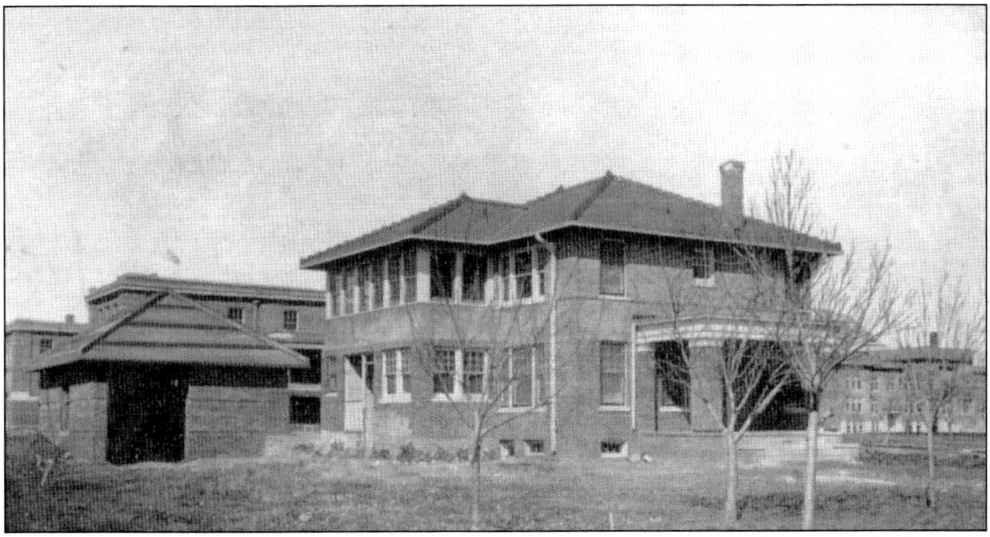

Part of the early campus construction, the President's Home was completed in 1919. The house is one of eight buildings designed by Solomon Andrew Layton, famous for designing the Oklahoma State Capitol. Pres. George Washington Austin was the first resident of the home. Other presidents to live in the home included Charles Procter, Freeman Beets, Charles Grady, Robert Martin, Bruce Carter, Roy Troutt, and, after an elaborate, privately funded restoration in 2009, John Feaver.

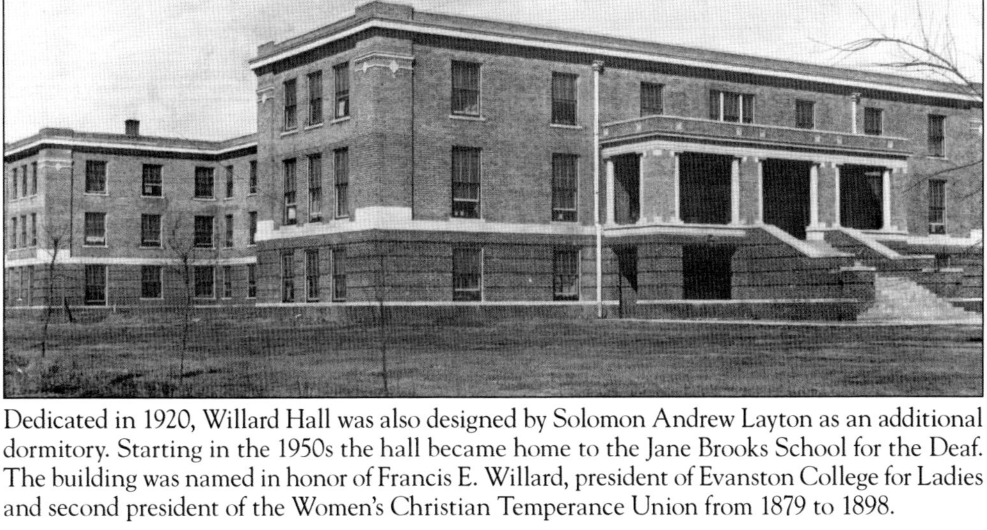

Dedicated in 1920, Willard Hall was also designed by Solomon Andrew Layton as an additional dormitory. Starting in the 1950s the hall became home to the Jane Brooks School for the Deaf. The building was named in honor of Francis E. Willard, president of Evanston College for Ladies and second president of the Women's Christian Temperance Union from 1879 to 1898.

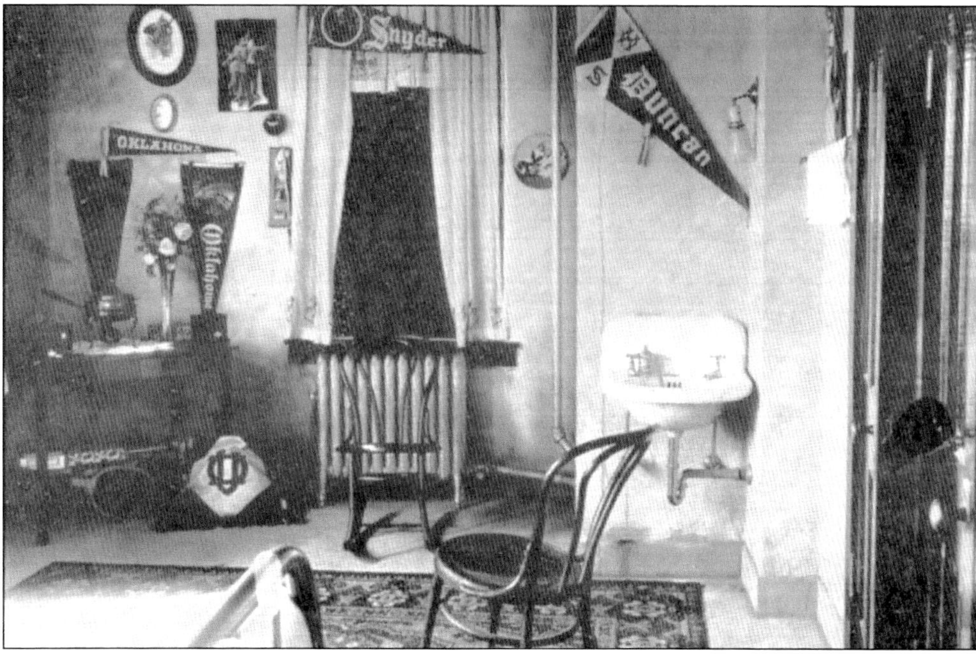

Shown is a typical dorm room in 1920. Discipline was tight in the early years of the school. The ladies of the college were expected to remain in their dorm rooms each night unless signed out by a guardian. They were also expected to wear their school uniform at all times, whether on or off campus.

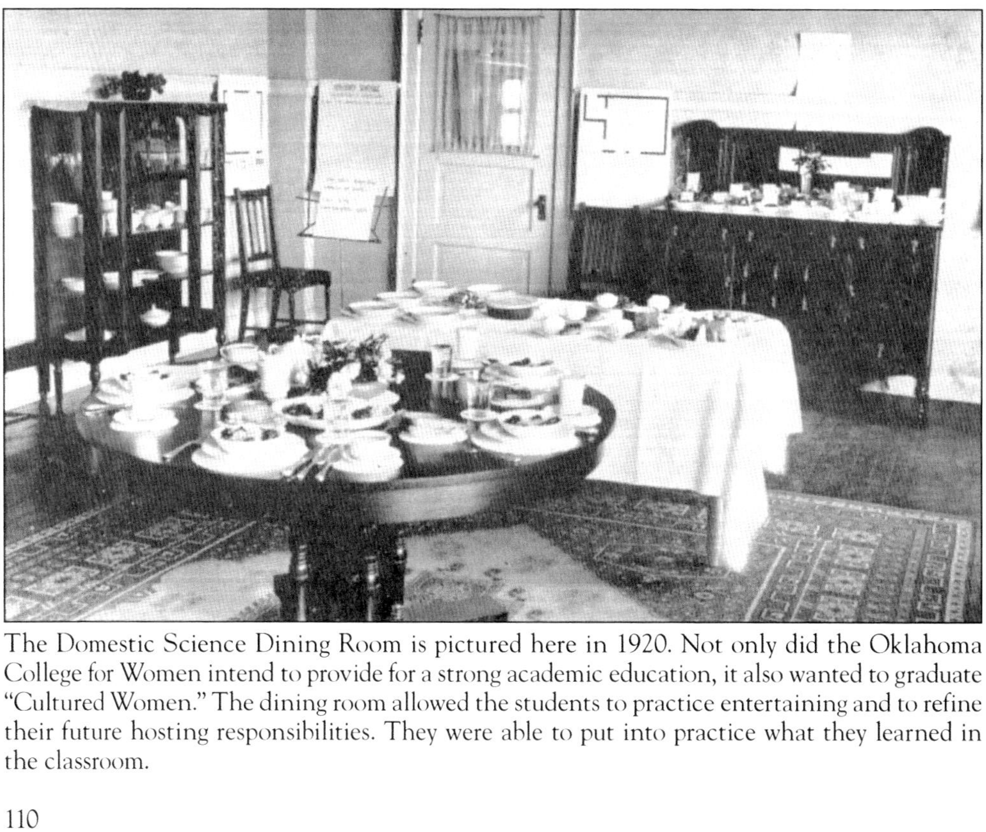

The Domestic Science Dining Room is pictured here in 1920. Not only did the Oklahoma College for Women intend to provide for a strong academic education, it also wanted to graduate "Cultured Women." The dining room allowed the students to practice entertaining and to refine their future hosting responsibilities. They were able to put into practice what they learned in the classroom.

The 1920 yearbook called the interurban waiting station on campus, "Our shield from the Sun and Rain, while waiting for the car. A gift from the Lions and the Rotarians." With over six miles of track and six cars, streetcars began operating in Chickasha in 1910.

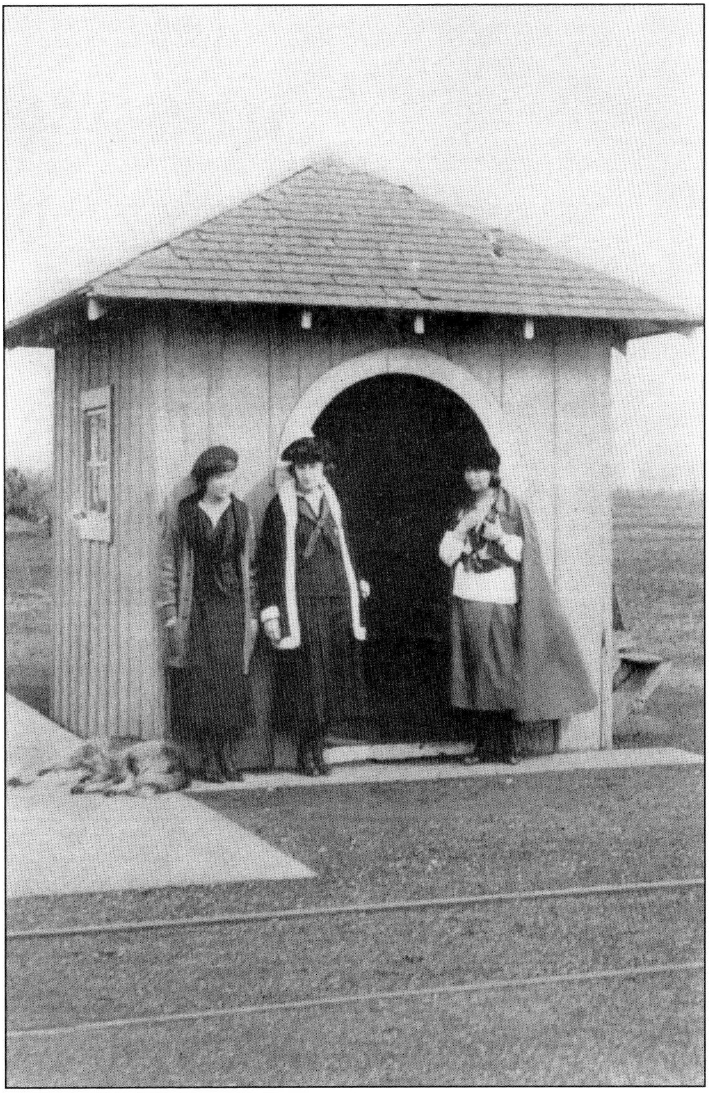

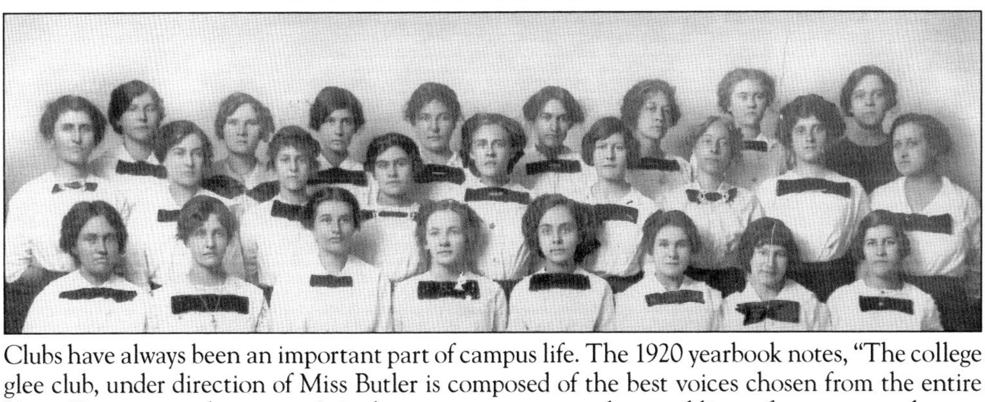

Clubs have always been an important part of campus life. The 1920 yearbook notes, "The college glee club, under direction of Miss Butler is composed of the best voices chosen from the entire Voice Department, by tryout. It is the custom to present three public performances each year. First Christmas, Spring performances and last commencement."

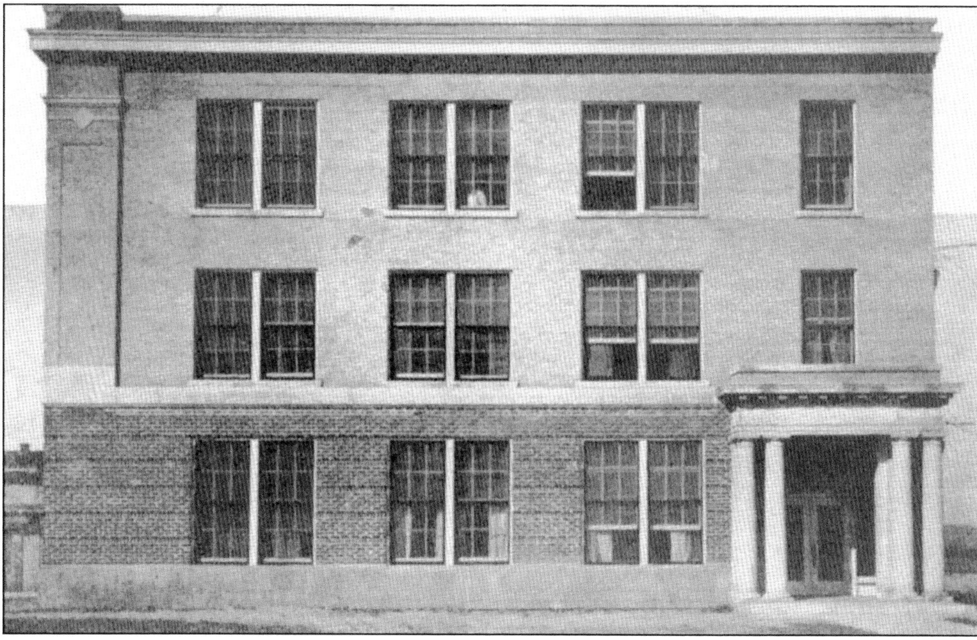

Built in 1921, the fine arts building held some of the earliest classrooms. The name was later changed to Davis Hall to honor Francis Dinsmore Davis. Davis served the Oklahoma College for Women for 44 years as both a faculty member and dean of fine arts. Today, Davis Hall houses most of the arts, social sciences, and humanities.

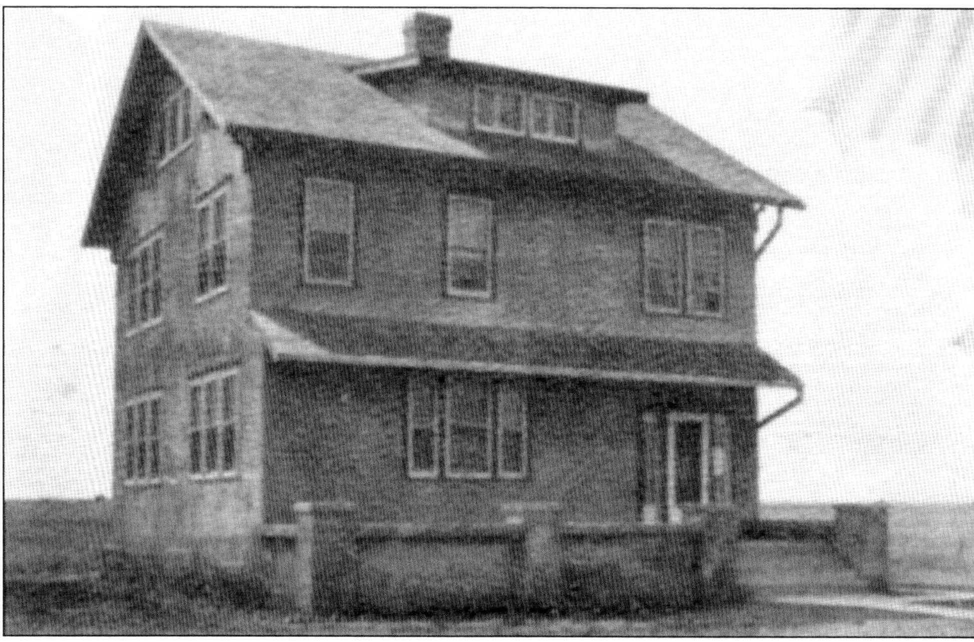

The yearbook describes the home economics house as "living at the practice house has an air of comfort and hospitality. Around this spot the students gather for popcorn parties . . . for more formal dinners, or just to sit quietly and dream after a busy day. Work is merely play in a beautiful kitchen. With the aid of the fireless cooker . . . work is shortened and the housekeepers become more efficient."

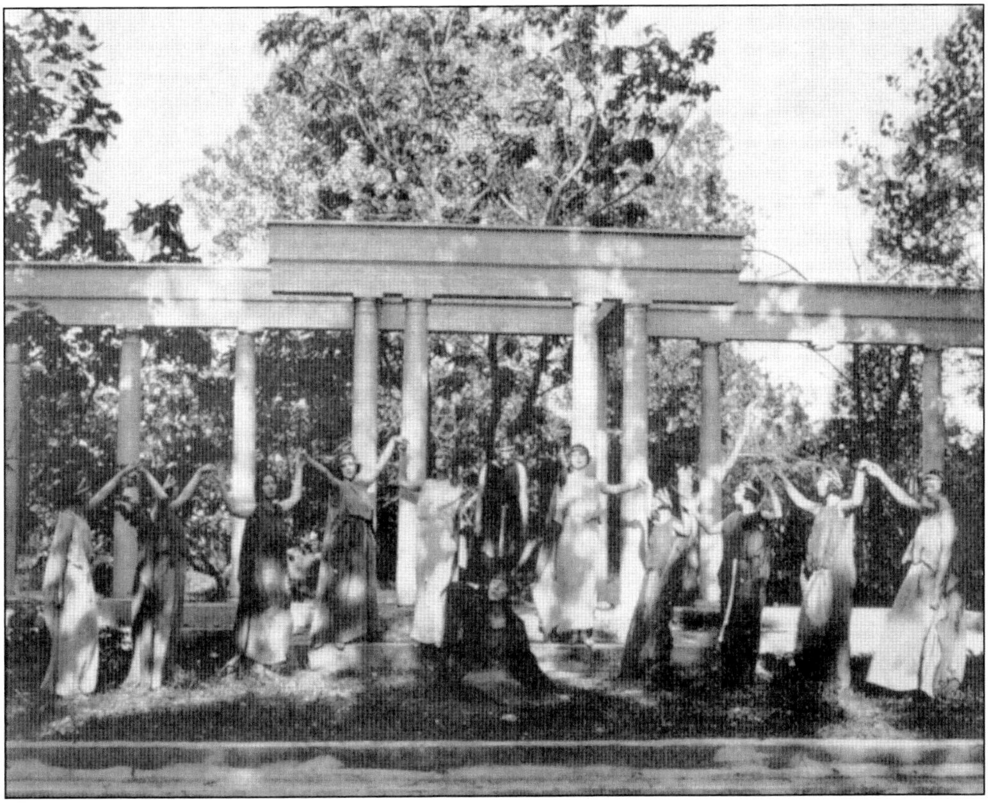

The Greek Theater was the site of many events. The 1926 yearbook reads, "The result from a mixture of mysterious hammerings and sawing, much canvassing for burlap sacks, and several afternoons of work with long needles and yarn, was a complete small stage which could easily be erected or taken down in fifteen minutes."

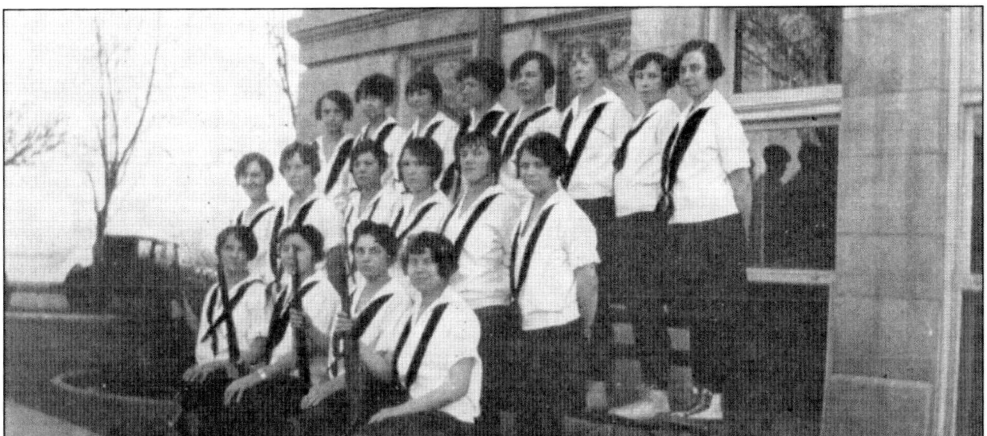

Posing in front of the administration building, the rifle club was first introduced in 1927. When the club first met, it was only open to physical education majors. Only a few colleges nationally were affiliated with the National Rifle Association and sponsored by the US Army. Henrietta Frey was the club's first president.

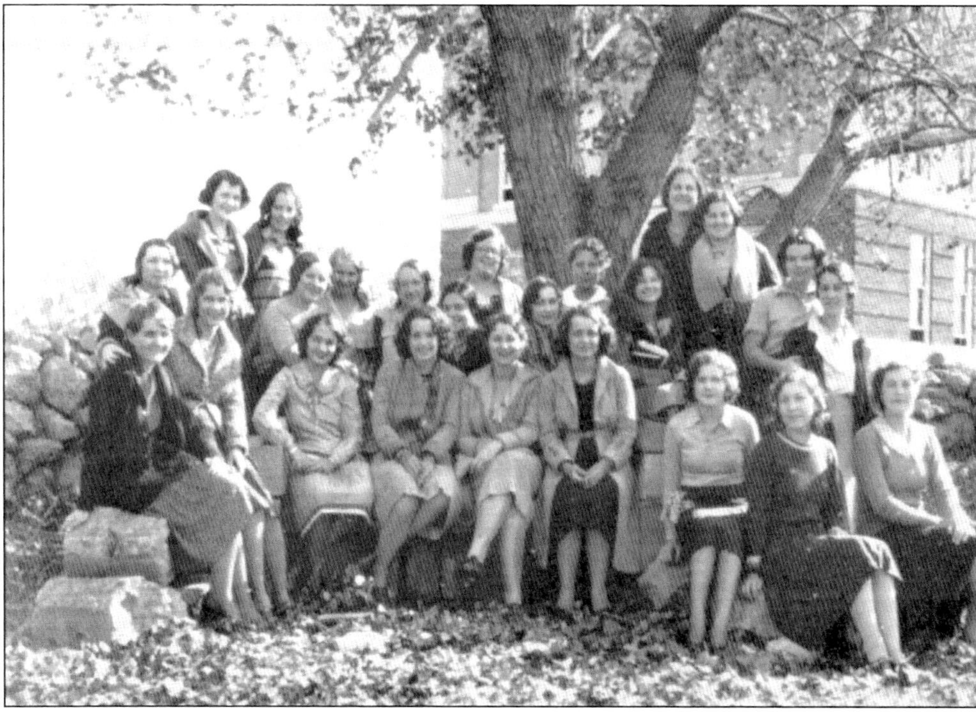

Members of the 1931 Kappa Z Club pose in Grimsley Gardens. Kappa Z was a society club founded in 1925. In the early years of the college, society clubs were very popular. Besides the Kappa Z, other popular clubs were the Em HI, "Q" Club, Be Si Ta, Tri D, and De Gamma Ve. The gardens were named in honor of J.H. Grimsley, who conceived the idea and began the planting.

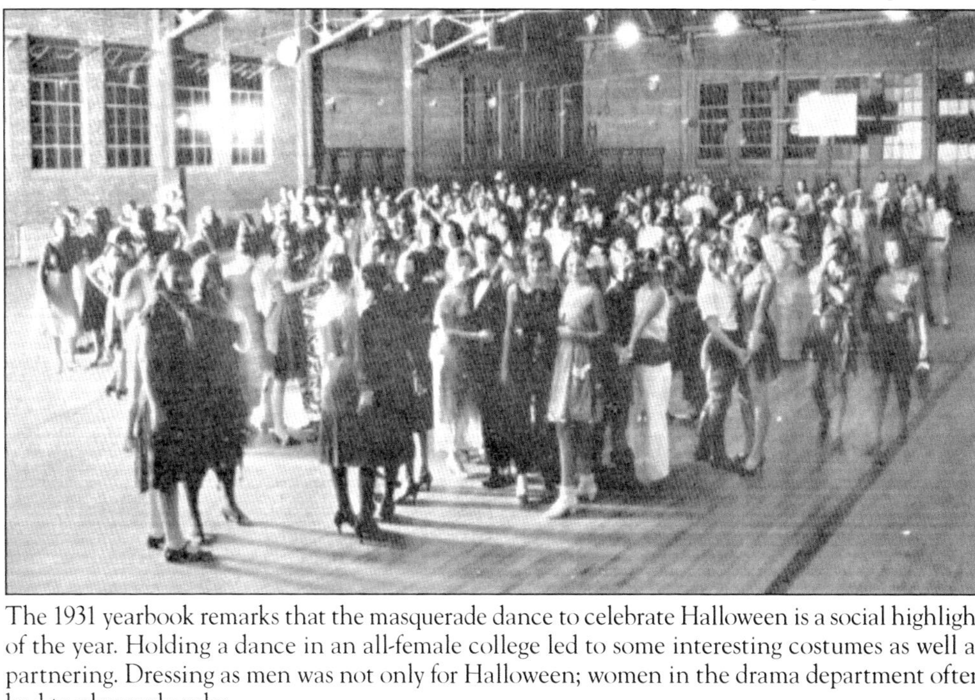

The 1931 yearbook remarks that the masquerade dance to celebrate Halloween is a social highlight of the year. Holding a dance in an all-female college led to some interesting costumes as well as partnering. Dressing as men was not only for Halloween; women in the drama department often had to play male roles.

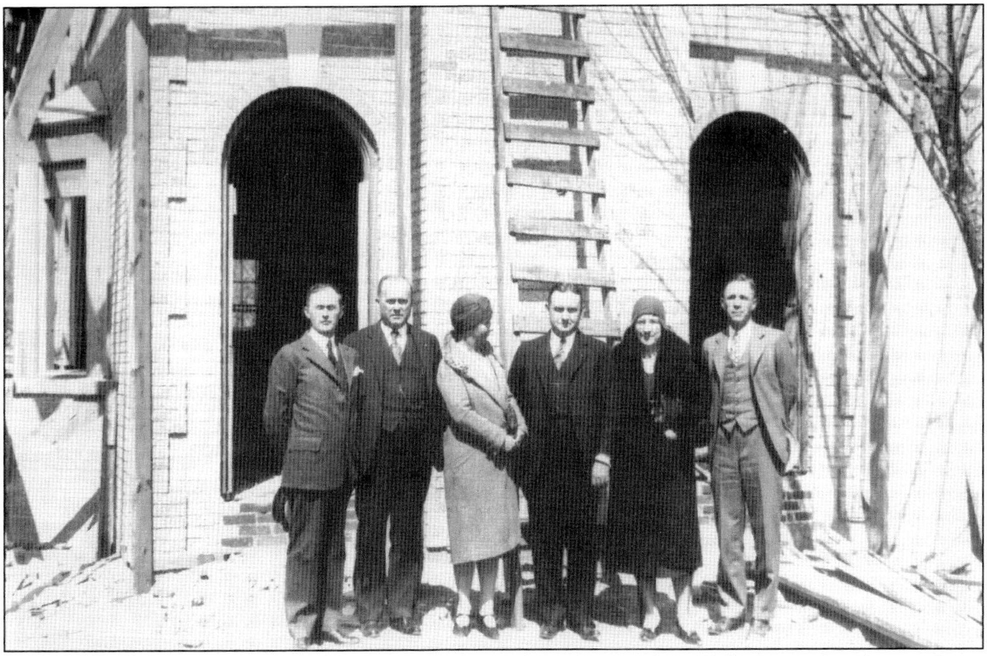

Completed in 1930, the Home Management House was designed as a laboratory for the teaching of domestic arts. Eight senior women, majoring in home economics, were to live in the building each semester. By living in the home full-time, they were able to apply the skills they learned. However, when the house was complete, the college was short of dorm space so they packed in 14 women instead. This picture was taken during the 1929 ground-breaking.

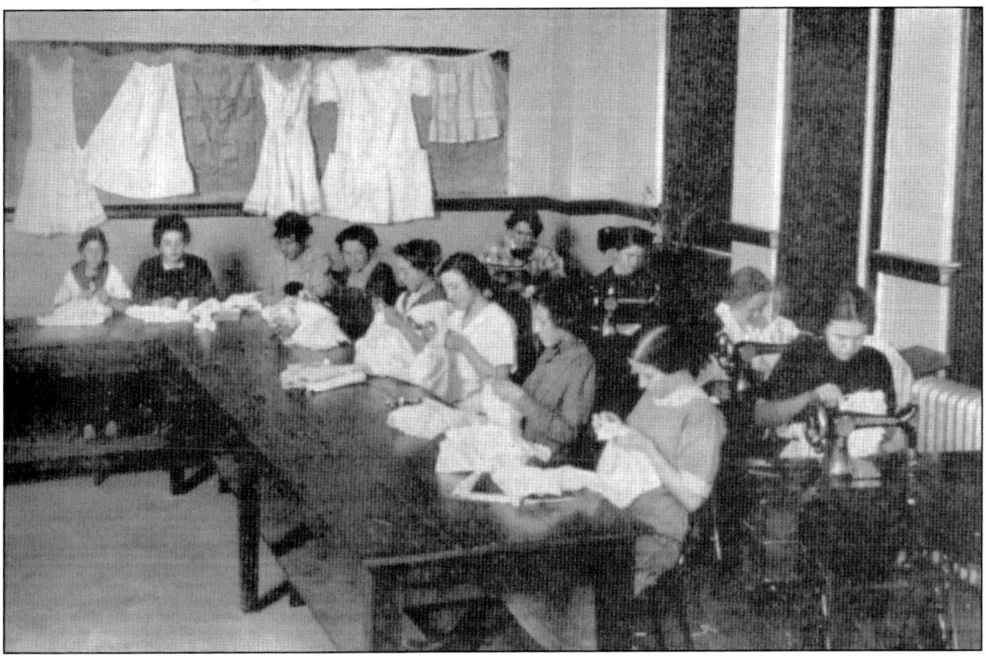

In 1916, the name of the school was changed to the Oklahoma College for Women. Pictured is a sewing class in 1933. During the Great Depression, the ability to make their own clothes was seen as an essential skill.

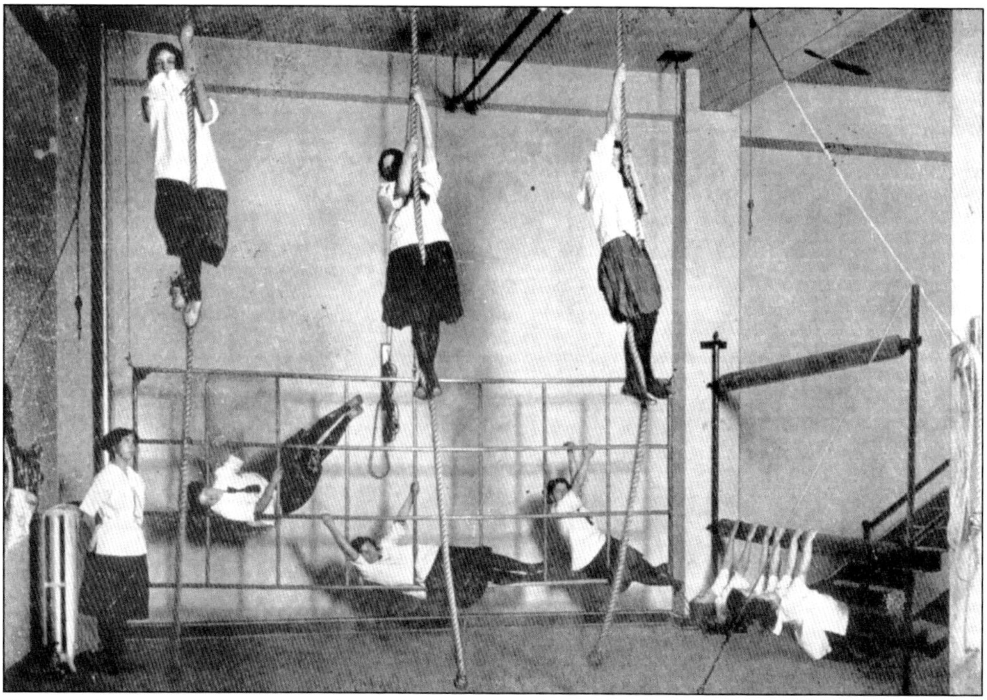

The 1933 yearbook describes physical education class as "when the gymnasium had a close resemblance to a torture chamber." In 1927, the yearbook gave a description of athletics on campus: "every afternoon, after regular classes are over, all girls interested in athletics meet on the athletic field or in the gym for participation in organized seasonal games . . . The entire student body is divided into two athletic tribes, the Kiowas-blue, and the Marathons-Red. All new students are affixed on the annual tag day. Hockey, soccer, basketball, tennis and track are hotly contested." As part of the curriculum, all the students were expected to swim and climb the rope.

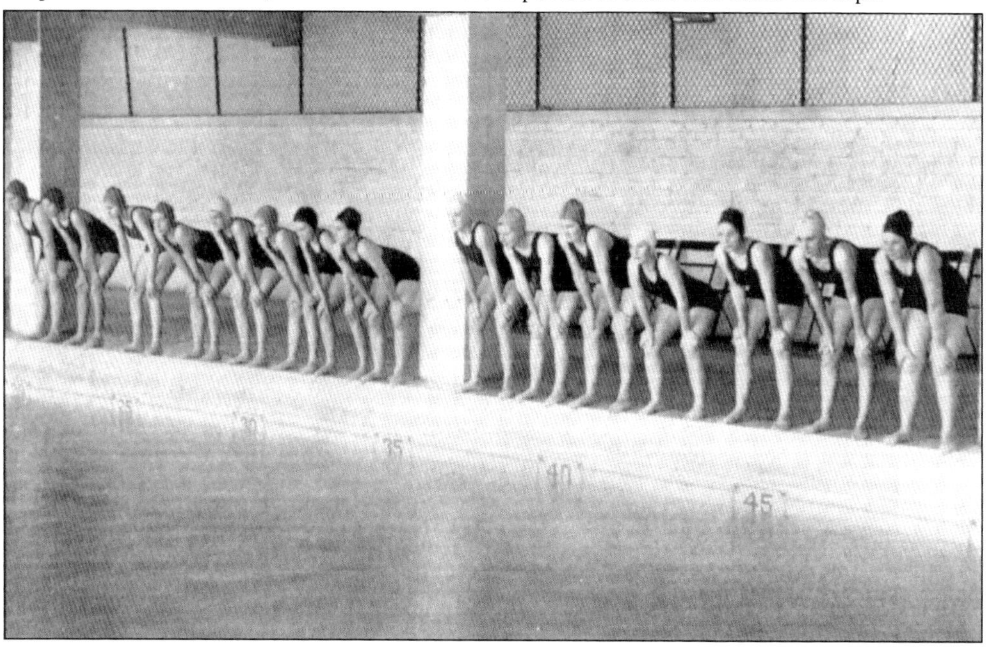

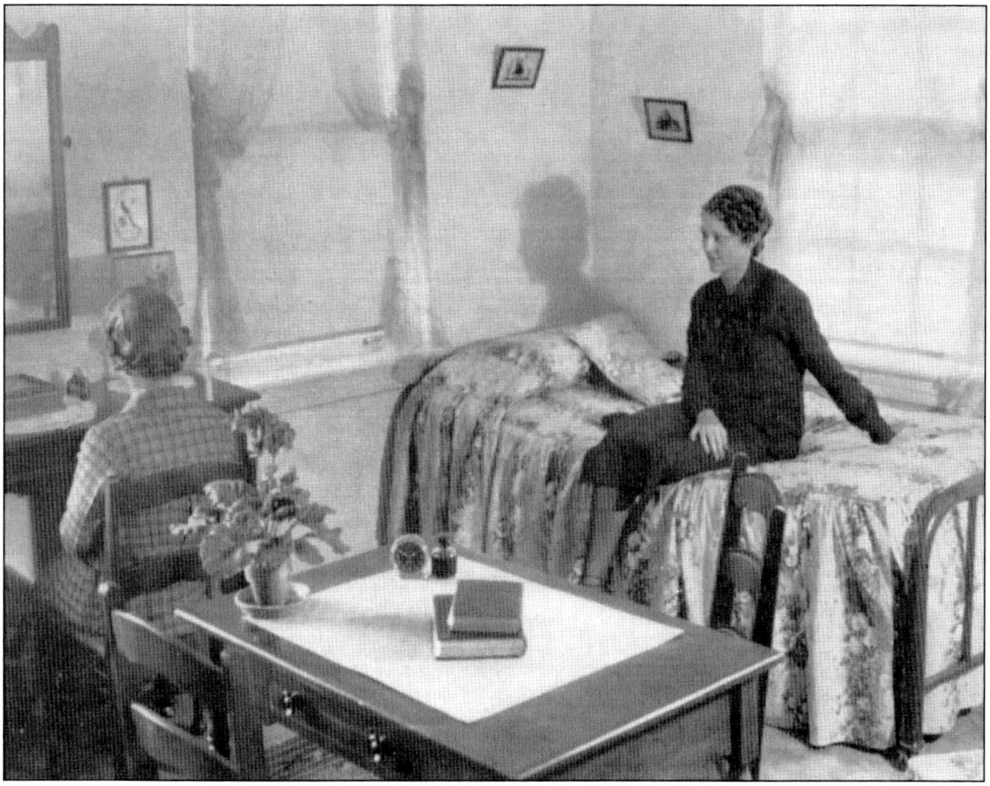

During the 1930s, several new structures were built on the Oklahoma College for Women campus, including the Home Management House, Mary Lyon Hall, the riding stables, Canning Hall, Lawson Hall, Robertson Hall, the nursery school, golf course, the college cabin, and Addams Hall. Pres. M.A. Nash, who took over the school in 1927, was famous for planting trees all over campus. It was said that his trees would grow for him even if planted in the desert. This 1934 aerial view below shows the growth of the campus during its first 25 years. Some of the new buildings are dorms that had new, updated rooms, as seen in the above 1936 yearbook picture.

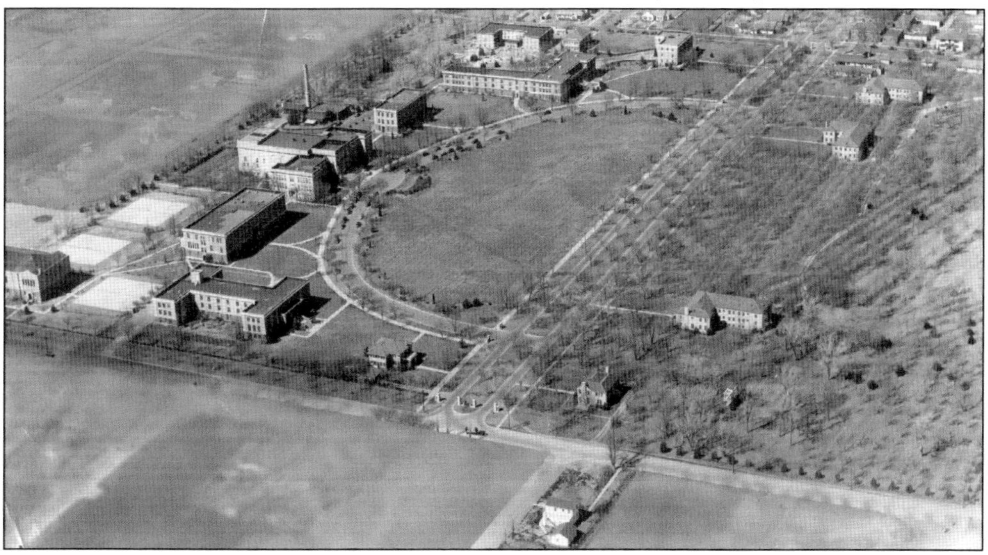

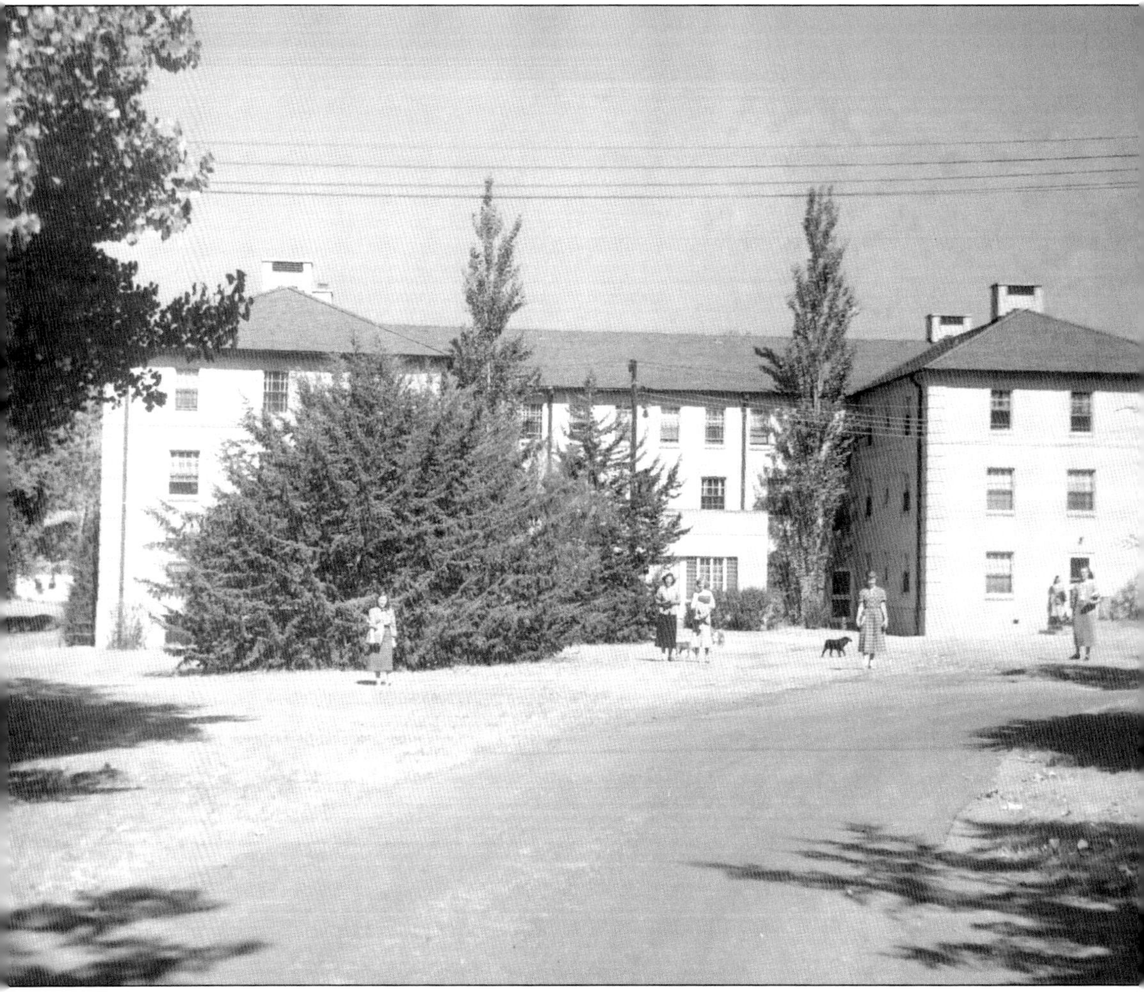

Jane Addams Hall, finished in 1939, was the last of the Great Depression–era dormitories. Part of the funding came from the Public Works Administration, a program during the Depression to fund public works and provide jobs. The dorm was constructed in an *H* shape, and it was the only building on campus that faced Alabama Avenue. It was originally built to house around 100 sophomore girls on campus, but the dorm was retired from service in the 1980s. It was named in honor of Jane Addams, the American social worker and 1931 Nobel Peace Prize winner. Addams, famous for her work with immigrants, built the model settlement house Hull-House in Chicago. Considered one of the founders of social work, Addams did research on the causes of poverty in order to try to solve many of the related issues.

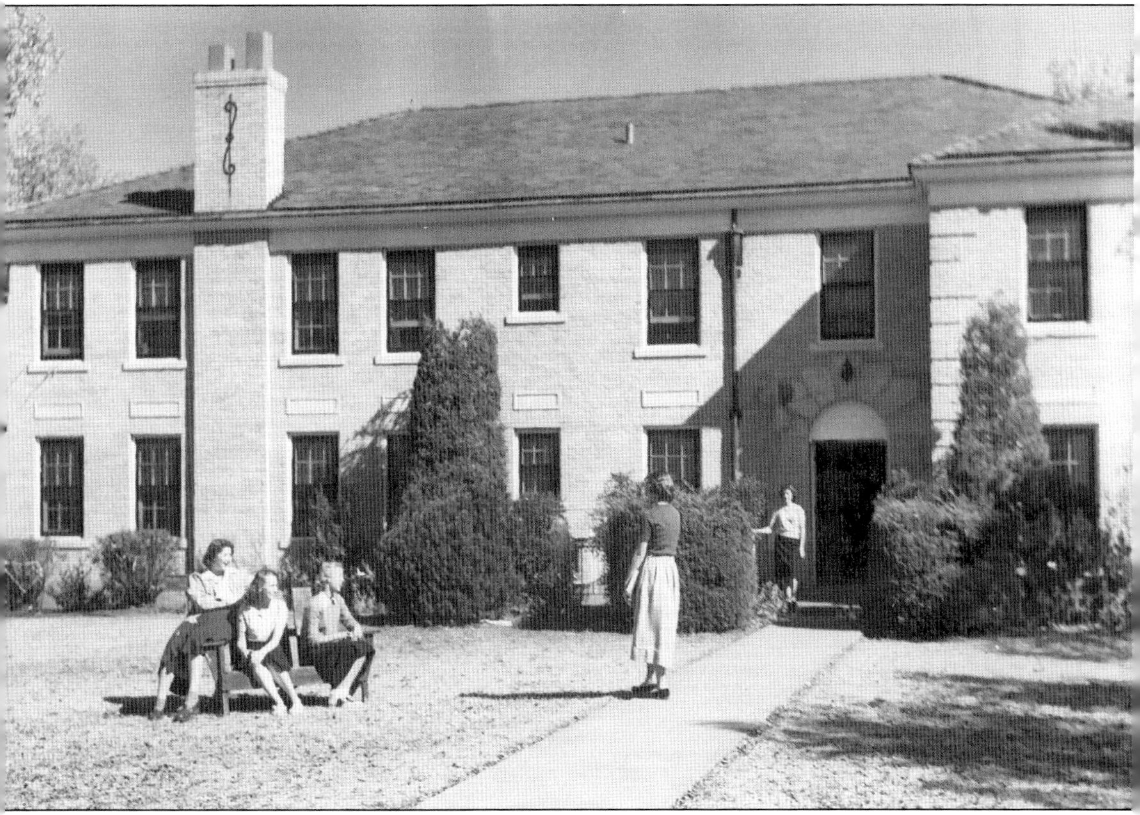

Finished in 1935, Canning Hall was built to house juniors and seniors. As one of the Great Depression building on campus, like Addams Hall, it was in part a project of the Public Works Administration. Along with Lawson and Robertson, it was one of the three matching dorms built on the east side of campus. All three dorms were designed by architect Paul Harris in the Spanish Eclectic style. The dorm was named in honor of Ruby John Canning, the first graduate of the Oklahoma College for Women. John was an active student in campus events, and with her musical gift she participated in all theatrical and musical events. She was also a member of the Utopia Literary Society. A native of Chickasha, John left to pursue a job teaching, but while home visiting family for Christmas break, she caught pneumonia and died in 1918.

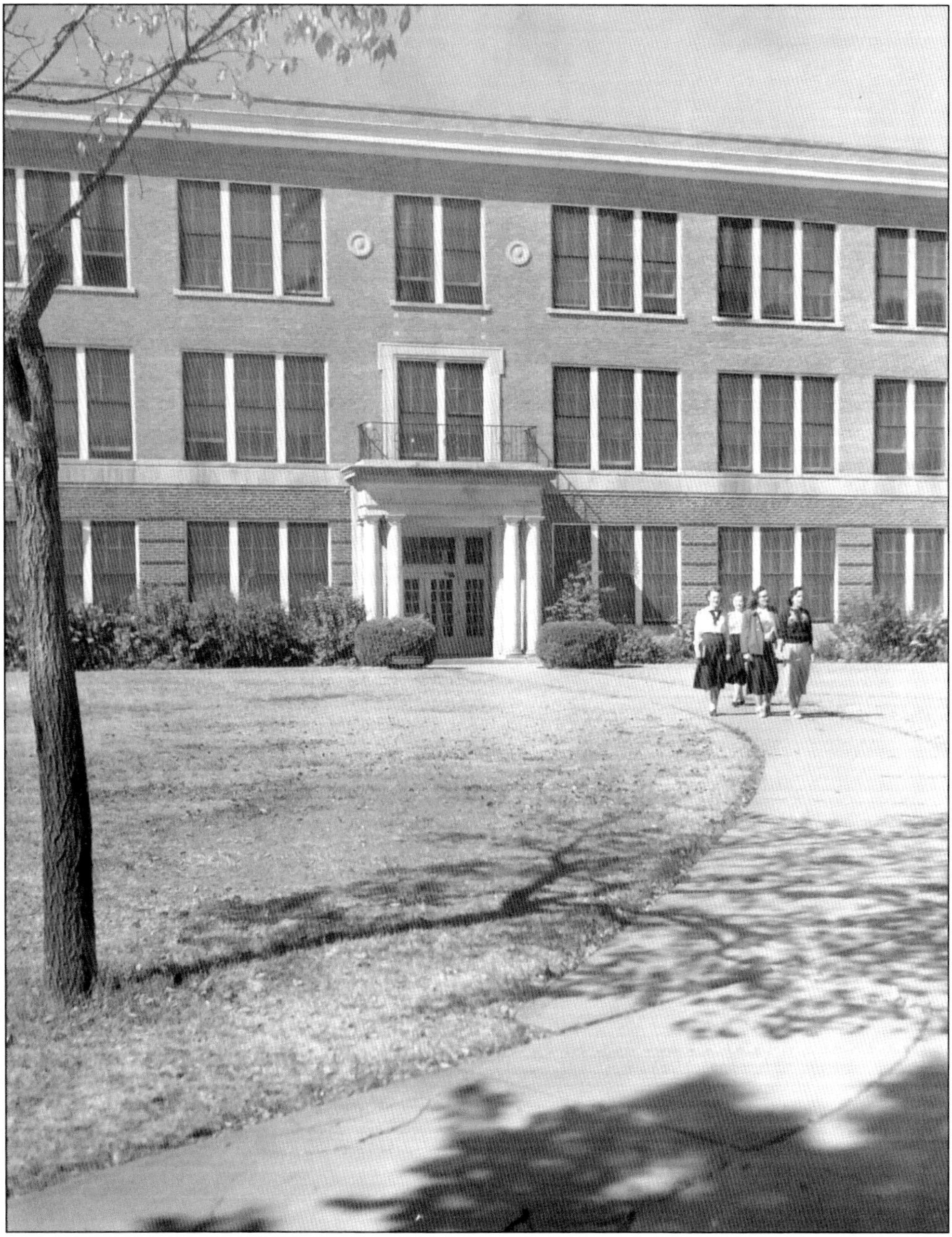

Originally known as the Home Economics and Science Building, Austin Hall was dedicated in 1924. The first floor was for cooking, the second for textiles, and the third for botany, chemistry, and physics. Today, Austin Hall is home to math and sciences. The building was named for George Washington Austin, the forth president of the college. During his tenure, the campus grew from 20 to 45 acres and from two to seven buildings.

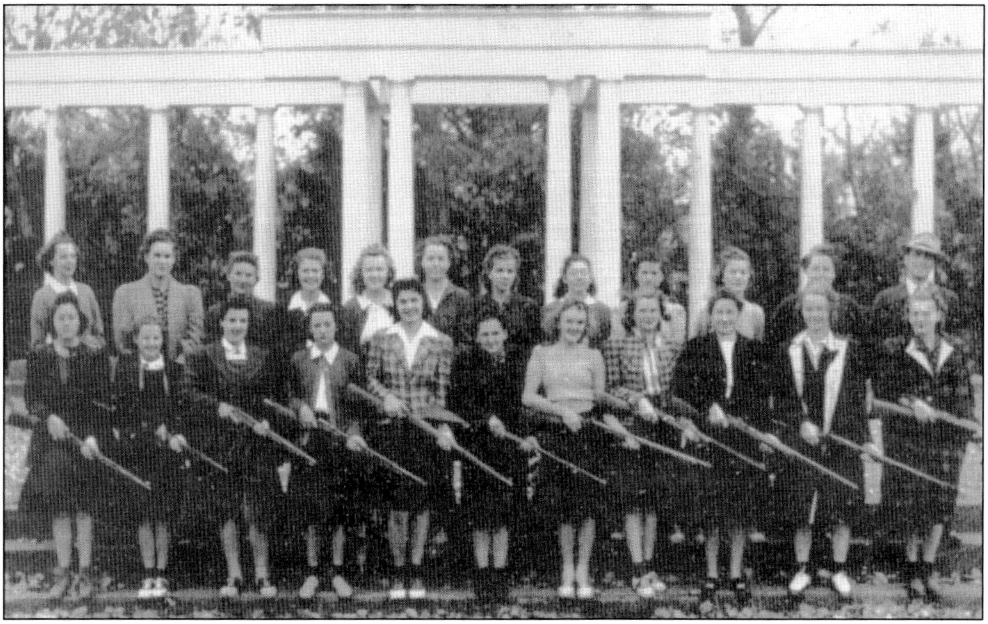

America was attacked in 1941 by the Japanese; in that same year, the Molly Stark Gun Club was organized. The yearbook states it was created by "a group of girls interested in learning how to shoot and how to improve their marksmanship. The use and care of firearms are also emphasized. Any student interested may join the club." Dorothy Jones served as the club's first president.

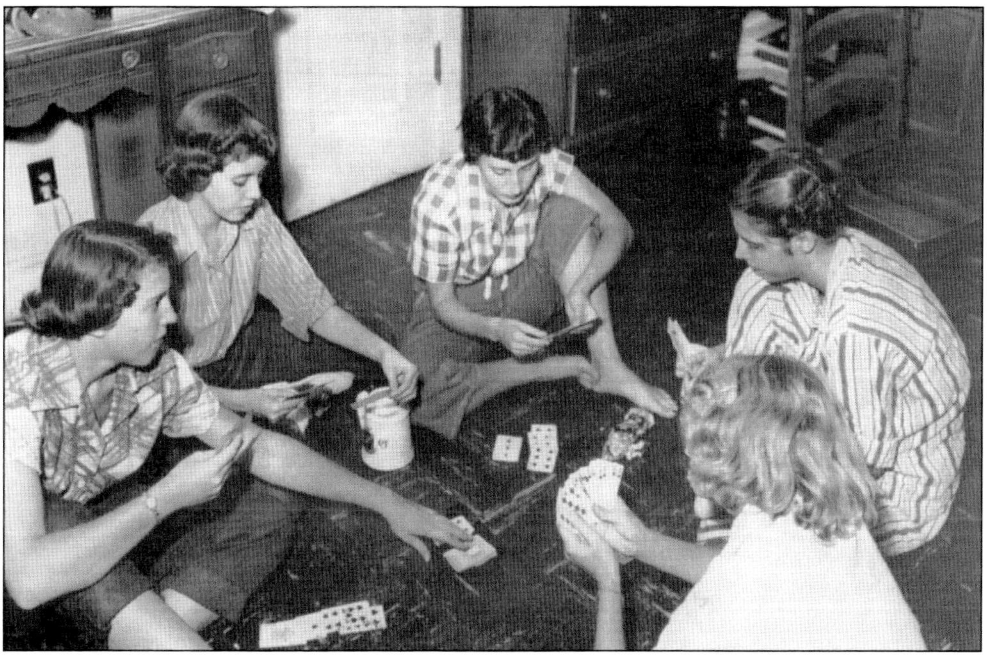

The 1951 yearbook describes this scene as "All work and no play makes Jane a dull girl . . . but there is no place for dull Janes at the Oklahoma College for Women. As important as the mad whirl of books, eight o'clock classes, term papers, and daily assignments, are the moments of relaxation-cards, cokes, and parties—dances, Play Days, and special entertainment. Result . . . from OCW emerge the more interesting, well educated ladies of tomorrow."

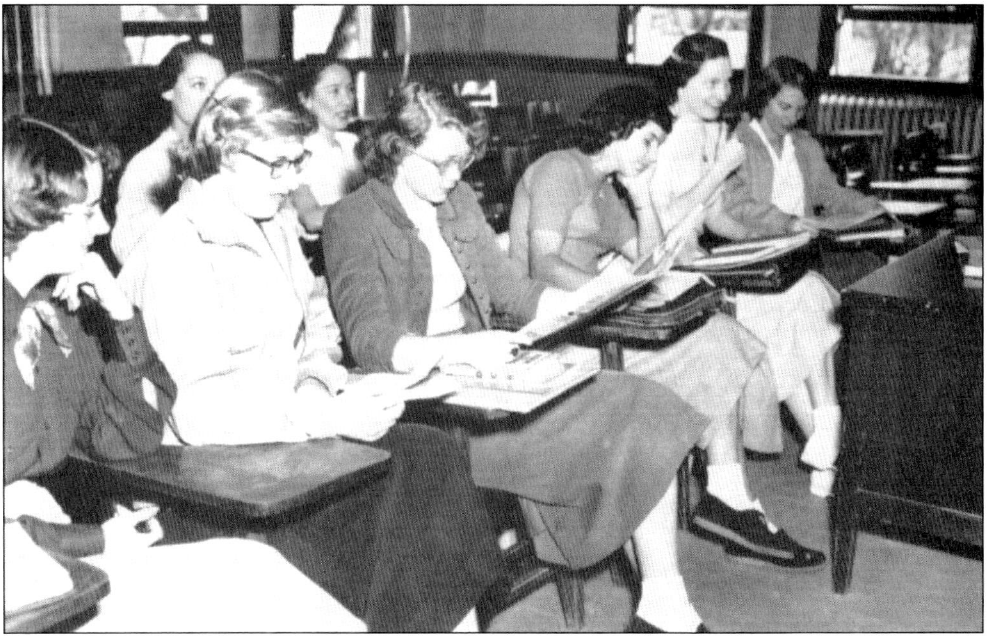

The 1950 yearbook states, "If the letters, magazines and conversations were only in French, Dr. Cole would probably let her students continue with them after class begins" (above) and "Rachel Vinyard tries to convince the others that they need not be so anxious about their turns in the shower, because the hot water has all been used" (below). With all the kidding aside, the 1950s also brought serious change. In 1954, the US Supreme Court declared an end to segregation in public schools. The next year, the regents of the Oklahoma College for Women agreed that in a progressive state like Oklahoma their school could no longer be for the sole benefit of white girls, and they opened their doors to girls of all races.

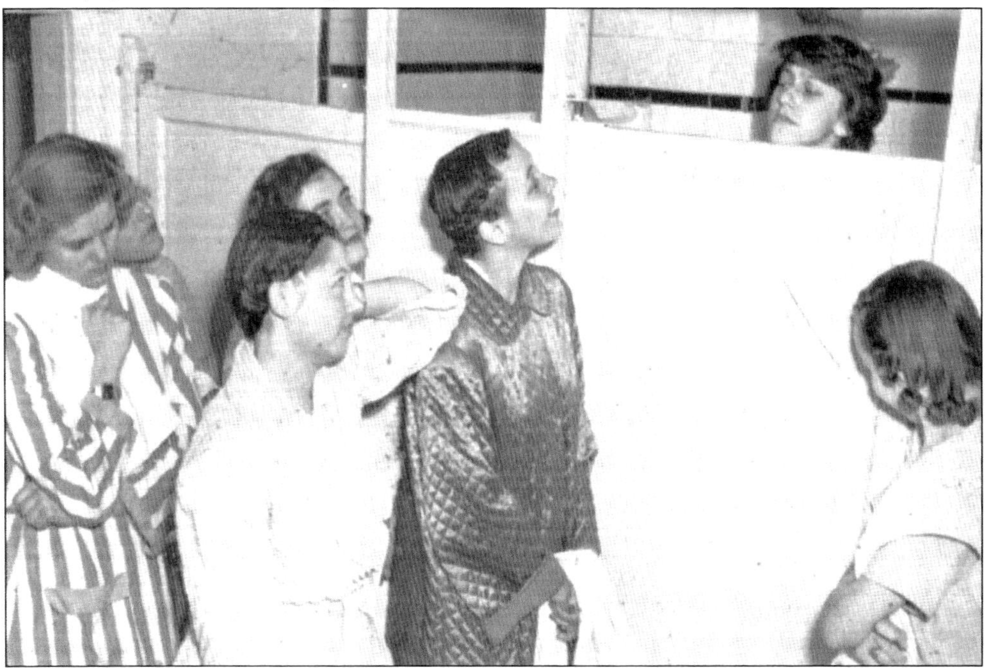

Written in the 1950 yearbook for the image at right is, "Geneva Tucker thinks she has the solution to term paper problems, but if her plan becomes popular before the opening of the new library the stacks are going to be crowded." Tucker would not have to wait long; the next year, 1951, the new Nash Library opened (below). The ladies of the college assisted with the opening by transporting over 10,500 books from the administration building in just half a day. The large grass field in front of the library was designed to hold convocations and commencement ceremonies. The library was named for the Mell Nash, fifth president of the college. Upon leaving the college, Nash served as Chancellor of the Oklahoma State System of Higher Education, and in 1935, was inducted into the Oklahoma Hall of Fame.

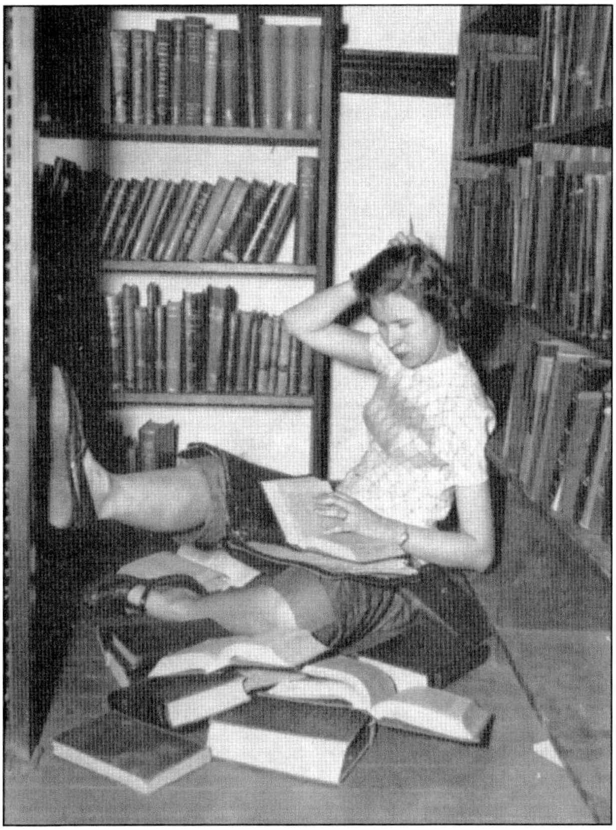

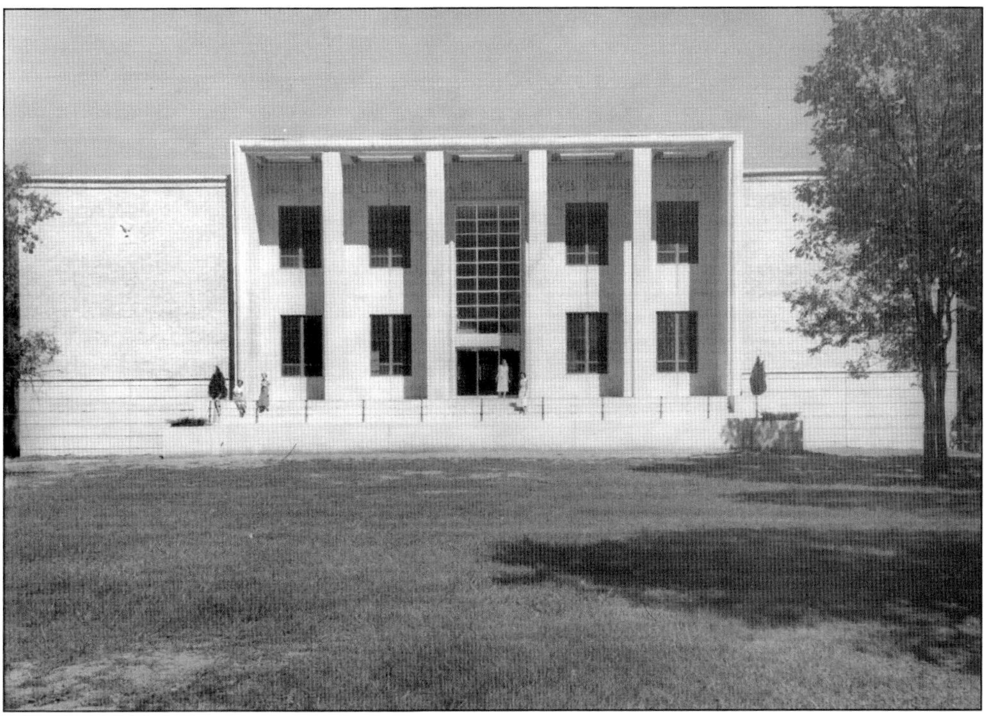

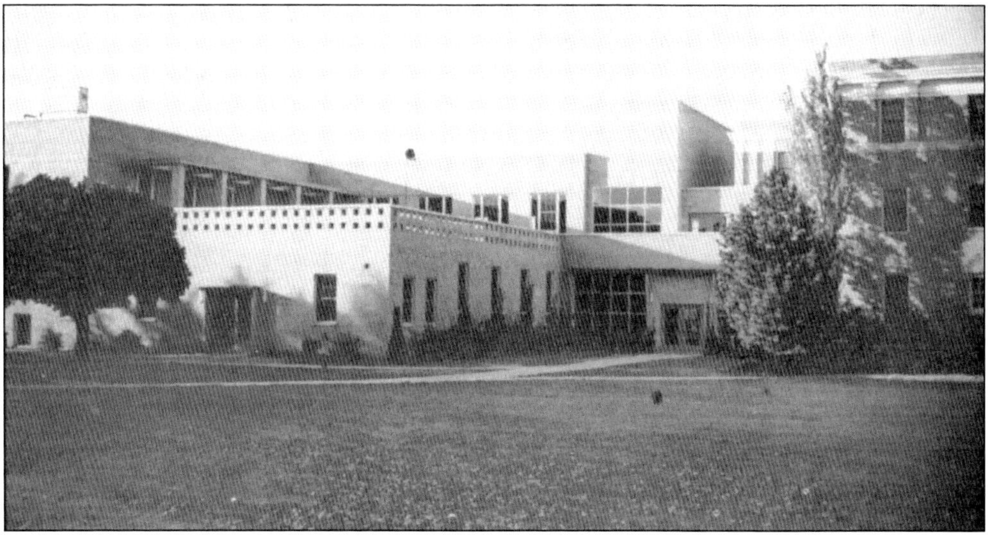

Finished in 1928, Senior Hall (right wing of building) was built to house upper-division students who were expected to take on leadership roles. In 1940, the name changed to honor Susan B. Anthony, the 19th-century women's rights leader and founder, along with Elizabeth Cady Stanton, of the Women's State Temperance Society. Anthony dedicated her life to securing the right to vote for women. In 1947, the student union (left side of building) was built, and the two wings attached became part of the union. The dorms were changed to a hotel for visiting parents and guests. Beginning in the 1960s, the old Senior Hall housed the student activities offices. Below, students of the Oklahoma College for Women enjoy dinner at the student union.

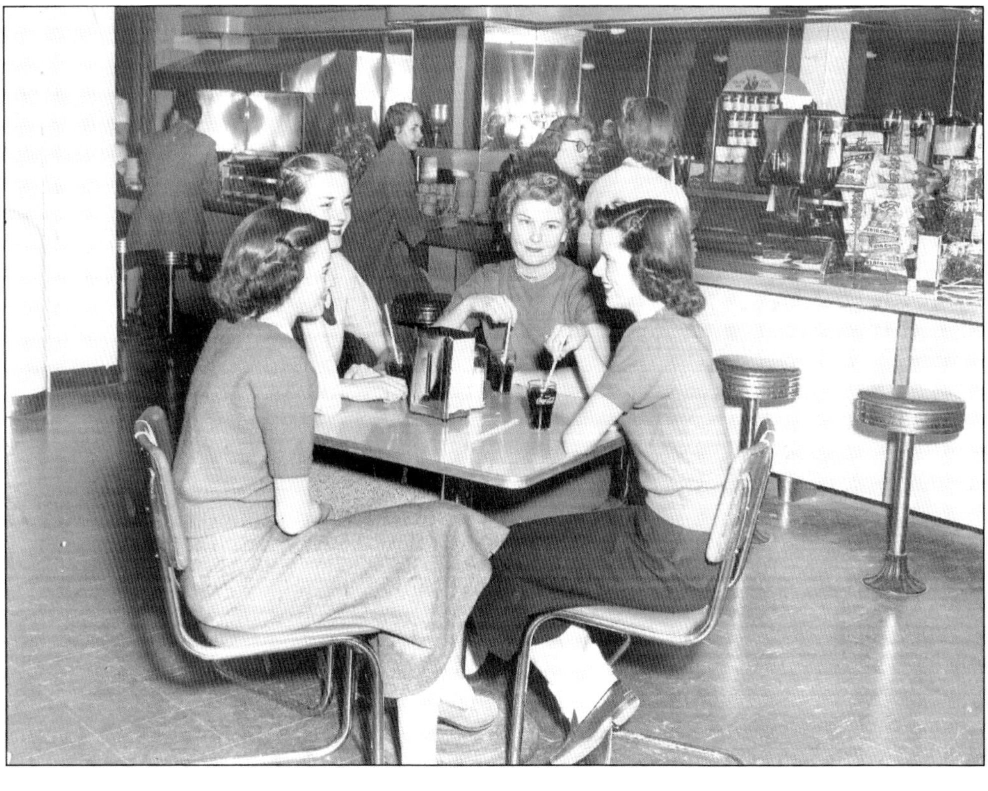

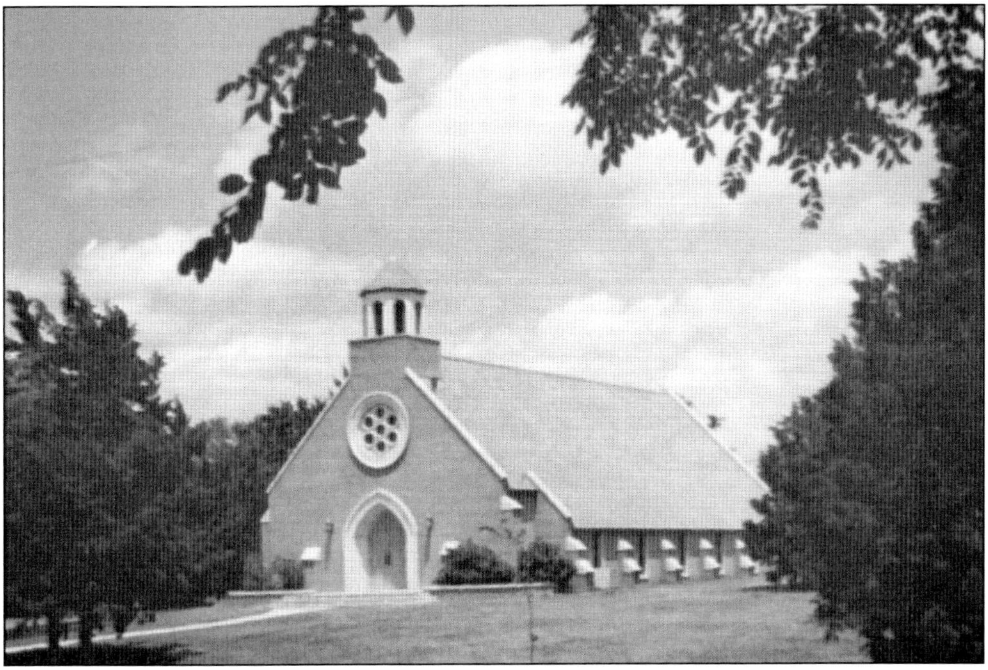

Completed in 1968, the Alumni Chapel was built for multidenominational use on campus. Over the years, the chapel has been used for weddings, funerals, and a variety of recitals. In 1968, an Allen Electric TC-38 organ, one of only five in the nation, was installed in the chapel. In 2002, the class of 1949 built the bridge that connects the campus to the chapel.

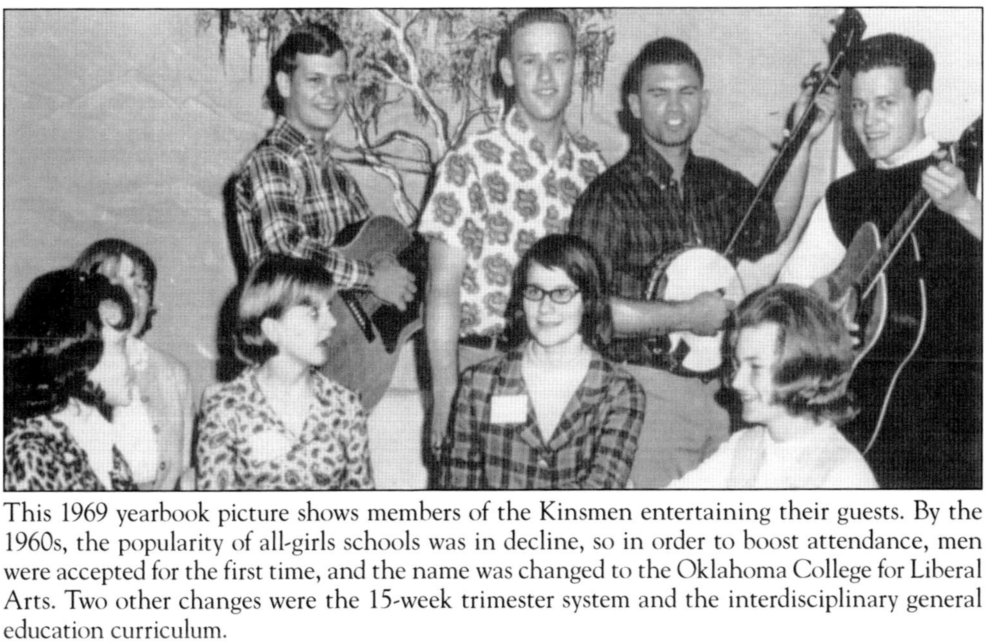

This 1969 yearbook picture shows members of the Kinsmen entertaining their guests. By the 1960s, the popularity of all-girls schools was in decline, so in order to boost attendance, men were accepted for the first time, and the name was changed to the Oklahoma College for Liberal Arts. Two other changes were the 15-week trimester system and the interdisciplinary general education curriculum.

BIBLIOGRAPHY

Chickasha Oklahoma 1892–1992. Chickasha: Chickasha Centennial Committee, 1992.

Dews, Maude. *Shacktown, Indian Territory, to Chickasha, Oklahoma*. Chickasha: University of Science and Arts of Oklahoma Foundation, 1990.

First Christian Church (Disciples of Christ) Chickasha, Oklahoma 1892–1991. Chickasha: First Christian Church, 1992.

Munn, Irvin. *Chickasha . . . A Journey Back in Time*. Chickasha: University of Science and Arts of Oklahoma Foundation, 1982.

———. *Chickasha: Another Journey Back in Time*. Chickasha: University of Science and Arts of Oklahoma Foundation, 1992.

About the Organization

The Grady County Historical Society (GCHS) was organized in 1973. Artifacts were originally stored in the upstairs portion of the *Express-Star* newspaper building until the Chickasha Public Schools gave the society permission to use the Auchincloss House. In 1995, the GCHS purchased the Dixie Department Store building, which was located in historic downtown Chickasha. First-floor renovations were completed in 1998, which resulted in museum exhibition and retail spaces. The retail rental spaces provide a portion of the funding for the museum and building maintenance.

The GCHS is dedicated to the acquisition, preservation, interpretation, and exhibition of information and materials primarily derived or relevant to the social and natural history of Grady County, Oklahoma. The museum collections are used for exhibition, research, and other educational purposes.

Some of the museum collections include the Geronimo Hotel murals painted by F.C. Peyraud; photographs and original documents; transportation, railroad, and farm equipment; personal clothing and military uniforms; furniture, appliances, and household items; medical equipment; scrapbooks, tax rolls, and newspapers; and natural history objects including a mastodon tusk.

The Grady County Museum is operated by a group of volunteer docents who watch the museum during visiting hours. A board of directors directs the oversight of the museum, and a volunteer director-curator provides supervision of museum activities.

The museum is located at 415 West Chickasha Avenue and is open Monday through Friday from 10:00 a.m. to 3:00 p.m. Admission is free.